ELDER CRIMES ELDER JUSTICE

David R. Snyder

JONES & BARTLETT
LEARNING

World Headquarters
Jones & Bartlett Learning
5 Wall Street
Burlington, MA 01803
978-443-5000
info@jblearning.com
www.jblearning.com

Jones & Bartlett Learning books and products are available through most bookstores and online booksellers. To contact Jones & Bartlett Learning directly, call 800-832-0034, fax 978-443-8000, or visit our website, www.jblearning.com.

Elder Crimes, Elder Justice is an independent publication and has not been authorized, sponsored, or otherwise approved by the owners of the trademarks or service marks referenced in this product.

This publication is designed to provide accurate and authoritative information in regard to the Subject Matter covered. It is sold with the understanding that the publisher is not engaged in rendering legal, accounting, or other professional service. If legal advice or other expert assistance is required, the service of a competent professional person should be sought.

Some images in this book feature models. These models do not necessarily endorse, represent, or participate in the activities represented in the images.

Production Credits
Publisher: Cathleen Sether
Acquisitions Editor: Sean Connelly
Editorial Assistant: Caitlin Murphy
Production Assistant: Leia Poritz
Marketing Manager: Lindsay White
Rights & Photo Research Assistant:
   Ashley Dos Santos
Manufacturing and Inventory Control
   Supervisor: Amy Bacus

Composition: Cenveo Publisher Services
Cover Design: Amy Snyder
PERLS Logo: Amy Snyder
Printing and Binding: Edwards
   Brothers Malloy
Cover Printing: Edwards Brothers Malloy

Library of Congress Cataloging-in-Publication Data
Snyder, David R.
   Elder crimes, elder justice / David R. Snyder. — 1st ed.
      p. cm.
   Includes bibliographical references and index.
   ISBN 978-0-7637-2859-5 (pbk.) — ISBN 0-7637-2859-4 (pbk.)
   1. Older people—Crimes against. 2. Crime analysis. I. Title.
   HV6250.4.A34S65 2013
   364.084'6—dc23
                              2012014227
6048

Printed in the United States of America
16 15 14 13 12   10 9 8 7 6 5 4 3 2 1

Dedication

To my wife Amy, for her unyielding love and support, for without it, this text would not have been possible.

Contents

Preface

Crime is one of the greatest problems in the United States today. It is one of the principal considerations that occupies our thoughts and shapes the way we live. The proportion of older people in society today is greater than ever before and growing faster than any other segment of the population. Law enforcement officers are increasingly called upon to manage the needs of the older population they serve. This creates a unique opportunity for the law enforcement community to understand and embrace the needs of the elderly.

In February 1977, Edward M. Davis, former President of the International Association of Chiefs of Police and Chief of Police of Los Angeles, California, stated the following regarding the study of crime and older people:

> Perhaps this lack of concern stems from the fact that we live in a rather plastic and disposable world. We shop at markets and buy convenience items that serve some immediate utility and when we are through with them, we throw them away. Can it be that people are treated in the same manner? Let's look at that possibility: A child is born and develops into a functional human being. As the child advances into adulthood and becomes a productive member of society, a certain utility is attached to that person's functioning and purpose. Once that same human being becomes older and retires and is no longer a producer, he or she loses utility. When that occurs, no one appears concerned. The elderly are neglected to a position of being isolated from the rest of society. They are discarded, as it were, to a place for old people. Their wisdom and their judgments are no longer solicited. No one cares for them and no one cares about them. They are lost in a new generation and they are alone.[1]

This poignant observation made by Chief Davis remains true today.

---

[1] Reprinted from *The Police Chief*, page 8, February 1977. Copyright held by the International Association of Chiefs of Police, 515 North Washington Street, Alexandria, VA 22314 USA. Further reproduction without express written permission from IACP is strictly prohibited.

There are several rationalizations for studying crime and gerontology. Among them are:

1. Of older people who live below the poverty level, the impact of any loss of economic resources is greater.
2. Older people are more likely to be victimized repeatedly, often the same crime by the same victimizer.
3. Older people are more likely to live alone, increasing their vulnerability to crime.
4. With increasing age, there is decreasing capacity.
5. Older crime victims who opt to defend themselves are more likely to suffer injury as a result.
6. Some older people who are victimized reside in high-crime neighborhoods.
7. Criminals are aware when monthly pension and social security checks are deposited. These criminals prey upon older people who bank at certain times of the month.
8. An awareness of their own susceptibility or the fear of being victimized may make some older people place themselves under "house arrest."
9. Elder abuse is now coming to the forefront of our nation's consciousness. It must be understood so that those who perpetrate this crime can be punished.
10. Older offenders make up only a small number of those who perpetrate crime. However, understanding older offenders will aid law enforcement officials to better deal with this cohort of offenders.

The United Nations Principles for Older Persons declares, "Older persons should be able to live in dignity and security and to be free of exploitation and physical and mental abuse."[2] These are principles we must embrace—for the standards that we set today will affect our lives tomorrow.

The study of crime is not new. The term *gerontology* was first used in 1903 at the Pasteur Institute in Paris. However, these two disciplines have not merged until now. *Elder Crimes, Elder Justice* seeks to bring together what is known about aging and crime. More importantly, the text serves to educate the law enforcement community on the important issues facing older people with regard to crime and victimization. It also presents an opportunity to embrace a cohort that is often overlooked.

Elder Crimes, Elder Justice addresses the special needs of older people and gives the law enforcement officer the confidence needed to understand the aging process, communicate effectively with older people, understand

---

[2] United Nations General Assembly. (1991). *United Nations principles for older persons.* Retrieved from http://www2.ohchr.org/english/law/olderpersons.htm.

the fears of older people, develop effective crime prevention strategies, and respond effectively to the older perpetrator.

Key features of the text include Case Studies, Attitude Tips, and Communications Tips. Each chapter contains multiple case studies that prompt the law enforcement officer to think about what they might do if they encountered a similar situation in the field. Attitude Tips help law enforcement officers appropriately handle calls involving older people, and also help address myths or stereotypes. Communication Tips remind the law enforcement officer of communication issues and how to communicate effectively. Key terms are defined comprehensively in a glossary at the end of the text.

Those who are taking the time to study crime and older people are to be commended for their effort. By doing so, when older people are victims of crime or are in need of assistance, someone will care for them and about them, and they will not be alone in their time of crisis.

I would like to acknowledge Jones & Bartlett Learning for recognizing the need for this most important topic in law enforcement and the editors and staff in the production of the text.

—David R. Snyder

Acknowledgments

We would like to thank the following individual for reviewing the text:

Detective Gary T. Childs
Criminal Investigation Division, Homicide Unit
Baltimore County Police Department
Towson, Maryland

Chapter One

Social Gerontology for Law Enforcement

LEARNING OBJECTIVES

1. Discuss aging in society today, including demographic trends.
2. Discuss the integration of law enforcement with the needs of older people.
3. Understand social gerontology as it relates to law enforcement—specifically the social aspects of aging, including ageism, retirement, lifestyles, family, social roles, and the financial status of older people.
4. Demonstrate sensitivity to the negative stereotyping of older people and be able to educate others about stereotyping.
5. Describe the living arrangements of older people.
6. Discuss the opportunities for positive changes that exist when serving the needs of older people.

Attitude Tip—It is an honor to be involved in the life of an older person in any way.

Case Study 1

You have recently graduated from a large metropolitan police academy, and you are assigned to a precinct that contains a large older population. Included in your post are several high-rise senior apartment complexes and a senior citizens center. You are eager to serve the population in your precinct.
How can you make a difference?
What should you do?

OLDER PEOPLE AND THE LAW ENFORCEMENT OFFICER

Aging is part of the lifecycle. As a law enforcement officer, you see older people in the community every day. Have you ever wondered what older people think about themselves? About the community? About crime? What the attitudes of older people toward law enforcement are? As a law enforcement officer, what are your views about aging? How do these views affect your perceptions about the older people you serve?

The later half of the 20th century has often been referred to as "the graying of America." As the Baby Boom generation approaches retirement age, the average age of Americans continues to rise. By the year 2010, the number of Americans over age 65 increased to 13% of the population (40.2 million). It is estimated that by the year 2030, those 65 and older will account for more than 20% of the overall population.[1]

One of the major issues for those who study or work with older people is defining what constitutes "old" or "old age." Depending upon what discipline one is working in or what text one is reading, old or old age can be defined as age 55 (as in prison populations), 60, or 65. This textbook defines older people as age 65 or older. It must be stated that older persons are different than younger adults. Variability increases dramatically with age. Whereas most 50-year-old adults are quite similar to most other 50-year-old adults, an 85-year-old person is quite different from another 85-year-old adult. In fact, the over 65 population is the most heterogeneous of all **cohorts**.

Historical Development

Societies have long recognized the need to protect themselves, to develop laws and ordinances governing behavior, and to punish those who are lawbreakers. The history of law enforcement can be traced back to ancient times when the family, tribe, or clan assumed responsibility for protecting its members.[2]

The ancient Greeks were the first to develop the practice of city policing. Modern municipal policing originated in New York City in 1844.

The history of aging had its origins in the Archaic period, or the beginning of recorded history. The ancient civilizations of China, India, and Asia Minor bore the hallmarks of their patriarchs in which aging personified achievement. Ironically, just as the ancient Greeks were the first to develop city policing, the Greek physician Galen used the term "gerocomy" in the 1st century A.D. for the medical care of the elderly. **Gerontology** is the modern term used for the study of aging, which was coined in 1903 at the Pasteur Institute in Paris.

Law enforcement programs and the historical development in the field of aging have gone unparalleled until now. What then does aging mean for law enforcement? Life expectancy in 2009 was 78.5 years for both sexes (76.0 for males and 80.9 for females). At age 65 in 2009, additional life expectancy was 19.2 years for both sexes (17.6 for males and 20.3 for females).[3] This represents a gain of more than 30 years in just one century. This gain in life expectancy is unparalleled in the history of mankind.

Historically, like other professions, police training programs usually grew out of problem identification—that is, when enough people are affected by a problem, the response is to solve it.[4] Law enforcement has embraced this concept since police–community relations training programs began in the 1940s.

While one would hardly call the emerging older population in America a "problem," it is a social and societal phenomenon that warrants special attention. There also exists an *opportunity*—the opportunity to respond more effectively to the special needs of older people. Not only do law enforcement officers respond to the criminal victimization of older people, but to their social, psychological, and environmental problems as well. No other age group served by law enforcement presents such unique challenges. With proper training and an attitude of compassion and caring, law enforcement officers can have a profound positive impact on the lives of older people.

THE PERLS SCALE

In responding to the needs of older people, it is important to remember certain key concepts. **PERLS** is an acronym created to help you remember unique law enforcement issues when responding to the needs of older people. PERLS will appear throughout the text whenever one of the five aspects of PERLS is being discussed.

- ***P*** *stands for prevention.* What are the crime prevention programs and strategies that are best suited for the population you are serving? How can they be implemented?
- ***E*** *stands for the elder population.* What are the distinct things that you must remember about this population in order to respond to its needs effectively? The first thing you should think of when responding to a

situation involving an older person is that older people are different and will present differently than younger adults, and will have specific fears and concerns. You will need to remember the changes that occur with age, and how to effectively communicate with the older person. Just as important, remember that an older person is just as human as a child or younger adult. Treat older persons with respect and dignity.

- **R** *stands for responsiveness, resources, and referrals.* Be responsive to older people's needs. They have lived a lifetime and should not have to live the end of their lives in any fear or deprivation. What resources are available for older people? Be aware of what services your local municipality and state have to offer older people and make the necessary referrals. The time you take will help to improve the quality of the lives of your senior citizens.

- **L** *stands for life issues.* What are the unique characteristics of the older population you are serving? Are there ethnic considerations? Issues of poverty? Access to transportation problems? Understanding what these life issues are will better prepare you to serve the older population's needs in your area.

- **S** *stands for social issues.* Older people may have less of a social network, due to death of a spouse, family members, or friends. This can lead to depression. The older person may need help with **activities of daily living (ADLs)**. Activities of daily living are defined as basic everyday activities needed to sustain life, such as feeding oneself, walking, dressing, getting up from a chair, and toileting. You will need to find out if the older person has sufficient social support to care for both physical and emotional needs. Evaluate the older person's surroundings, and be on guard for the possibility of elder abuse and neglect. If during your observations of the older person's social issues, you observe deficiencies, make appropriate referrals or take appropriate action (see **Table 1-1**).

Remembering the components of PERLS will provide you with a concise way of remembering the important issues regarding older people. Keep it in mind whenever you are involved with older people, and as you read this text. Using this concept will help you identify important issues, and, if necessary, make appropriate referrals. As a result, you will help the older person maintain, or even improve, his or her quality of life.

ATTITUDE

Older people have unique needs and problems that must be managed with skill and compassion. In order to properly manage these needs, you must educate yourself about the issues involving older people in your precinct

Table 1-1 The PERLS Scale

	P Prevention • What are the crime prevention programs and strategies that are best suited for the older population? • How can they be implemented?
	E Elder Population • Treat the older person with respect and dignity. • Older people are different and will present differently than younger adults. • Older people have specific fears and concerns. • Think about the changes that occur with age. • Remember how to effectively communicate with the older person.
	R Responsiveness, Resources, Referrals • Be responsive to the older person's needs. • What resources are available for older people? • Taking the time to make referrals will help to improve the quality of the lives of older people.
	L Life Issues • What are the unique characteristics of the older population you are serving?
	S Social Issues • Does the older person have a social network? Does the older person have ways to interact socially with others on a daily basis? • Evaluate activities of daily living (eating, bathing, dressing, toileting). • Evaluate the older person's surroundings, and be on guard for the possibility of elder abuse and neglect.

or district. Most importantly, you must have the appropriate attitudes when managing the needs of older people.

It is an honor to be involved in the life of an older person in any way. Your attitude as a law enforcement officer must reflect this. Just as it is your responsibility to manage a crime involving the older person, it is also your responsibility to manage the social, psychological, and environmental needs of the older person as well. With an attitude of caring and compassion, you can have a profound positive impact on the lives of older people.

> Attitude Tip—With an attitude of compassion and caring, you can have a profound positive impact on the lives of older people.

Ageism

Dr. Robert Butler coined the term **ageism** in 1969. As Butler originally defined it:

> Ageism can be seen as a systematic stereotyping of and discrimination against people because they are old, just as racism and sexism accomplish this with skin color and gender. Old people are categorized as senile, rigid in thought and manner, old fashioned in morality and skills . . . Ageism allows the younger generation to see older people as different from themselves; thus they subtly cease to identify with their elders as human beings.[5]

Even use of the terms "honey," "dear," or "pops" or addressing older persons by their first name without their permission are subtle forms of ageism. It is never appropriate to refer to the older person using these or similar terms, even if you think the older person cannot hear or understand you. The reality of aging is that older people are healthy, active, and continue to be engaged in society long after retirement (see **Figure 1-1**).

> Communication Tip—Referring to the older person as "honey," "dear," or "pops" or addressing older persons by their first name without their permission are subtle forms of ageism.

Using derogatory terms, speaking in a condescending tone, and having a negative attitude toward older people will undermine the trust that older people have in law enforcement. There may be instances where you are disgusted

Figure 1-1 The majority of people are healthy, active, and continue to be engaged in society after retirement.
Source: © Pixland/Thinkstock.

or disturbed by what you see on a scene. This is no excuse for a negative attitude. It unjustly punishes the person simply for being old—something over which the person has no control. Additionally, if the older person has just suffered a loss or has been the victim of crime, it further adds to the emotional aguish he or she is experiencing.

> Attitude Tip—Assess your own attitudes about older people, and improve or change them if indicated.

As human beings, we must understand and accept aging as part of the lifecycle, and as a society, we must reverse the attitude that aging is an affliction. As law enforcement professionals, we must manage the special needs of older people, and educate older people about crime prevention strategies that promote and enhance the quality of life. Law enforcement officers should not treat older people with disdain and disgust, but rather with an understanding of their situations and needs and with the respect they have earned.

When thinking about older people, keep this in mind: A person age 90 has experienced the Great Depression, two World Wars, the Korean and Vietnam conflicts, the Cold War, the civil rights movement, the peace movement, the space age, and the terrorism on our own soil. Older people are unique individuals with a lifetime of experiences. Take time to get to know some of the older people on your beat or in your sector—it will enrich your life. By providing an example of a caring and compassionate attitude toward older people, the law enforcement community can begin to win the battle against ageism.

THE OLDER POPULATION

To understand the older population, you need to understand the demographics of the older population as a whole. This section provides a brief overview of the older population in the United States.

Geographic Distribution

The 13 states with the highest percentage of resident population age 65 and over are as follows:[6]

1. Florida, 17.3%
2. West Virginia, 16.0%
3. Maine, 15.9%
4. Pennsylvania, 15.4%
5. Iowa, 14.9%
6. Montana, 14.8%
7. Vermont, 14.6%

8. North Dakota, 14.5%
9. Arkansas, Delaware, Rhode Island, 14.4%
10. Hawaii, South Dakota, 14.3%

Currently, 12.9% of the U.S. population is 65 years of age and older. Twenty-three states have population percentages of persons over 65 years of age that are higher than the national average. The states with the largest populations of people over the age of 65 are shown in **Figure 1-2**. It is estimated that 50% of older people live in suburbs, 27% live in cities, and 23% live outside of a metropolitan area.[7]

> Attitude Tip—Always attempt to serve as an advocate for older people. Be a positive role model and force for positive changes in the attitudes of others and in the quality of services provided to older people.

Rate of Aging

The number of people over 65 has dramatically increased over the last century. **Table 1-2** illustrates this.

The older population will continue to grow significantly in the future and will burgeon between 2010 and 2030 when the Baby Boom generation reaches age 65. The population 65 and older will increase to 55 million in 2020 and to 72.1 million in 2030. The age 85 and above population is expected to increase

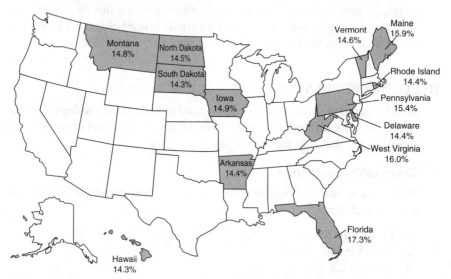

Figure 1-2 The states with the largest populations of people over the age of 65 are highlighted.

Source: Modified from © Dr_Flash/ShutterStock, Inc.; Data from US Census Bureau. (2011, November). *The Older Population: 2010*. 2010 Census Briefs. Retrieved from http://2010.census.gov/news/pdf/20111130_slides.pdf.

Table 1-2 Number of Older Adults in the United States in 2008

Age	Number of People	Increase Since 1900
65–74	20.8 million	9.5 times more
75–84	13.1 million	17 times more
85 and older	5.6 million	46 times more

Source: Data from *A Profile of Older Americans: 2010*. Administration on Aging, U.S. Department of Health and Human Services.

from 5.8 million in 2010 to 6.6 million on 2020. Minority populations are projected to increase from 8.0 million in 2010 (20.1% of older people) to 12.9 million in 2020 (23.6% of older people). Between 2010 and 2030, the white population 65 and older is projected to increase by 50% compared to 160% for older minorities, including Hispanics (202%); African Americans (114%); American Indians, Eskimos, and Aleuts (145%); and Asians and Pacific Islanders (145%).[8]

Case Study 2

You are dispatched to the scene of a motor vehicle crash in a residential neighborhood. The fire department and emergency medical services (EMS) are already on location, reporting no injuries. Your scene observations reveal a car that has struck a residence. The car was driven by an 84-year-old female. Your investigation reveals that the driver of the vehicle, while attempting to back the car out from her driveway, accidentally depressed the gas pedal instead of the break, causing the vehicle to careen backward across the street into the neighbor's house. The woman's 90-year-old husband is also on location, and both of them appear to be very distraught.

How do you proceed?

What are your interventional decisions?

Living Arrangements

Older people live in a variety of settings—with family, alone, and in institutions. Each type of living arrangement brings with it a distinct set of concerns which law enforcement officers are called upon daily to manage. For example, those who live alone might fear they are targets for victimization; those who live with family may be the victims of elder abuse and neglect; and those who reside in institutional settings are at the mercy of staff members for their care.

Over half (55.1%) of older non-institutionalized persons lived with their spouse in 2010. About 29.3% of all non-institutionalized older persons lived alone in 2010.[9]

There are a variety of living facilities for older people that provide an array of care, with all of which law enforcement officers must interact.

Active Adult Communities

Active adult communities have become very prevalent in the United States. They are also known as active adult living and active retirement communities. Fees are paid by private funds only. These communities offer age-restricted housing specifically created for seniors who enjoy participating in physical and social activities. The communities boast resort-type amenities, such as golf courses, tennis courts, pools, education classes, bike paths, and restaurants. Often, these facilities have their own private security.

Attitude Tip—Older adults are vital, generally healthy, contributing members of society and the community.

Independent Living in Senior Apartments

There are a number of rental developments that contain multiple units restricted to lease to those over the age of 55. Individuals who reside in these facilities may want additional physical or emotional security, or prefer to live with other seniors. These complexes often have restricted access and may have someone on duty, such as a desk clerk, 24 hours a day.

Independent Living in Congregate Housing

Independent living in congregate housing may contain convenience services for the residents of the community. Some of the provisions may include meals, housekeeping services, transportation, or social events. Residents may have minor health concerns. They may need the added security of having staff and other residents. This type of housing is typically paid for on a monthly basis by private funds. Independent living is unlicensed and may vary greatly.

Assisted Living

Assisted living is also known as residential care, board and care, and boarding house. Residents residing in these facilities require assistance with one or more of the activities of daily living, or 24-hour supervision to maintain safety. Residents tend to need assistance with medication administration, but not more significant daily medical care. They enjoy the security of 24-hour staffing. Some facilities specialize in the care of Alzheimer's patients or those with other dementias. Fees may be paid for with private funds, supplemental security incomes (SSI), long-term care insurance, or Medicaid. These facilities are typically licensed by each state, and licensing varies by each state. Assisted living facilities may be built as such, or may be contained in regular

Figure 1-3 Example of an assisted living facility.
Source: © Myrleen Pearson/PhotoEdit, Inc.

neighborhood homes (see **Figure 1-3**). Law enforcement should be familiar with the location of such facilities in their posts or sectors, as these facilities can be an easy target for criminals.

Alzheimer's Care Facilities

Alzheimer's care facilities are specialized care facilities for those with signs of Alzheimer's disease or other dementias. The residents of these facilities typically exhibit signs of impaired cognitive ability, forgetfulness, and/or wandering. The facility is designed to prevent residents from wandering off and to maintain safe activities. This may include features such as alarm systems on all doors and hallways that allow residents to wander in a continuous path without obstacles. Private funds, Medicaid, and long-term care insurance typically pay the fees associated with Alzheimer's care facilities. Law enforcement officers may be called to this type of facility for aggressive behavior on the part of a resident or to assist in locating a resident who has wandered off.

Nursing Homes

The term **nursing home** is also known as a skilled nursing facility, convalescent home, or long-term care facility. Residents require 24-hour nursing care and are unable to ambulate without the assistance of a walker, wheelchair, or the assistance of another person in most cases. Residents cannot perform their activities of daily living without assistance. A resident may need therapeutic or rehabilitative services, including speech therapy, physical therapy, occupational therapy, respiratory therapy, or wound care.

In 2009, there were approximately 15,700 nursing homes in the United States comprising some 1,705,808 nursing home beds. Both the federal and state government regulate these facilities to ensure quality of care. Private funds, long-term care insurance, Medicare, and Medicaid pay for the fees associated with long-term care. Out of all persons 65 years of age or older, 4.1% (1.6 million) live in an institutional setting (see **Table 1-3**).[10] The rate of institutionalization increases with age. Law enforcement officers may be called to this type of residence to investigate abuse and neglect issues.

Income and Poverty

Almost 8.9% (3.4 million) of those 65 and older were below the poverty level in 2009. This number is below the poverty level of 12.9% for those between the ages of 18 and 64. Another 5.4% (2.1 million) of older people were classified as "near poor." Older women are more likely to be impoverished than older men.[11] Income and poverty levels can affect older people's eating habits, upkeep of their homes, and their health care.

Overall Health

In 2009, 41.6% of non-institutionalized older persons assessed their health as excellent or very good (compared to 64.5% for all persons aged 18–64 years). There was very little difference between the sexes on this measure. Most older persons have at least one chronic condition and many have multiple conditions. In 2007–2009, the most frequently occurring conditions among older persons were:[12]

1. Hypertension, 38%
2. Diagnosed arthritis, 50%
3. All types of heart disease, 32%
4. Any cancer, 22%
5. Diabetes, 18%
6. Sinusitis, 14%

Some type of disability (e.g., difficulty in hearing, vision, cognition, ambulation, self-care, or independent living) was reported by 37% of older persons in 2009. Some of these disabilities may be relatively minor, but others cause people to require assistance to meet important personal needs. In 2005, almost 37% of older persons reported a severe disability and 16% reported that they

Table 1-3 Percentage of Older People Living in Institutions

Age in Years	Percentage Living in Institutions
65–74	1.1%
75–84	3.5%
85 and over	13.2%

Source: U.S. Department of Health and Human Services, Administration on Aging. (2011). *A profile of older Americans: 2011.* Retrieved from http://www.aoa.gov/aoaroot/aging_statistics/Profile/2011/docs/2011profile.pdf.

needed some type of assistance as a result. Reported disability increases with age: 56% of persons over age 80 reported a severe disability and 29% of the over 80 population reported they needed assistance. There is a strong relationship between disability status and reported health status. Among those age 65 and older with a severe disability, 64% reported their health as fair or poor.[13]

A study focusing on the ability to perform specific ADLs found that more than 25% of community-resident Medicare beneficiaries over age 65 in 2007 had difficulty in performing one or more ADLs. By contrast, 83% of institutionalized Medicare beneficiaries had difficulties with one or more ADLs and 67% of them had difficulty with three or more ADLs. Limitations in activities because of chronic conditions increase with age.[14] Law enforcement officers may be called to assist emergency medical services personnel with an older person, or may be managing a situation involving an older person on their own.

Use of Healthcare Services

In 2007, about 12.9 million persons aged 65 and older were discharged from short-stay hospitals. This is a rate of 3,395 for every 10,000 persons over age 65, which is about three times the comparable rate for persons of all ages (which was 1,149 per 10,000).[15]

The **old-age dependency ratio** depicts the dependency individuals place on society as they age. It is defined as the number of older people for every 100 adults (potential caregivers) between the ages of 18 and 64. In 2010, there were 22 older people for every 100 "caregivers." By the year 2030, it is projected that there will be 35 older people for every 100 caregivers.[16] The supply of caregivers is not keeping pace with the growth of the older population. The need for caregivers is going to increase, and society is going to have difficulty keeping up with the demand for services as the population continues to age.

SOCIOLOGY OF AGING
Attitudes and Perceptions of Crime and Law Enforcement

What are the attitudes and perceptions of crime by the elderly? Of law enforcement?

These questions are difficult to quantify within the confines of this text. Although the aged have the lowest crime victimization rates, there is disagreement among researchers about the specific fears and perceptions among older people. Some research suggests that older people fear crime less and are more confident in the police than other age groups; other studies report a general fear of crime among both urban and rural older people. There is also research that suggests that older people are aware of crime and alter their lifestyles to avoid becoming victims (e.g., by direct deposit of social security and retirement checks, increased security measures in their homes, and avoidance of being on the street after dark). Other research suggests further that older people feel that the courts are too lenient with sentencing of criminals.[17]

Perhaps this research is difficult to quantify because those over 65 represent the most heterogeneous of all cohorts. For example, those who live in a secured continuing care retirement community may not perceive crime as a daily threat as compared to a widowed elderly woman who lives alone in either an urban or rural setting. There is one question that deserves further thought: If older people are socialized into perceiving themselves as especially vulnerable by society, do these perceptions become self-evident to older people?[18]

Research on the attitudes of the elderly toward the police is also mixed. Some studies suggest that older people who have direct contact with the police hold generally favorable attitudes (regardless of whether this contact was in response to criminal or noncriminal events). Yet, other researchers have found that the greater the frequency of contact with the police, the less favorable were older people's attitudes toward them. One researcher suggests that the indifference to the problems of older people may be at the root of older people's dissatisfaction with police.[19]

The mixed research on the fear of crime and the perceptions of the elderly toward the police gives further credence to the notion that there exists an *opportunity*—the opportunity to understand aging, the fears and concerns of older people, and a chance to quell these fears and intervene with appropriate crime prevention programs. Of particular interest to criminologists and gerontologists is why, after a lifetime of conformity and being law abiding, older people commit criminal offenses for the first time. A discussion of the sociology of aging is offered in order to gain an understanding of the issues affecting individuals as they age.

Lifespan Issues

How individuals perceive life as they grow older has a large effect on their aging process. People who have a healthy attitude may be running marathons when they are 90 years old. Conversely, people who fear growing older may feel useless and depressed. This concept is particularly relevant when considering crime, and the older person's fear of crime. Those who perceive (not falsely) that their neighborhood is safe, and that the police take an active role in community crime prevention programs and who are attentive to the older person's needs, may feel more engaged in society, and, more specifically, in the community in which they live.

Throughout the stages of life, people have emotional reactions to the aging process, especially during major life events. For example, parents who build their lives around their children may have difficulty when their children grow older. The difficulties they may have in dealing with their new lifestyle as the children grow can lead to uncertainty and depression, which have an adverse effect on the aging process. On the other hand, if parents have a healthy attitude and enjoy watching their children grow into adulthood, they will see their role in their children's lives as evolving, not ending. Having a positive outlook on major life events can make the aging process smoother.

Later in life, women undergo **menopause**, and men undergo the lesser known "male menopause," or **andropause**—a time of lessening of testosterone and sexual hormone activity. Just as every individual is unique, these changes affect each individual differently. Individuals in some instances alter their lifestyle, which alters their aging process.

Views about retirement also have an effect on aging. People retire at different ages for different reasons. Economic reasons may influence the choice for some of when to retire. Once people stop working, they need to find another purpose in life. Those with hobbies and interests are better able to enjoy their retirements. Those who feel they have lost their purpose with retirement age more rapidly and with greater difficulty.

The Self in Later Life

As aging occurs, coping with life's changes can be more difficult. How a person controls and copes with the aging process is an important factor in emotional reactions. The personality of the individual determines how well he or she will react to the aging process. How one expects the aging process to occur directly influences the individual's aging process.

End-of-Life Issues

There are several controversial issues with regard to ending one's life to honor the individual's modesty, dignity, self-esteem, and independence. Many feel they should have the right to determine how and when they will die. Late-life suicide often results from the loss of a spouse or the lack of wanting to continue to live with a terminal illness. Euthanasia has been legalized in a few states, but continues to be controversial. The right-to-die movement has focused on all of the various issues; however, not all are accepted.

Law enforcement officers will be involved in deaths concerning older people, or to assist fire and EMS providers at the scene of a cardiac arrest or of an older person who has expired. One document that the law enforcement officer should familiarize him- or herself with is the **do not resuscitate (DNR) order**. Most states have prehospital DNR orders which emergency medical technicians and paramedics are bound by state law to honor. Most DNR orders give specific direction for the EMS provider to follow. To simplify, these DNR orders specify (based on the patient's or the patient's physician's request) the type of care that the EMS provider is able to render. Care may range from palliative (or comfort measures) only to advanced life support procedures up until cessation of breathing and/or pulselessness occurs. As a law enforcement officer, you should familiarize yourself with the type of DNR orders that are in use in your state.

Influences in the Life Course

A variety of factors influence the process of aging. The following sections give an overview of some of these.

Social Class and Life History

The social class and the environment in which a person lives directly influence how that person deals with the aging process (and one would surmise that this also influences the older person's perception and fear of crime). Social institutions and their policies dictate how issues of modesty, dignity, self-esteem, and independence are accepted within the institution's walls.

Race and Ethnicity

Our society is diverse in its ethnic culture. A person's race, ethnicity, and culture will influence how he or she deals with issues (see **Figure 1-4**). In different cultures, the gender of an individual may alter the way the aging process is viewed. In neighborhoods where service is provided to a specific ethnic older group, or a diversified older group, it may be wise to contact community leaders and arrange training so that, as a law enforcement officer, you can understand how the ethnic older population in your precinct or areas perceives the aging process, itself, crime, and law enforcement. In this way, you will gain a better understanding of the population you serve and be better prepared to respond effectively to its needs.

Older Persons on Their Own

As they age, individuals want to maintain their independence as long as they possibly can. As a law enforcement officer, you must be sensitive to the need, and take the older person's wishes for independence into consideration when faced with situations that could negatively impact their independence.

Aging and the Family

The family needs to consider its responsibility to its aging members and take distance of the members into consideration. The nuclear family is often extended miles apart, and younger family members may not be in close proximity to their aging members.

Figure 1-4 Our society is diverse in nature.
Source: © Bob Daemmrich/PhotoEdit, Inc.

Older People Making Choices

The ability of the older person to make sane and rational decisions decreases as the mental capacity of those afflicted by certain ailments, such as dementia, diminishes. When older people make bad decisions, it may cause financial and health problems.

Case Study 3

You are dispatched to an intersection of a reported struck pedestrian. Upon your arrival, EMS is on the scene treating an 82-year-old female who is bleeding from the arm. The injured older woman was attempting to cross the street with the light when a vehicle traveling approximately 20 miles per hour struck her. You note that this is the third time this month that a pedestrian has been struck at this intersection. Your observations reveal a newly opened senior apartment building on one side of the street and a grocery store on the other side of the street.
What are your thoughts?
What are your intervention decisions?

SUMMARY

Older people are a special group in American society who require police assistance. By taking the time to study the issues involved in the aging process, and how crime impacts older people, you are increasing your knowledge beyond that of your initial academy and preparing yourself to properly manage the diverse needs of the older population you serve. One day, you and your parents, siblings, friends, and extended family will be part of the older population, perhaps needing the services of law enforcement. The measures you take to improve the law enforcement response to the needs of the older population today will shape the law enforcement response you may receive tomorrow. By being aware of opportunities for prevention, you can have a positive impact on the lives of the older population you serve.

Attitude Tip—"One hallmark of a civilized society," it was said, "is its willingness to care for its poor, ill, elderly . . . and handicapped."
—Saturday Review, May 1970

CASE STUDY SUMMARIES

Case Study 1 Summary

Wanting to make a difference with the population you serve is the first step. Given that you have a large number of older people in your precinct, including several high-rise senior apartment complexes and a senior center, there are several things that you (and your department) can do to have a positive impact on the older people in your precinct. One thing that can be done is to visit each of the senior high-rise complexes. This will give the management at these facilities a chance to meet you and for you to get to know them. This will result in developing a positive rapport. It will also provide you with the opportunity to review the security measures in place at the facilities and to make necessary recommendations for improvement. You may also have the opportunity to meet some of the residents, and hear their concerns and fears about crime. It will also show the residents that you are concerned for their wellbeing. When visiting the senior center, find out when it will have a fair or expo, and involve your department by displaying a booth with crime prevention literature.

Case Study 2 Summary

There are several ways you could proceed with this incident, one of which is to charge the driver with failure to control her vehicle (and any other applicable statute) and clear the scene. But would this get to the cause of *why* this accident occurred? It may not, and it would not prevent a reoccurrence. There may be some underlying disease process that caused the driver to pass out, or the driver's reaction time may be impaired. A more judicious way to proceed may be to take both driver and spouse back to their home and evaluate alternatives to the woman driving without threatening her independence. Inquire if there are adult children or other family who could do errands. This will also allow evaluating what other services both may need to maintain themselves in the community. Make any necessary follow-up calls for services that may be necessary. Unfortunately, though, this may be a case where you will have to intervene with the state motor vehicle administration for the person's own safety, and for the safety of others. If this is the case, an attitude of caring and compassion will make it easier.

Case Study 3 Summary

Your observations at the scene revealed a newly opened senior apartment complex on one side of the street and a grocery store on the other side of the street. This should arouse your suspicion that perhaps the traffic light at the intersection is not long enough for older pedestrians to cross, or that there may be obstructions to motorists. In this case, there is an excellent opportunity to prevent a potentially serious or fatal pedestrian accident from occurring. Contact the local or state bureau of highways so that an evaluation of the intersection can be made. The solution may be as simple as extending the time allowed in the crosswalk.

ENDNOTES

1. U.S. Census Bureau. (2011, November). *The older population: 2010.* 2010 Census Briefs. Retrieved from http://2010.census.gov/news/pdf/20111130_slides.pdf.
2. Palmiotto, M. J. (1997). *Policing—Concepts, strategies, and current issues in American police forces.* Durham, NC: Carolina Academic Press; p. 5.

3. National Center for Health Statistics. (2012, May). *Health, United States, 2011: With special feature on socioeconomic status and health.* Hyattsville, MD. Retrieved from http://www.cdc.gov/nchs/data/hus/hus11.pdf#listfigures.
4. Radelet, L. A. (1986). *The police and the community* (4th ed.). New York: Macmillan and Company; p. 14.
5. Enright, R. B. Jr. (Ed.). (1994). *Perspectives in social gerontology.* Needham Heights, MA: Allyn and Bacon; p. 3.
6. U.S. Census Bureau. (2011, November). *The older population: 2010.* 2010 Census Briefs. Retrieved from http://2010.census.gov/news/pdf/20111130_slides.pdf.
7. Ibid.
8. Administration on Aging, U.S. Department of Health and Human Services. (2011). *A profile of older Americans: 2010.* Retrieved April 10, 2012, from http://www.aoa.gov/aoaroot/aging_statistics/Profile/2011/docs/2011profile.pdf.
9. Ibid.
10. Ibid.
11. Ibid.
12. Ibid.
13. Ibid.
14. Ibid.
15. Ibid.
16. U.S. Census Bureau. (2011, November). *The older population: 2010.* 2010 Census Briefs. Retrieved from http://2010.census.gov/news/pdf/20111130_slides.pdf.
17. Davis, S. K., & Troy, R. (1986). Perceptions by the aged of crime, criminals, and the criminal justice system. *Perceptual and Motor Skills, 63*(3), 1149–1150.
18. Brogden, M., & Nijhar, P. (2000). *Crime, abuse, and the elderly.* Portland, OR: Willan Publishing; p. 63.
19. Rothman, M. B., Dunlop, B. D., & Entzel, P. (Eds.). (2000). *Elders, crime, and the criminal justice system, myths, perceptions, and reality in the 21st century.* New York: Springer; pp. 8–9.

RESOURCES

Administration on Aging (www.aoa.gov)

Aging Network Services (www.agingnets.com)

Alzheimer's Association (www.alz.org)

American Association for Retired Persons (www.aarp.org)

American Federation for Aging Research (www.afar.org)

American Geriatrics Society (www.americangeriatrics.org)

American Senior Fitness Association (www.seniorfitness.net)

American Seniors Housing Association (www.seniorshousing.org)

American Society on Aging (www.asaging.org)

Assisted Living Federation of American (www.alfa.org)

Children of Aging Parents (www.caps4caregivers.org)

Family Caregiver Alliance (www.caregiver.org)

Gerontological Society of America (www.geron.org)

Hospice Foundation of America (www.hospicefoundation.org)

Indian Health Service (www.ihs.gov)

Leading Age (www.leadingage.org)

National Aphasia Association (www.aphasia.org)

National Asian Pacific Center on Aging (www.napca.org)

National Association of Area Agencies on Aging (www.n4a.org)

National Association of State Units on Aging (www.nasua.org)

National Caucus and Center on Black Aged (www.ncba-aged.org)

National Center on Elder Abuse (www.ncea.aoa.gov)

National Council on Aging (www.ncoa.org)

National Hispanic Council on Aging (www.nhcoa.org)

National Indian Council on Aging (www.nicoa.org)

National Institute on Aging (www.nih.gov/nia)

National Stroke Association (www.stroke.org)

The National Consumer Voice for Quality Long-Term Care (www.theconsumervoice.org)

U.S. Census Bureau (www.census.gov)

KEY TERMS

active adult community: A community that offers age-restricted housing specifically for seniors who enjoy participating in physical and social activities; also called active adult living and active retirement community

activities of daily living (ADLs): Basic, everyday activities needed to sustain life, such as feeding oneself, walking, dressing, getting up from a chair, and toileting

ageism: Stereotyping of, and discrimination against, people who are old

Alzheimer's care facilities: Specialized facilities for those with signs of Alzheimer's disease or dementia

andropause: A lessening of testosterone and sexual activity in males later in life; also known as male menopause

assisted living: A residential facility that provides residents with assistance with activities of daily living; also known as residential care, board and care, and boarding house

cohorts: Persons who experience the same significant life event (i.e., birth, marriage) within a specified period of time

do not resuscitate (DNR) order: Written documentation giving permission to medical personnel not to attempt resuscitation in the event of cardiac arrest

gerontology: The study of aging

menopause: The process later in a woman's life during which menstruation ceases

old-age dependency ratio: The number of older people for every 100 adults between the ages of 18 and 64

nursing home: A facility where residents receive 24-hour nursing care; also known as a skilled nursing facility, convalescent home, or long-term care facility

PERLS: A concept developed to assist the law enforcement officer when responding to calls for service to older people. PERLS has five components: P—prevention; E—elder population; R—responsiveness, resources, referrals; L—life issues; S—social issues

Chapter Two

Physical Changes with Age

LEARNING OBJECTIVES

1. Identify the general decline in organ systems in older people.
2. Explain how the decline in organ systems in older people affects the law enforcement response to older people.
3. List major diseases common in older people.

Case Study 1

You respond to a call for an assault and robbery. Upon your arrival, you encounter an 80-year-old female, Mrs. Smith, who states she was beaten and robbed of her money. You notice that Mrs. Smith has a large bruise on the back of the head and is bleeding slightly. You suggest having EMS respond to the scene to evaluate her, but Mrs. Smith declines, stating that she is fine and just wants to go home. What do you do?

INTRODUCTION

Understanding age-related changes will help you better understand the aging process. Age-related issues cannot often be separated into categories. How one ages is dependent on many factors, one of which is physical aging, or the changes to the body that occur as one ages.

Understanding the normal physical changes that take place with aging will help you when you encounter older persons and must manage their needs. Additionally, in many places the law enforcement officer is a trained first responder or emergency medical technician and often assists at the scene of emergencies involving older people. In some areas, law enforcement officers serve a dual role in that they provide law enforcement and emergency medical services (EMS). In either case, this chapter will provide an understanding of the aging process as it relates to body systems and common disease states in older people. There are also times when the older person, as the perpetrator, must be managed by law enforcement. Understanding the physical changes with age and disease processes will also aid law enforcement when the latter occurs.

INTEGUMENTARY SYSTEM (THE SKIN)

Wrinkling and loss of resiliency of the skin are the most visible signs of aging. Wrinkling occurs because the skin becomes thinner, drier, less elastic, and more fragile. Subcutaneous fat becomes thinner, making a loosened outer cover for the body. **Elastin**, the substance that makes the skin pliable, and **collagen**, the substance that makes the skin strong, both decrease with age.

The tightened skin of youth allows the **tamponade** (closing/blockage and stopping of bleeding) of subcutaneous injuries (injuries under the skin). With aging skin, however, bleeding may go unnoticed or uncontrolled, producing large hematomas underneath the skin. Injuries to the skin are slow to heal because of diminished capillary blood flow. Sebaceous glands produce less oil, making for dryer skin. Sweat gland activity also decreases, hindering the body's ability to sweat and help regulate heat. With aging, hair follicles produce less **melanin**. Melanin is a pigment that provides color to the skin and hair. Without color, the hair is gray. Hair also becomes thinner.

Pressure Ulcers

Pressure ulcers, also called decubitus ulcers or pressure sores, occur when older people remain stationary, allowing the weight of the body to compress the already thinned skin. With little blood flow to regenerate the cells damaged by the pressure, tissue dies and a sore results.

Pressure ulcers occur mainly in immobile or debilitated persons. Currently, an estimated 1.5 million or more Americans are affected. They are a frequent problem in older adults, and can cause pain and distress for the patient and family. Pressure ulcers are usually localized in areas close to a bony prominence (hard site). Pressure affects blood flow and oxygenation of the tissues between bony prominences and the skin. It first causes failure to oxygenate and deliver nutrients in the area, then accumulation of waste products, and finally tissue damage or death (necrosis). Time is an important factor in this process, as well as pressure. The damage also depends on the person's general health and type of tissue affected. For example, muscle tissue damage can occur after applying enough pressure to affect the blood flow for approximately 2 hours. But with higher pressure, the time required to cause damage decreases. Muscle and subcutaneous tissue are more susceptible to pressure and hydration than epidermal tissues. Therefore, damage usually occurs in the underlying tissues first and will not be clearly visible in the epidermis.

Pressure ulcers commonly occur in areas around the sacrum, greater trochanter, ischial tuberosity, heel, scapula, and fibular head (see **Figure 2-1**). Approximately 95% of pressure ulcers occur in the lower part of the body. Three key factors in addition to pressure contribute to development of pressure ulcers: friction, moisture, and shearing forces (forces sliding past each other in opposite directions). For example, shearing forces and friction occur when a person slides down in bed, stretching subcutaneous tissues and compromising blood supply. Moisture, often from **incontinence** or perspiration, is another important factor. This can lead to **maceration** that makes the skin more susceptible to pressure, friction, or shearing forces.

Any factor that increases exposure to pressure in the hard sites of the body increases the risk for pressure ulcers. Conditions that affect mobility, such as spinal cord injury, brain injury, or neuromuscular disorder, or any acute illness that makes the person less active, increases the risk for a pressure ulcer. Problems with nutrition, fecal or urinary incontinence, and neuropathies also can significantly increase the risk for pressure ulcers.

Pressure ulcers can be classified in four different stages, describing the severity of the sore (see **Table 2-1**). Stage I is **nonblanching erythema**. To evaluate this stage, gently apply pressure to the area of tissue redness with a finger; this will not produce a blanching (whiteness) as a rash does. It is important

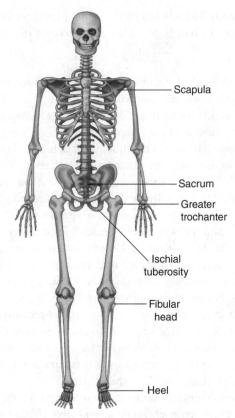

Scapula

Sacrum

Greater
trochanter

Ischial
tuberosity

Fibular
head

Heel

Figure 2-1 Pressure ulcers commonly occur in areas around the scapula, sacrum, greater trochanter, ischial tuberosity, fibular head, and heel.

to note that, in stage I, the damage occurs under the skin, which will be intact. In stage II, the damage extends through the epidermis and dermis. This could appear as a superficial ulcer or blister. In stage III, the epidermis, dermis, and subcutaneous tissues are affected. Fat is visible at the base of the ulcer. In stage IV, the ulcer extends into muscle, tendons, or bone. On occasion, ulcers cannot

Table 2-1 Pressure Ulcer Stages

Stages	Description
I	Nonblanching erythema; damage beneath the skin
II	Blister or ulcer affecting the epidermis and dermis
III	Ulcer exposing the fat down to the fascia
IV	Ulcer exposing muscle or bone

Stages of Pressure Ulcer

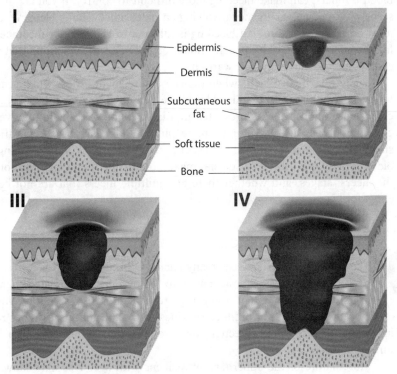

Figure 2-2 A pressure ulcer, or decubitus ulcer, develops when pressure compromises blood supply and thus oxygenation to an area of tissue.
Source: © Alila Sao Mai/ShutterStock, Inc.

be classified because of scar tissue formation or a covering of black dead tissue, **eschar**, which makes it difficult to know how deep the ulcer is. In all cases, in addition to the stage of the ulcer, it is important to describe the surrounding structure, location, appearance, and size (see **Figure 2-2**).

Issues for Law Enforcement

When managing the needs of older persons, care must be taken with the skin. Skin tears can occur easily. If an older person must be taken into custody, care should be taken when applying handcuffs over thin, frail skin, as skin tears can occur. If possible, handcuffs should be applied over sleeves of clothing. If this is not possible, handcuffs should be applied loosely, so as not to cause pressure on the skin. If an older person must be housed or incarcerated, the older person should be provided with a padded surface on which to sit or lie for extended periods. Certain medications, such as warfarin (Coumadin), or other blood thinners, can make bleeding more difficult to control. If you are on the scene of a medical emergency involving an older adult who is bleeding, care must be taken to ensure that bleeding is fully controlled. Since subcutaneous fat becomes thinner, older people should be provided with clothing that will enable them to maintain their warmth.

There may be occasions when the law enforcement officer will be called to investigate cases of possible elder abuse and neglect. A full discussion of elder abuse and neglect is presented in a later chapter. Evaluate the overall condition of the patient's skin: Are there multiple skin tears, bruises in various stages of healing, infestations, rashes, or pressure ulcers? When evaluating an older person with decubitus ulcers, make note of the following: location of the ulcers, stages, and whether there are multiple ulcers that are not being cared for.

RESPIRATORY SYSTEM

The respiratory system sees many changes throughout the lifecycle. All parts of the respiratory system are affected by aging. Age-related changes in the respiratory system result in a predisposition to respiratory illness. Normal activities can produce shortness of breath that necessitates resting. A minor respiratory infection may propel the older person into a life-threatening episode.

Musculature of the upper airway weakens with age. This may allow the tongue and soft tissue of the **oropharynx** to close in easily, narrowing the airway when the older person becomes overtaxed or less responsive. Changes in bones and teeth can alter the shape of the face and mouth. Many older people require dentures or dental appliances to eat. Improperly fitted dental appliances can create an airway obstruction. If an older person is lying on either his/her back or stomach, check the person for loose-fitting dental appliances. If found, these appliances should be removed.

The loss of mechanisms that protect the upper airway is a concern in older adults. These can include a decreased ability to clear secretions, as well as decreased cough and gag reflexes. The cilia that line the airways lessen as one ages, and the innervation of the structures in the airway provide less sensation. Without the ability to maintain the upper airway, aspiration and obstruction are more likely.

The smooth muscle of the lower airway also weakens with age. When a younger person inhales, the airway maintains its shape, allowing air to enter. As these muscles weaken with age, strong inhalation can make the walls of the airway collapse inward and cause inspiratory wheezing. Conversely, strong exhalation can cause expiratory wheezing. The collapsing airways result in low flow rates because less air can move through the smaller airways, and air trapping (incomplete expiration) because air does not completely exit the **alveoli**.

By age 75, the **vital capacity** can decrease to 50% of what it was in younger adulthood. This occurs because of the loss in respiratory muscle mass, increases in the stiffness of the thoracic cage, and decreases in the available surface area for the exchange of air.

Physiologically, vital capacity decreases and **residual volume**, which is the amount of air left in the lungs after the maximum possible amount of air has been expired, increases with age. This leaves stagnant air resting in the alveoli and hampers good gas exchange, which can produce a relative **hypercarbia** and related **acidosis**, even at rest. The spine, ribs, breastbone, and muscles work together to pump air in and out of the lungs—this is **ventilation**. Aging adversely affects ventilatory function. The muscles of the chest wall and the diaphragm weaken with age.

Issues for Law Enforcement

When managing the needs of older people or when the older person is taken into custody, care must be taken to ensure that any respiratory medications the older person is taking are brought along with the individual. Many times, older people who have chronic obstructive pulmonary diseases require supplemental oxygen. If an older person who is on supplemental oxygen requires transport, the person must be transported with his or her oxygen. Older people, especially older persons with preexisting respiratory conditions, should not be transported lying down. Pepper spray should never be used on an older individual. In those older people with existing respiratory conditions, stressful situations can make worse already compromised breathing. A calm approach by the law enforcement officer can have a significant positive impact on the older person's respiratory condition. Older persons who experience any sign of respiratory difficulty should be referred to EMS for evaluation.

CARDIOVASCULAR SYSTEM

Cardiac function declines with age consequent to anatomic and physiologic changes that are largely related to the high incidence of coronary disease caused by **atherosclerosis**. In this disorder, cholesterol and calcium build up inside the walls of the blood vessels, forming plaque. The accumulation of plaque eventually leads to partial or complete blockage of blood flow. Atherosclerotic disease affects more than 60% of people over age 65. Age-related changes typically include a decrease in heart rate, a fall in **cardiac output** (the amount of blood pumped out of the heart in 1 minute) secondary to lowered **stroke volume** (the amount of blood pumped out of the heart in one beat), and the inability to elevate cardiac output to match the demands of the body. **Arrhythmias**, or irregular or abnormal heart rhythms, are common as aging alters the heart's electrical system.

With age, the vascular system becomes stiff, resulting in increases in the systolic blood pressure. As the pressure of systole increases with age, the left ventricle works harder and becomes thicker, similar to what happens to a muscle when it is trained. The muscle also looses its elasticity in this process. The thickening and stiffening of this muscle decreases, filling in the ventricle, thus decreasing the cardiac output. This stiffening also occurs in the heart valves, which may impede normal blood flow into and out of the heart.

Issues for Law Enforcement

As in older persons with an underlying respiratory condition, older people who must be transported by law enforcement or taken into custody should be asked about existing cardiovascular disease. In particular, those with a pre-existing heart condition who require medication must have this medication transported with them.

NERVOUS SYSTEM

Nervous system changes can result in the most debilitating of age-related ailments. The central and peripheral nervous systems see significant changes during life. The brain weight will **atrophy** (shrink) 10–20% by age 80. This age-related shrinkage provides room for the brain to move around when stressed. The shrinkage also produces stretching of the bridging veins that return blood from inside the brain to the **dura matter**. If trauma moves the brain forcibly, the bridging veins can tear and bleed (see **Figure 2-3**). Bleeding can empty into this void, resulting in a **subdural hematoma**, and go unnoticed for some time. This is due to the age-related change—it takes longer for blood to accumulate in the brain before the older person will become symptomatic, unlike a younger adult where signs may be present within minutes (as there is no brain shrinkage in younger adults). Increased intracranial pressure is required for signs of head trauma to be present. Until the void space has been filled, signs will not be present.

There is a selective loss of 5–50% of **neurons**—the cells that make up nerve tissue and receive and transmit impulses—and the remaining neurons shrink in size. Peripheral nerve function slows with aging. Sensation becomes diminished and misinterpreted. This makes for slow reflexes, a contributing cause of trauma. Nerve endings deteriorate, and the ability of the skin to sense the surroundings becomes hindered. Therefore, hot, cold, sharp, and wet items can all become dangerous because the body cannot sense them

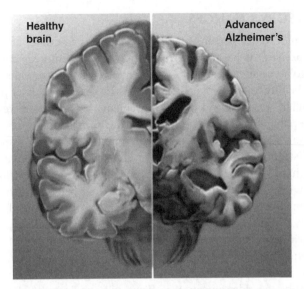

Healthy brain

Advanced Alzheimer's

Figure 2-3 Brain atrophy with age can make tearing of the bridging veins more likely with trauma, as well as creating a space into which bleeding can occur without immediate signs of increased intracranial pressure.

quickly enough. Because of changes in the nervous system, older people do not experience pain in the same fashion as younger adults. For example, pain from an injured area may not be felt in the affected tissue, but rather in the surrounding areas. As another example, the classical presentation of a cardiac event—chest pain with radiation to the neck or arms—may not be the presenting problem in the older adult. Older adults experiencing a cardiac event may present with vague symptoms such as fatigue, nausea, or vague complaints of chest discomfort.

Implications for Law Enforcement

When responding to a call for an assault involving an older person, particularly an older person who has been struck in the head, have the patient evaluated by EMS. There is one important point to keep in mind regarding older people involved in traumatic events: *Less mechanism equals more significant trauma.* In other words, it takes less force to an older person to create significant injury. Additionally, older people who have sustained significant trauma to the head may not present with classic signs of head trauma immediately. Depending upon the severity of the injury, it may take hours or days to manifest. Therefore, any older person with even a minor head injury should be evaluated by EMS.

SENSORY CHANGES

At times, older persons may be eyewitnesses to crime, or crime victims themselves. As part of an investigation, the law enforcement officer must try to ascertain a description of a perpetrator from an older person. This can be difficult due to age-related sensory changes in older people.

Pupillary reaction and ocular movements become more restricted with age. The pupils are generally smaller in older people, and opacity of the eye's lens lowers visual acuity and makes the pupils sluggish to respond to light. Visual distortions are also common in older people. Thickening of the lens makes it harder for the eye to focus, especially at close range. If the older person is a witness, ascertain how far away the older person was from the scene or incident. Peripheral fields of vision become narrower and there is greater sensitivity to glare, which leads to a constricted visual field.

Hearing loss is about four times more common than loss of vision. Older people often have the greatest loss at high frequencies. With age, changes in several structures of hearing produce loss of high frequency hearing. When interrogating the older person, the officer with the deepest voice may do best! If the older person wears a hearing aid, allow the older person to put it in before beginning any questioning.

MUSCULOSKELETAL SYSTEM

The musculoskeletal system weakens and atrophies with age. Muscle fibers become smaller and fewer, motor neurons decline in number, and strength declines, but most older people maintain the ability to carry out daily activities. The ligaments and cartilages of the joints lose their elasticity. Cartilage also goes through degenerative changes with aging, contributing to arthritis.

Muscle mass decreases over time and is replaced by fat. This increase in fat also alters the body's capacity to use some drugs. Alcohol is distributed in lean tissue. Because there is less lean tissue in older adults, the blood level rises more quickly.

The stooped posture of older people comes from atrophy of the supporting structures of the body. Two out of every three older people will show some degree of **kyphosis**. Kyphosis is what gives some older people a humpback appearance (see **Figure 2-4**). Lost height in older people generally results from compression in the spinal column, first in the disks, and then from the process of **osteoporosis** in the vertebral bodies. Osteoporosis occurs as the skeleton ages. Postmenopausal osteoporosis is by far the most common form. Clinically significant postmenopausal osteoporosis, present in one-third of older women, is the basic cause of vertebral body collapse, hip fractures, and forearm fractures in this group.

Figure 2-4 Kyphosis is seen to some degree in two of three older people.
Source: © Walker & Steps/Thinkstock.

MEDICAL CONDITIONS COMMON IN OLDER PEOPLE

This section discusses medical conditions common in older people.

Dementia

Disease is not a normal part of aging. So too, cognitive decline is not a normal part of aging. Dementia is defined as an acquired persistent impairment in intellectual function that affects three or more of the following areas:

- Memory
- Emotions/personality
- Visual-spatial skills
- Language
- Cognition (calculation, intelligence, judgment)

Dementia is a disorder that can go unrecognized, as it has a slow, gradual progression that is often mistaken for growing old. It is estimated that dementia affects 10% of people over age 65, 20% of people from age 75 to 84, and almost 50% of people over age 85.[1] The most common primary type of dementia is Alzheimer's disease. Sadly, Alzheimer's is a progressively debilitating disease. **Table 2-2** compares early warning signs of Alzheimer's disease with normal mental lapses.

Table 2-2 Alzheimer's Disease Versus Normal Behavior: Warning Signs

Normal Behavior	Symptoms of Disease
Temporarily forgetting things	Permanently forgetting recent events; asking the same questions repeatedly
Inability to do some challenging tasks	Inability to do routine tasks, such as making and serving a meal
Forgetting unusual or complex words	Forgetting simple words
Getting lost in a strange city	Getting lost in one's own block
Becoming momentarily distracted and failing to watch a child	Forgetting that a child is in one's care and leaving the house
Inability to balance a checkbook	Forgetting what the numbers in a checkbook mean and what to do with them
Misplacing everyday items	Putting things in inappropriate places where one cannot usefully retrieve them, e.g., a wristwatch in a fishbowl
Occasional mood changes	Rapid, dramatic mood swings and personality changes; loss of initiative

Source: Data from Papalia, D. E., Camp, C., & Feldman, R. D. (1996). *Adult development and aging.* New York: McGraw-Hill; p. 138.

Alzheimer's Disease and Law Enforcement[2]

Instances where the law enforcement officer might encounter an Alzheimer's patient include:

- *Wandering*—can be lost anywhere, even on their own street as they can no longer learn landmarks
- *Indecent exposure*—will react to feelings, take off clothes if too warm, urinate when needed, etc.
- *Shoplifting*—will forget to pay for things, accuse others of stealing
- *Appear intoxicated*—has problems with language, poor coordination
- *Automobile accidents*—poor judgment; cannot remember directions; may leave the scene of an accident, forgetting what happened
- *False reports*—may report an intruder who turns out to be a spouse; may report thefts that did not occur

How to recognize an Alzheimer's disease patient:

- *Identification labels*—look for Safe Return bracelet, clothing labels, etc.
- *Confusion/disorientation*—nothing is familiar, may be agitated
- *Inappropriate dress*—not dressed according to weather, buttons mismatched

- *Repeated response*—"I need to go to work," "What time is it?"
- *Delusions*—persistent incorrect belief, may believe spouse is trying to hurt them or steal from them
- *Problem with short-term memory*—present address not known
- *Age*—usually over age 65, but can strike in people in their 50s

General helping strategies:

- Keep the climate "cool," be nonthreatening, reassuring
- Avoid restraints, if possible
- Talk one-on-one, avoid crowds
- Make communication simple
- Ask questions that can be answered with a simple "yes" or "no"
- Don't offer choices as the person can no longer reason
- If attempts at communications are not successful, wait a few minutes and try again
- Be patient

General suggestions when encountering a lost or wandering Alzheimer's patient:

- Make the person as comfortable as possible. He or she may be inappropriately dressed and cold, or need to go to the bathroom. If the person has been missing for some time or out in the cold, he or she may need medical attention. Consider the need for EMS.
- If possible, get the person's name and address. However, this may not be correct, as he or she may give childhood information.
- If unable to determine the person's address, make a description of the person, and contact local nursing homes, day care centers, hospital emergency rooms, or the local Alzheimer's office. The local Alzheimer's office may have the lost person's information on file.
- When reuniting the lost person with family members, suggest the importance of the Safe Return bracelet and refer the family to the local Alzheimer's office.

The Alzheimer's Safe Return program helps identify, locate, and return persons who are memory impaired due to Alzheimer's disease or related disorders. The programs provides: an identity bracelet or necklace, clothing labels, and wallet cards to identify the memory impaired person; registration in a national database; a 24-hour toll-free 800 number to contact when a person is lost or found; access to the National Crime Information Center's electronic clearinghouse of crime data (see **Figure 2-5**).

Malnutrition

Older Americans, due to many environmental, social, economic, and physical changes of aging, are at disproportionate risk for poor nutrition with

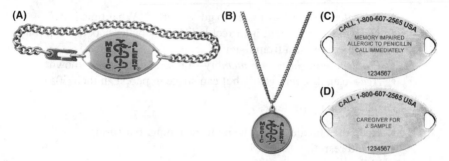

Figure 2-5 MedicAlert + Alzheimer's Association Safe Return program. (A) Bracelet. (B) Necklace. (C) Back of emblem for person with Alzheimer's disease. (D) Back of emblem for caregiver.

corresponding adverse affects on their health and vitality. A report of the U.S. Senate Committee on Education and labor stated that 85% of the older population has one or more chronic conditions that have been documented to benefit from nutrition interventions.[3]

Malnutrition is the condition that develops when the body does not get the right amount of the vitamins, minerals, and other nutrients it needs to maintain healthy tissues and organ function. Determination of when a food or fluid problem exists in an older person can present a challenge. When malnutrition or dehydration is suspected, it is useful to ask the older person, or his/her caregiver about symptoms of illness, such as weight loss, poor appetite, fever, confusion, or diarrhea; about chewing or swallowing problems; about the presence of illness that may affect oral intake such as depression, dementia, or stroke; about ill-fitting dentures; and about the use of alcohol or medications that affect eating and body water.

One of the most common reasons for undernutrition in the community-dwelling older person is a social one: Ask the person if he or she has difficulty getting groceries, preparing meals, paying for groceries, or frequently eats alone. If this is the case, know what resources are available in your community, and make the appropriate referrals.

Cardiovascular Disease

Cardiovascular diseases are the most common causes of morbidity and mortality among people age 65 and older. Coronary artery disease and congestive heart failure are at the top of the list. Coronary artery disease accounts for approximately 70–80% of deaths among men and women of this age group. Congestive heart failure is the most common cause of hospitalizations among older people.[4]

When an occlusion of a coronary artery occurs due to a rupture and thrombosis of an atherosclerotic plaque, decreased blood flow to the heart muscle causes a decrease in oxygen perfusion to the tissue. This can produce ischemia, pain, or, if the decreased perfusion is substantial and sustained, death of the heart muscle—**myocardial infarction (MI)**. Older people tend to be able to tolerate ischemia better than younger people due to collateral circulation, which is the development of new blood vessels around tissue that is subjected to low flow rates of blood. The purpose of collateral circulation is to increase perfusion. The new vessels allow blood to shunt around occluded areas and supply ischemic tissue with oxygen. Older people may not have the typical presentations of MI as younger adults may have, such as chest pain with radiation to the jaw or arm. Atypical MI presentations in older people can manifest with such symptoms as difficulty breathing, worsening of heart failure, fluid in the lungs, fainting, stroke, dizziness, sudden onset of confusion, palpitations, persistent nausea and vomiting, altered thinking process, excessive weakness, and changes in eating patterns.

Congestive heart failure is a disease process in which the heart is not able to maintain an output adequate to meet the metabolic needs of the body. Essentially, the heart muscle fails to pump sufficiently. This occurs as the aging heart and vessels undergo structural and physiological changes, particularly stiffening of the muscle. There are many ways to categorize congestive heart failure, but for our purposes here, the easiest is left and right sided. Right-sided heart failure manifests as excess fluid backing up into the body. The signs of right-sided hear failure include distention of neck veins, enlarged liver, fluid in the abdomen, and **peripheral edema**. The most common cause of right-sided failure is left-sided failure. Left-sided heart failure causes fluid to back up into the lungs and, eventually, to the right side of the heart. The primary sign of left-sided heart failure is **pulmonary edema** (a build up of fluid in the lungs).

The most common complaint with acute or worsening congestive heart failure is shortness of breath. Individuals may also experience peripheral edema, cough, or fatigue. A person may report difficulty breathing when lying down or on exertion, as well as recent weight gain.

If you observe any of these symptoms when encountering an older person, have EMS respond to the scene. The patient will require prehospital treatment (oxygen, medications for fluid overload, and cardiac monitoring), as well as definitive hospital treatment.

Stroke

Stroke is the most prevalent of the primary neurological problems in older people, and is a leading cause of death. The risk of stroke doubles with every decade over the age of 55. The main risk factors for stroke are both preventable and treatable. High blood pressure, heart disease, smoking, diabetes, and high levels of fats in the blood, including cholesterol, are the most common and significant contributors to risk of stroke. Other important risk factors are also controllable, such as obesity and sedentary lifestyle.

There are two main types of stroke: ischemic and hemorrhagic. About 70–80% of all strokes are ischemic, and the other 20–30% are hemorrhagic.[5] Hemorrhages occur when a blood vessel within the brain tears and produces bleeding in or around the brain. Although hemorrhagic stroke is less common than ischemia, it is often more lethal. Ischemic stroke typically occurs when a clot obstructs blood flow in an artery that supplies a portion of the brain. The clot may have formed within the artery at a specific site, or develop elsewhere—in the heart, for example—and broken off, traveled, and finally lodged in an artery serving part of the brain. Brain tissue supplied by this artery is thus deprived of oxygen and glucose, resulting in immediate brain tissue death.

The symptoms of ischemic stroke include:

- Weakness or paralysis on one side of the body
- Numbness on one side of the body
- Slurred speech
- Aphasia (inability to speak or inappropriately naming words)
- Confusion
- Convulsions
- Visual disturbances
- Incontinence (loss of bladder control)
- Numbness of the face
- Headache
- Dizziness

The symptoms of hemorrhagic stroke include:

- Headache (often described as the worst headache of the person's life)
- Nausea and vomiting
- Change in mental status (the person may become restless, agitated, or confused)
- Mental status changes may progress from alert to lethargic

Ischemic stroke may develop slowly, whereas hemorrhagic stroke may develop rapidly. Both forms of stroke can be life threatening. It is important to determine the exact onset of symptoms. This can be vital to stroke treatment. A mini-stroke, or **transient ischemic attack (TIA)** is an episode of cerebral dysfunction that lasts from several minutes to hours. A TIA is an important indication of an impending stroke. The signs and symptoms of a TIA are the same as that of a stroke—weakness, paralysis, speech disturbances, and numbness to the face.

Law enforcement officers can play a pivotal role in the outcome of stroke patients. The American Stroke Association has developed a Stroke Chain of Survival consisting of four components:

1. Rapid recognition and reaction to stroke warning signs
2. Rapid start of prehospital care

3. Rapid EMS system transport and hospital notification
4. Rapid diagnosis and treatment at the hospital

As a law enforcement officer, being able to rapidly recognize the signs and symptoms of a stroke and initiating EMS can have a profound impact on the outcome of the stroke patient. The important point to keep in mind is this: *time is brain.*

Issues for Law Enforcement

When you encounter a medical emergency in the older person, rapid recognition and prompt initiation of EMS will prove valuable. There are other valuable things that you can do while awaiting EMS. Ascertain from the older person, family, or caregiver the older person's complete medical history. Gather together and make a list of the older person's medications (including prescription, over-the-counter, and herbal medicines). Also inquire if the person has any allergies to medicines. If time permits, find out how long the person has been experiencing his or her signs and symptoms, and what the person's normal activity level is. Just doing these simple things will save time and be of great service to the EMS providers, and ultimately, to the older person themselves.

Chronic Obstructive Pulmonary Disease (COPD)

Chronic obstructive pulmonary disease (COPD) is a slow process of dilation and disruption of the airways and alveoli caused by chronic bronchial obstruction. An estimated 12.1 million adults 25 years or older are reported to have the diagnosis of COPD. It is the fourth leading cause of death.[6] Three conditions are commonly associated with COPD—chronic **bronchitis, emphysema**, and **asthma**. Chronic bronchitis is an ongoing irritation of the **trachea** (the windpipe; the main trunk for air passing to and from the lungs) and **bronchi** (the two main branches leading from the trachea to the lungs). With bronchitis, excessive mucous is constantly produced, obstructing small airways and alveoli. Protective cells and lung mechanisms that remove foreign particles are destroyed, further weakening the airways. Chronic oxygenation problems can also lead to right-sided heart failure and fluid retention, such as **edema** (the presence of large amounts of fluid between the cells in body tissues, causing swelling of the affected area) to the legs. Pneumonia develops easily when the air passages are persistently obstructed. Ultimately, repeated episodes of irritation and pneumonia cause scarring in the lungs and some dilation of the alveoli, leading to COPD.

Emphysema is a loss of the elastic material around the air spaces as a result of chronic stretching of the alveoli when inflamed airways obstruct easy expulsion of gases. Normally, lungs act like a spongy balloon that is inflated; once they are inflated, they will naturally recoil because of their elastic nature, expelling gas rapidly. However, when they are constantly obstructed or when the "balloons'" elasticity is diminished, air is no longer expelled rapidly, and the walls of the alveoli eventually fall apart, leaving large "holes" in the lung that resemble a large air pocket or cavity.

Most patients with COPD have elements of both chronic bronchitis and emphysema. Some people will have more elements of one condition than the other; few people will have only emphysema or bronchitis. Therefore, most people with COPD will chronically produce sputum, have a chronic cough, and have difficulty expelling air from their lungs, with long expiration phases and wheezing.

Asthma is an acute spasm of the smaller air passages associated with excessive mucous production and with swelling of the mucous lining of the respiratory passages. Asthma produces a characteristic wheezing as people attempt to exhale through partially obstructed air passages. These same air passages open easily during inspiration. In some cases, the airways are so blocked that no air movement can be heard.

When encountering people with COPD who are in distress, EMS should be called to evaluate the person.

Parkinson's Disease[7]

Parkinson's disease is a progressive neurologic disorder caused by a degeneration of neurons in the brain. The disease commonly occurs in older people, although it can occur in younger adults. Parkinson's disease occurs throughout the world in all populations. Men have a slightly higher prevalence rate than women. The mean age of onset is approximately 60 years. It usually occurs in people over 50 years of age; onset before age 25 is uncommon. The four main features that clinically characterize Parkinson's disease are:

1. Resting tremor (shaking back and forth when the limb is relaxed)
2. **Bradykinesia** (slowness of movement)
3. Rigidity (stiffness, or resistance of the limb to passive movement when the limb is relaxed)
4. Postural instability (poor balance)

Other common signs include shuffling gait, stooped posture, difficulty with fine coordinated movements, and **micrographia** (small handwriting). Other features include constipation, sweating, cognitive decline (dementia), depression, and sensory complaints, including pain in muscles.

Approximately 60–90% of those with Parkinson's disease exhibit speech or voice abnormalities, including reduced volume, diminished articulation, and decreased variation in tone, tremor, or hoarseness. Those with Parkinson's may lose clarity of speech, and articulation of consonants is less precise. Particularly difficult are the sounds of the letters k, g, f, v, s, and z, as there is loss of dexterity in the muscles involved in articulation. Decreased control and strength of airflow and rigidity of the laryngeal (voice) muscles may also contribute to speech difficulty.

ASSESSING FUNCTIONAL ACTIVITY

Being able to perform one's **activities of daily living (ADLs)** is essential to the wellbeing of the older person. Activities of daily living include the ability to perform basic, everyday functions needed to sustain life, such as feeding oneself, walking, dressing, getting up from a chair, and toileting (see **Figure 2-6**). If, during your interaction with the older person, you observe that the older person is not able to perform one or more of these functions, you should refer the older person for appropriate services, or arrange for in-home services. As a law enforcement officer, whenever you encounter an older person, you should assess the older person's ability to perform his or her activities of daily living. An inability to perform one or more of these daily functions can significantly diminish the older person's quality of life. Making appropriate referrals for in-home care, meals, or other services will significantly improve the quality of elderly lives.

Figure 2-6 Being able to perform activities of daily living are essential to the older person.
Source: Courtesy of John Valentini, Jr.

Case Study 2

While patrolling a suburban neighborhood on a Sunday afternoon in December, you notice an elderly man wandering the street. The man is dressed only in a bathrobe and slippers. The temperature is a chilly 42°F. When you approach the elderly man, he states he is on his way to work. He has no identification, and does not know where he lives. Your dispatcher advises that there is no report of a missing subject. You suggest that he come with you to the precinct, but the elderly man becomes agitated and insists that he must go to work.

What do you do?

SUMMARY

As we get older, our body undergoes many changes. These changes alter the way the body can compensate for the stress of illness and injury. It is important for the law enforcement officer to understand the physical changes associated with normal aging in order to better anticipate the older person's response to changing conditions.

CASE STUDY SUMMARIES

Case Study 1 Summary

Though Mrs. Smith is conscious, and states that she is fine and just wants to go home, you must insist that she be evaluated by EMS and ultimately transported to the emergency department. This is recommended primarily from a medical perspective, because this 80-year-old woman has experienced age-related changes to her nervous system that may prevent immediate signs and symptoms of a head injury, even a relatively severe blow to the head. Secondarily, you want to have the injuries documented by the emergency department physician.

Case Study 2 Summary

The first thing you must do is keep the situation calm, and try to effectively communicate with the older person. This may be difficult, since you are not familiar with the older person. Obviously, the man is not dressed appropriately for the weather, and does not know where he is. You have two concerns: What underlying medical problem does this person have, and how long has he been outside dressed in this fashion? You know that as a condition of aging, the subcutaneous fat becomes thinner. You should be concerned about hypothermia as well. Every attempt should be made to have the older person come with you either to the precinct, or to the local emergency department for evaluation—preferably to the emergency department, since you do not know what medical condition led this person to engage in wandering behavior—that is, is there something acute happening, or is this an expected occurrence of a preexisting condition?

While you never want to lie to anyone you encounter in the course of your duties, you have to tell this person that you will drive him to work, while ensuring that you end up at the emergency department. If this person has a chronic medical problem, the emergency department staff may know him. Once at the emergency department, you can begin the search for his residence.

In your investigation to find the older man's residence, you contact the Alzheimer's Association to provide the city where the person was found and a description. The older person is registered under the Safe Return program, and you are able to ascertain an address. In the meantime, a family has reported a missing person matching your victim's description. You advise your dispatcher to have the family report to the emergency department. What you learn is that while the family was attending church services, the older person simply wandered out of the house. The family says that he has some dementia, but has never done this before.

This is a common scenario. While your duty has been fulfilled in reuniting family with the lost person, you must take things a step further. Since you know that Alzheimer's is a progressively debilitating disease, you must stress to the family the importance of supervision of their older family member, and the criticalness of never leaving the person alone.

ENDNOTES

1. Dial, L. K. (1999). *Conditions of aging.* Baltimore, MD: Lippincott, Williams & Wilkins; p. 29.
2. Alzheimer's Association. (2006). *Safe return: Alzheimer's disease guide for law enforcement.* Chicago, IL: Alzheimer's Association. Retrieved from http://www.alz.org/national/documents/safereturn_lawenforcement.pdf.
3. U.S. Congress, Committee on Education and Labor. (1995, May 16). *Compilation of the Older Americans Act of 1965 and related provisions as amended through Dec. 29, 1981.* 97th Congress, First Session.
4. National Center for Health Statistics. (2011, February). *Health, United States, 2010: With special feature on death and dying.* Hyattsville, MD. Retrieved from http://www.cdc.gov/nchs/data/hus/hus10.pdf.
5. Atlas of Stroke Mortality. *Racial and ethnic disparities in stroke.* Centers for Disease Control and Prevention. Retrieved from http://www.cdc.gov/dhdsp/atlas/stroke_mortality_atlas/docs/Section_one.pdf.
6. American Lung Association Lung Disease Data: 2008. *Chronic obstructive pulmonary disease (COPD).* Retrieved from http://www.lung.org/assets/documents/publications/lung-disease-data/ldd08-chapters/LDD-08-COPD.pdf.
7. Hauser, R. A., & Zesiewicz, T. A. (2000). *Parkinson's disease: Questions and answers* (3rd ed.). Pine Grove, FL: Merit Publishing International.

RESOURCES

Alzheimer's Association (www.alz.org)
American Stroke Association (www.strokeassociation.org)

KEY TERMS

acidosis: An actual or relative increase in the acidity of blood due to an accumulation of acids or an excessive loss of bicarbonate; the hydrogen ion concentration of the fluid is increased, lowering the pH

activities of daily living (ADLs): Basic, everyday activities needed to sustain life, such feeding oneself, walking, dressing, getting up from a chair, and toileting

alveoli: Air sacs in the lungs

arrhythmia: An abnormal or irregular heart rhythm resulting from an electrical disturbance in conduction

asthma: An acute spasm of the smaller air passages, called bronchioles, associated with excessive mucous production and with swelling of the mucous lining of the respiratory passages

atherosclerosis: A disorder in which cholesterol and calcium build up inside the walls of the blood vessels, forming plaque, which eventually leads to partial or complete blockage of blood flow. An atherosclerotic plaque can also become a site where blood clots can form, break off, and embolize elsewhere in the circulation

atrophy: Wasting or shrinkage of an organ

bradykinesia: Slowness of movement

bronchi: The two main branches leading from the trachea to the lungs

bronchitis: An acute or chronic inflammation of the lung that may damage lung tissue; usually associated with cough and production of sputum and, depending on its cause, sometimes fever

cardiac output: Amount of blood pumped out of the heart in 1 minute

chronic obstructive pulmonary disease (COPD): A slow process of dilation and disruption of the airways and alveoli caused by chronic bronchial obstruction

collagen: The substance that makes the skin and other connective tissues strong; both collagen and elastin decrease with age

dura matter: A fibrous connective tissue membrane, the outermost of the meninges covering the spinal cord and brain

edema: The presence of large amounts of fluid between the cells in body tissues, causing swelling of the affected area

elastin: The substance that makes the skin pliable; both elastin and collagen decrease with age

emphysema: A disease of the lungs in which there is extreme dilation and eventual destruction of the pulmonary alveoli with poor air exchange of oxygen and carbon dioxide; it is one form of chronic obstructive pulmonary disease

eschar: A covering of black, dead tissue; this can form over a pressure ulcer, making it difficult to determine how deep the ulcer is

hypercarbia: Increased carbon dioxide in the bloodstream

incontinence: Involuntary leakage of urine or feces

kyphosis: A condition in which the back becomes hunched over due to an abnormal increased curvature of the spine

maceration: The process of softening a solid by steeping in a fluid

melanin: The pigment that provides color to the hair and skin

micrographia: Small handwriting

myocardial infarction (MI): Death of heart muscle caused by hypoxia as a result of obstruction of blood flow to the heart

neurons: Cells that make up nerve tissue and receive and transmit impulses

nonblanching erythema: Tissue redness that does not blanch (turn white) when pressed with a finger

oropharynx: The central portion of the pharynx (the passageway for air from the nasal cavity to the larynx and for food from the mouth to the esophagus) lying between the soft palate and the upper portion of the epiglottis (the uppermost cartilage of the larynx, located immediately posterior to the root of the tongue)

osteoporosis: A condition characterized by a decrease in bone mass, leading to a reduction in bone strength and a greater susceptibility to fracture, even after minimal trauma

peripheral edema: Swelling in the abdomen or lower extremities; can be a sign of right-sided heart failure

pulmonary edema: A build up of fluid in the lungs, usually as a result of congestive heart failure

residual volume: The amount of air left in the lungs after the maximum possible amount of air has been expired

stroke volume: The amount of blood pumped out of the heart in one beat

subdural hematoma: Bleeding into the area between the brain and the meningeal layer called the dura matter

tamponade: Closing or blockage in order to stop bleeding

trachea: The windpipe; the main trunk for air passing to and from the lungs

transient ischemic attack (TIA): A disorder of the brain in which brain cells temporarily stop working because of insufficient oxygen, causing stroke-like symptoms that resolve completely within 24 hours of onset

ventilation: Movement of air in and out of the lungs produced by chest wall motion

vital capacity: Volume of air moved during the deepest inspiration and expiration

Chapter Three

Psychosocial Issues of Aging

LEARNING OBJECTIVES

1. Understand the psychosocial changes that occur with age.
2. Understand depression in older people.
3. Discuss suicide in the older population.
4. Understand issues involving the older driver.
5. Understand alcoholism and drug abuse in the older population.
6. Discuss death and dying in the older population.

Case Study 1

You are dispatched along with EMS to a nursing home for a reported cardiac arrest. You are the first to arrive on the scene. As you enter the patient's room, you encounter Mr. Smith, an 87-year-old man, lying in bed; he is unconscious, unresponsive, not breathing, and has no pulse. You see a bracelet on Mr. Smith's wrist indicating do not resuscitate (DNR) status.
What should you do?

INTRODUCTION

As a law enforcement officer, you respond daily to the needs of older people. But how does aging affect one's perception of things—particularly of crime, and of being a victim? What are some of the social issues that, as a law enforcement officer, you will encounter with older people? How will you respond to these issues? This chapter will provide an understanding of what the psychosocial issues are and offer solutions in their management.

PSYCHOLOGICAL CHANGES WITH AGE

The psychology of aging is a complicated subject. Many factors that influence and complicate the psychology of aging, including normal age-related psychological changes, disease processes (both physical and emotional), and how society views the aging process. If an older person is viewed as more rigid and cautious than a younger person, is this an age-related psychological change or a generational difference? Consider the older person who has lived through the depression and is hesitant or resistant of a financial investment, even when the return is predictable and stable. This hesitation may be a cohort difference relating to an earlier time in life.

Cognition

Cognition refers to mental processes used for perceiving, remembering, and thinking. Cognitive abilities are the greatest when people are in their 30s and 40s. Cognitive abilities stay about the same until the late 50s and early 60s, at which point they begin to decline, but only to a small degree. The effects of cognitive changes are not usually noticed until the 70s and beyond. It should be noted that these changes do not happen to everyone. Within each age group, however, there were wide variations in cognitive ability. Disease processes and overall intellectual ability will have a bearing on cognition in later life, and vary from person to person. Remember, older people are the most heterogeneous of all cohorts.

Memory

Memory is a complex function that has been divided into different types. Only some of these are affected by age. Difficulties that occur with memory are usually small and vary widely from person to person, making generalizations difficult.

Further complicating the memory picture are the different methods by which different researchers categorize memory. However, it is widely believed that one type of memory, called working memory, is most affected by age. Working memory is the retention of information that must be manipulated or transformed in some way.

Conscious mental processing goes on in working memory. It requires taking information from the environment and from memory stores and accomplishing a mental task. An example is paying a restaurant check. The amount of the check is kept in memory while figuring out which bills to use to pay the check, how much change is due, and how much tip to leave. Everyone has limits on how much they can keep in working memory at one time. As people get older, complex mental tasks can become more difficult if they require too much information to be held in memory in order to process it.

Some researchers postulate that problems with working memory are related to reduced speed of information processing, which reduces the efficiency of working memory. One popular method for categorizing memory divides it into *implicit memory* and *explicit memory*. Implicit memory is the retention of skills and reflexes that have been acquired, such as the procedures for driving a car. Implicit memory generally remains intact throughout life. Explicit memory is the conscious remembering of facts and events. These memories are more vulnerable to age-related decline.

Older adults may have increasing difficulty with word retrieval—that is, recalling the name of a familiar person or object. The reasons for this are unknown. In general, memory tasks that are complex and require manipulating a lot of new information quickly become more difficult to retrieve from memory. However, knowledge that has been accumulated over a lifetime is generally retained. Well practiced skills and abilities remain intact. Vocabulary usually continues to increase throughout life.

Personality

Personality, like intelligence, is complex—hard to define and measure. Personality is generally defined as the essence of a person—what makes someone a unique, recognizable individual. Longitudinal studies of personality traits found that personality traits remain relatively constant throughout one's adult life.

One thing to keep in mind is that disease is not a normal part of aging. Do not assume that because someone is old that he or she cannot reason and discuss issues intelligently. Older people in distress, however, do require more time to process information and respond to questions.

Attitude Tip—Disease is not a normal part of aging.

DEPRESSION

Depression is a common, often debilitating psychiatric disorder experienced by approximately 5 million older American adults. It should be noted that depression is not a normal part of aging any more than it is at any age. Aging is a time of loss. Losses in the older person include the death of a spouse, other family members, and friends; loss of employment through retirement or disability; loss of strength, stamina, or mobility; loss of a lifelong home; loss of sensory ability; and loss of social support, power, purpose, and independence. These losses can lead to depression. Some of these losses are discussed in the following sections.

Table 3-1 is a modified geriatric depression scale that law enforcement officers can use as a guide in evaluating depression in older adults. Respondents should give the best answer for how they have felt over the past week.

SUICIDE

The highest rates of suicide in America occur in the older population. The suicide rates for men rise with age, most significantly after age 65. The rate of suicide in men age 65 and older is seven times that of females who are 65 and older. The suicide rates for women peak between the ages of 45–54 years old, and again after age 75. It is estimated that as many as half of all suicides committed by older people go unreported, mistakenly classified as accidents, death by natural causes, or some other form of trauma.[1] **Table 3-2** lists the suicide rate (per 100,000 persons in each age group) by age (65 and older) and sex for 2007.

Most of the Southern and Western states have rates that are higher than the U.S. average rate for those 65 and older. **Figure 3-1** shows state suicide rates for ages 65 and older (per 100,000 population).

Older people who attempt suicide choose much more lethal means than younger victims and generally have diminished recuperative capacity to survive an attempt. For the young, it is estimated that there are 100 to 200 attempts for every committed suicide; in the older population, that figure drops to only four attempts to one completion.[2] More than 71% of completed suicides in

Table 3-1 Geriatric Depression Scale

1. Are you basically satisfied with your life?	Yes/**No**
2. Have you dropped many of your activities and interests?	**Yes**/No
3. Do you feel that your life is empty?	**Yes**/No
4. Do you often get bored?	**Yes**/No
5. Are you in good spirits most of the time?	Yes/**No**
6. Are you afraid that something bad is going to happen to you?	**Yes**/No
7. Do you feel happy most of the time?	Yes/**No**
8. Do you often feel helpless?	**Yes**/No
9. Do you prefer to stay home most of the time rather than go out and do new things?	**Yes**/No
10. Do you feel that you have more problems with memory than most?	**Yes**/No
11. Do you think that it is wonderful to be alive now?	Yes/**No**
12. Do you feel pretty worthless the way you are now?	**Yes**/No
13. Do you feel full of energy?	Yes/**No**
14. Do you feel your situation is hopeless?	**Yes**/No
15. Do you think that most people are better off than you are?	**Yes**/No

Scoring: Answers in **bold** indicate depression. Score 1 point for each bolded answer.
A score > 5 points is suggestive of depression.
A score ≥ 10 points is almost always indicative of depression.
A score > 15 points should warrant a follow-up comprehensive assessment.

Source: Adapted from the University of Rochester from Yesavage, J. (1986). Use of the self-rating depression scale in the elderly. In L. W. Poon (Ed.), *Handbook for clinical memory assessment of older adults.* Washington, DC: American Psychological Association.

Table 3-2 Suicide Rate (per 100,000 Persons in Each Age Group) by Age and Sex, United States, 2007

Age	Total	Sex	
		Male	Female
All ages	13.27	21.34	5.51
65–69 years	12.85	22.40	4.48
70–74 years	12.33	22.66	3.88
75–79 years	16.38	33.12	4.05
80–84 years	16.03	35.80	3.54
85 years and older	15.56	41.81	3.10

Source: Data from U.S. Department of Health and Human Services, Centers for Disease Control and Prevention, National Center for Injury Prevention and Control.

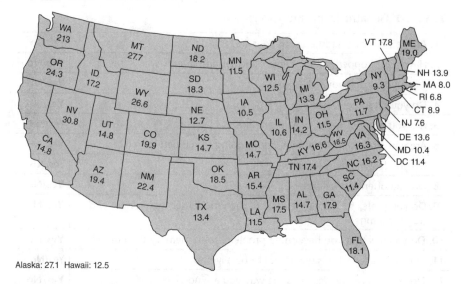

Figure 3-1 State suicide rates ages 65 and above, 2007 (per 100,000 population).
Source: Data from Centers for Disease Control, 2007.

older persons involve firearms, as compared to just over 55% in the general population.[3] **Table 3-3** lists the firearm suicide rate (per 100,000 persons in each age group) for those age 65 and older from 2000–2007.

Table 3-3 Firearm Suicide Rate (per 100,000 Persons in Each Age Group) by Age, United States, 2000–2007

	Total	65–69 years	70–74 years	75–79 years	80–84 years	85 years and older
2000	6.86	8.30	10.26	12.37	14.04	13.16
2001	6.87	8.99	10.25	12.36	14.14	12.16
2002	6.89	8.83	10.69	12.32	14.35	12.10
2003	6.74	8.55	10.07	11.86	13.09	11.85
2004	6.61	7.98	9.83	12.17	12.32	11.08
2005	6.65	8.17	9.89	11.92	13.57	11.29
2006	6.54	8.54	9.40	11.77	12.19	10.93
2007	6.65	8.75	8.81	12.52	11.72	10.99

Source: Data from U.S. Department of Health and Human Services, Centers for Disease Control and Prevention, National Center for Injury Prevention and Control.

Table 3-4 Methods of Completed Suicides in Older Persons

Type	Percent
Firearms	71.9%
Poisoning	11.1%
Suffocation (hanging)	10.8%
Falling	1.7%
Drowning	1.1%
Fire	0.5%

Source: Data from Centers for Disease Control, 2007.

Males of all age groups are more than four times more likely to complete suicide than females, yet females attempt suicide three times as often. The discrepancy in the attempts to completions ratio arises because males tend to use firearms more than 60% of the time, whereas females use other, less lethal means (such as an overdose) in most of their attempts. Widowed white males are at particularly high risk, with suicide rates almost double the average for all groups. **Table 3-4** shows the methods of completed suicides in older persons.

Characteristics of elderly suicide include:

- Fewer warnings of intent
- Attempts are more planned, determined
- Less likely to survive a suicide attempt due to use of more violent and immediate methods
- More likely to have suffered from a depressive diagnosis prior to their suicide compared to younger counterparts

Major depression is a significant predictor of suicide in older people, and is a widely underrecognized and undertreated medical disease (see **Figure 3-2**). Several studies have found that many older people who commit suicide have visited a primary care physician very close to the time of the suicide: 20% on the same day, 40% within 1 week, and 70% within 1 month.[4]

There are no published studies reporting base rates or documentation of the characteristics of homicide–suicide cases involving older adults. The anecdotal literature has described homicide–suicides in older couples, interpreting them as dual suicide pacts, dyadic deaths, or homicide–suicide with altruistic motives attributed to the perpetrator.[5]

Etiology of Suicide

Suicide can happen in any family, regardless of socioeconomic class, culture, race, or religious affiliation. Research suggests that some circumstances increase the risk of suicide in the older adult.

Figure 3-2 Major depression is a significant predictor of suicide.
Source: © Yuri Arcurs/ShutterStock, Inc.

Death of a Loved One

As adults reach later years of life, loss of significant people in their lives, including family, friends, and spouses, becomes inevitable. Often, the surviving person is left with feelings of abandonment, guilt, fear, and loneliness. Loss of a spouse or significant other, often one who has shared the person's life for decades, can be especially devastating.

Physical Illness

Physical illness common in older adults can affect mood, self-esteem, independence, and sense of wellbeing. Along with the psychological pressures associated with physical illness often come economic insecurity and reliance on some form of public assistance, which may deepen feelings of diminished self-worth and dependency.

Hopelessness

Although usually difficult to quantify, hopelessness seems to be the biggest risk factor for suicide in all age groups. No matter how bad a current situation appears, if one can see resolution to a situation (or multiple situations), suicide becomes less of an option. The older person who truly believes his or her life situation is hopeless is at an extremely high risk of suicide.

Isolation

Many older adults have difficulty with mobility due to physical illness. This can lead to social isolation and feelings of diminished self-worth. Death of friends and relatives may further isolate older people. Loneliness resulting from social isolation has also been shown to contribute to suicidal thoughts.

Alcohol Abuse and Dependence

A direct relationship exists between alcoholism and suicide. Studies indicate that risk of suicide in alcoholics is 50–70% greater than in the general population. Between 40–60% of the alcoholics suffer from depression as well as alcoholism; the combination of these risk factors is especially concerning.[6] Alcohol use and the older person are discussed later in this chapter.

Loss of Meaningful Life Roles

Significant changes in one's life roles often result in feelings of hopelessness and low self-esteem associated with suicide. Retirement, moving out of long-time family homes, and inability to continue in community projects and work often contribute to a sense of isolation by many older adults.

Suicide Among Older People in Long-Term Care Facilities

Functional incapacity, loneliness, loss of control, lack of a strong family support network, limited visitation by friends and family, and social withdrawal are all factors that can lead to depression and suicide. These elements, combined with a sense of helplessness, hopelessness, and loss of power in decision making about one's own life in the present and future, can lead to suicide. Thus, the following factors are contributory to suicide for individuals in long-term care facilities:

1. *Loss*—a major contributing factor for suicide. Significant losses include loss of a spouse, friends, pets, money, control, independence, physical mobility, and sensory/perceptual losses.
2. *Depression*—environmental stress seems to be a primary factor in precipitating depressive symptoms. When older people are helpless to control significant events in their environment, feelings of lowered self-concept and self-esteem result.
3. *Family dynamics*—family rejection, abandonment, and lack of informal supports are important factors contributing to suicidal behavior among residents of long-term care facilities.
4. *Physical and functional loss*—loss of physical function, especially seeing, hearing, speech, mobility, and ability to perform activities of daily living, may contribute to a sense of helplessness and loss of control.
5. *Moves*—frequent moves within and out of the facility serve to increase personal and psychological pain for vulnerable adults.[7]

National statistics are not clear on the prevalence of suicides in nursing homes. Very little information has been published; however, there are studies that give insight into this issue. The majority of suicides in nursing homes are male patients, and appear to be from hanging or a long fall.

Special Situations Involving Suicide and the Older Adult

"Police-precipitated suicide" (or "suicide by cop") has been used by those bent on suicide as an alternative for ending one's *own* life by forcing police into a no-win situation by perpetrating acts of violence against the police or others with lethal means. Police have no alternative but to respond accordingly. Given that older people have the highest rates of suicide, this phenomenon may be encountered by law enforcement (see **Figure 3-3**).

In a study of 1,912 incidents of hostage taking or barricades, nearly 2% of the subjects were 65 years of age or older. Some 13% previously had attempted suicide one or more times, and a significant number used alcohol or other drugs. Forty-eight percent used alcohol or other drugs during the incident, with alcohol being the overwhelmingly largest number (33%), and 44% had significant histories of substance abuse. In separate studies of suicide by cop, subjects were mostly male (94–96%), intoxicated (40–50%), depressed (60%), armed with firearms (46–63%), and previously had attempted suicide (38–50%).[8] Given these statistics, law enforcement officers must learn to recognize the dangers that older people may pose in similar circumstances.

Figure 3-3 Law enforcement officers may encounter an older person determined to end their life by police precipitated suicide.

Source: © iStockphoto/Thinkstock.

Medical facilities should be identified within the community that can provide both geriatric medical and psychiatric evaluation and management. Subjects should be transferred to these facilities in order to receive optimal treatment.[9]

Intervention

As a law enforcement officer, you see older people in a variety of settings for crisis events. Recognizing the threat of suicide allows you the opportunity to provide intervention and make appropriate referrals that may prevent a suicide and allow the older person to regain a sense of control or self-worth.

As some older people retire, or become ill, they disengage from society. Many churches, synagogues, and other places of worship have outreach programs for seniors. Additionally, there may be an opportunity for the older person to participate in senior center programs. A number of local municipalities even provide transportation to and from senior centers. Some older people may not know that these programs exist or may be reluctant to inquire about them. Inquire of older persons if they would like to participate in such programs, and make the initial contact on their behalf. How one ages is often directly proportional to his or her outlook on life. Maintaining social contact is extremely important (and necessary) for healthy, productive aging. Remember, older people are just as human as a child or younger adult, and socializing remains important for them. Unfortunately, life-altering events often prohibit older persons from remaining socially engaged. Helping to re-engage older persons into society will enhance their overall wellbeing.

Sometimes, though, more drastic measures must be taken, such as referring the older person for evaluation and potential counseling or hospitalization. The alternative may be an unnecessary, violent death.

Case Study 2

You are dispatched to the home of a 76-year-old male who is possibly suicidal. You learn from the dispatcher that the subject called 911 asking if suicide was illegal. The dispatcher (who is still on the line with the subject) states that the subject is possibly intoxicated. The dispatcher also informs you that the subject is armed with a handgun.[10]

What are your thoughts?

What is your course of action?

THE OLDER DRIVER

The issue of the older driver is a politically charged discussion. A full discussion of the topic is beyond the scope of this text. However, there are some basic statistics and information that the law enforcement officer should know regarding older drivers.

Statistics[11]

There were 31 million older licensed drivers in 2007—a 19% increase from 1997. In contrast, the total number of licensed drivers increased by only 13% from 1997 to 2007. Older drivers made up 15% of all licensed drivers in 2007, compared with 14% in 1997.

In 2008, 183,000 older individuals were injured in traffic crashes, accounting for 8% of all the people injured in traffic crashes during that year. These older individuals made up 15% of all traffic fatalities, 14% of all vehicle occupant fatalities, and 18% of all pedestrian fatalities.

Most traffic fatalities involving older drivers in 2008 occurred during the daytime (80%), occurred on weekdays (72%), and involved other vehicles (69%). Of all adult drivers, older drivers involved in fatal crashes had the lowest proportion of total drivers with blood alcohol concentration (BAC) of .08 grams per deciliter (g/dL) or higher. Among all fatally injured adult pedestrians, older pedestrians also made up the lowest proportion of total pedestrians with BAC of .08 g/dL or higher. Over three-fourths (77%) of all older occupants of passenger vehicles involved in fatal crashes were using restraints at the time of the crash, compared to 63% for other adult occupants (18 to 64 years old).

For older people, 64% of pedestrian fatalities in 2008 occurred at non-intersection locations. For other pedestrians, 79% of fatalities occurred at non-intersection locations. In two-vehicle fatal crashes involving an older driver and a younger driver, the vehicle driven by the older person was nearly twice as likely to be the one that was struck (58% and 35%, respectively). In 48% of these crashes, both vehicles were proceeding straight at the time of the collision. In 22% of these crashes, the older driver was turning left—four times more often than the younger driver (see **Table 3-5**).

Table 3-5 Driver Involvement in Fatal Crashes and Pedestrian Fatalities in the Older Population by Age Group, 2008

	Age Groups (Years)					
	65–69	70–74	75–79	80–84	85+	All Ages
Drivers involved in fatal crashes	1,592	1,321	1,116	858	682	5,569
Pedestrian fatalities	203	157	148	149	146	803

Source: National Highway Traffic Safety Administration, *Traffic Safety Facts: 2008 Older Population.*

Cues for Law Enforcement

Older drivers are seeking to keep autonomy and mobility. Many older drivers, who do not reside with immediate family and/or cannot be reached by sparse or nonexistent governmental social services, view their driving privileges and their motor vehicle as the last vestige of independence. This independence is difficult to relinquish. Older drivers want to drive safely. They are not opposed to fair and unbiased evaluations. *However, evaluations should be based on performance, not age.* Self-evaluation and self-assessment of driving ability are essential elements in the decision to restrict or eliminate certain styles of driving. Older drivers may avoid limited access roadways, scale back or eliminate nighttime driving, and rarely operate a motor vehicle in inclement weather.

Law enforcement officers can perform an integral part in assessing older driver capability. The law enforcement community must work with established civilian and governmental agencies to develop alternatives to the mobility needs of older persons. This can be accomplished by collaborating with other agencies, providing materials, training, information programs, and self-assessment techniques for the older driver. This approach must be positive. Law enforcement should take the lead and initiate actions that promote remedies. Law enforcement agencies can conduct educational programs and seminars at town meetings and senior citizen centers. Additionally, older driver assistance groups can be created. By doing these things, the law enforcement community is providing a sincere commitment to the community in addressing the concerns of the older driver.

Barriers to Safe Mobility

Older drivers face a multitude of medical and nonmedical barriers that may affect their safe operation of a motor vehicle. Some of the medical barriers that confront older drivers and impede their ability to operate a motor vehicle include:

- Alzheimer's disease
- Other dementia such as multi-infarction
- Field of vision loss, low vision, cataracts, and the onset of glaucoma
- Arthritis, Parkinson's disease, and stroke
- Slowed reaction time due to advanced age and/or poor physical condition

Nonmedical barriers to safe driving operation also hinder older drivers. These include:

- Interior design of a motor vehicle:
  - Seats that cannot be adjusted to accommodate a driver's shape, size, or medical condition
  - Interior seating that does not provide for the comfort of the operator
  - Illogical dash design and displays
  - Seat belt/shoulder harness placement that is difficult to reach

- Exterior design of motor vehicles:
  - Motor vehicle exterior doors that are heavy and cumbersome
  - Visibility problems due to poor pillar placement
  - Motor vehicles that are large in overall design
- Engineering barriers to safe operational mobility:
  - Small width on all inner, outer, and center highway divider lines
  - Worn, damaged, missing roadway markings and signs
  - Illegible and unreasonably sized fonts on traffic control devices
  - Work zone areas that are not distinctly marked with official traffic control devices
  - No warning of substandard width of lanes, slower posted speed, pedestrian traffic, etc.
  - Traffic control devices that, due to placement off the roadway, are not effective

Regarding the category of engineering barriers to safe operational mobility, the law enforcement officer can be particularly effective. You are out in the community and can observe for these barriers and make appropriate requests and recommendations for changes or improvements.

Safe Operational Detection Cues

Law enforcement officers must analyze a steady flow of clues when conducting any traffic encounter. Older drivers present a mix of operational mobility cues law enforcement officers should recognize. Understanding these cues will assist the law enforcement officer in assessing the continued safe operational needs of the older drivers that they may encounter. Older operators can have an abundance of medical and nonmedical barriers to safely operating a motor vehicle. A dialogue with persons, as well as visual clues, will assist in determining if the person will require further evaluation of driving mobility. Cues include:

- Does the driver know the current:
  - Time of day?
  - Day of the week?
  - Month of the year?
  - Year?
- Does the driver recall where he or she is coming from?
- Does the driver know his or her destination?
- Is the driver far from his or her residence?
- Does the driver:
  - Have difficulty communicating?
  - Stumble over words?
  - Ramble in short, unattached, meaningless sentences or give explanations of his or her driving ability?

- Is the driver's clothing:
    - Disheveled?
    - Non-matching?
    - Incomplete or too abundant for existing weather conditions?
- Does the driver exhibit poor personal hygiene?
- Does the driver launch into accusations of perceived victimization by criminals?
- Does the driver appear to be suffering from dementia, such as Alzheimer's disease?
- Is the driver wearing an identification bracelet or necklace indicating dementia that would affect safe driving mobility?
- Does the driver have large amounts of prescription medicines, pre-scribed by different doctors, visible in the motor vehicle?
- If the driver is out of the motor vehicle or exits the motor vehicle, does he or she have difficulty finding or removing a driver's license, motor vehicle registration, or insurance card from his or her wallet/purse, or producing other requested documents?
- Does the driver take long periods of time to walk a short distance, stumble/fall, shake excessively, or lack simple coordination when accomplishing simple tasks?

If the older driver experiences difficulty with any of the above cues, this may be a sign of a serious and evolving medical emergency. Emergency medical services should be requested to the scene immediately. The older driver may need further medical assessment, treatment, and transportation to the emergency department.

There may be times when the law enforcement officer confronts an older driver who must be removed from the roadway. Intervention does not have to be the beginning of administrative proceedings to punish the older driver. In extreme cases, when age is the only factor, the elimination of driving privileges *is* punishment. In cases when law enforcement intervention becomes necessary, the law enforcement officer's responsibility extends beyond just removing the older driver from the roadway (see **Figure 3-4**). Additional assistance comes in the form of:

- Referring the older driver to a local assistance agency that can coach and council older people on safe operational mobility
- Seeking information and assistance from family members of the older driver
- Recommending public transportation systems—and how to access them
- Coaching on restriction of certain types of motor vehicle operation, such as nighttime, inclement weather, interstate driving, etc.
- Offering the assistance of the law enforcement community in safe operational mobility learning exercises

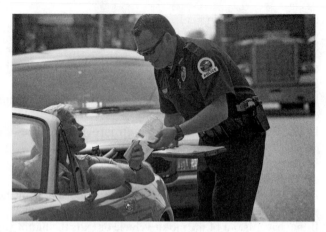

Figure 3-4 The law enforcement community can offer many resources to the older driver. *Source:* © Ariel Skelley/age fotostock.

- A reminder that self-assessment is an important step in maintaining safe operational mobility
- Resources are listed at the end of this chapter to support law enforcement in aiding the older driver

ALCOHOLISM AND DRUG ABUSE IN THE OLDER POPULATION

Alcohol, medication misuse, and use of illegal and illicit drugs can have serious consequences for older adults. Being able to recognize problems such as alcohol and drug misuse in older adults, and making appropriate referrals for treatment and counseling will help the older adults live more productive and healthier lives.

Alcohol Misuse

Changes in the life course can make older people more susceptible to alcohol use. Research shows general patterns of alcohol use in older people, such as:

- *Sleep problems.* Some older people consume alcohol prior to going to bed, because they may be having trouble sleeping. Alcohol may help them fall asleep faster, but will not improve sleep.
- *Gender.* Men tend to drink more than women do; however, women experience more negative effects of alcohol than men do. Women who drink tend to increase drinking later in life.
- *Family history of substance abuse.* People who have had or have a family member with a history of substance abuse are more likely to experience a problem with alcohol or drugs. People who had a substance abuse problem earlier in life are more likely to experience a relapse later in life.

- *Current or past psychiatric disorder.* People with psychiatric disorders are more likely to experience problems with drugs or alcohol.

A small percentage (2–4%) of older people meet current criteria for alcohol abuse or dependence. An additional 10–15% of older people meet criteria for at-risk drinking.[12] Older adults should not drink alcohol if:

- They are taking a prescription pain medication.
- They are taking sleeping pills or over-the-counter sleep medications.
- They are taking prescription medications for depression or anxiety.
- They have memory problems.
- They have a history of falls or unsteady walking.

Older persons can drink low amounts of alcohol and drink infrequently, and still experience problems. *Sensible* drinking in the older adult means no more than one drink per day.

Alcohol abuse is a more serious problem for older people because of their vulnerability to the effects of the drug. Biological sensitivity to alcohol increases with age. Metabolic and brain changes can make older people more susceptible to the effects of alcohol, including cognitive impairment, anxiety, depression, decreased tolerance, and physical symptoms.

A screening instrument specifically for older people that has particular utility in screening for alcoholism in older adults is the Michigan Alcoholism Screening Test—Geriatric Version (see **Table 3-6**).

Medication Misuse and Abuse

Medication misuse is an unintentional or willful use of a medication in a way that differs from its prescribed dose or intent. Examples include:

- Taking several old or unused antibiotic pills for a sore throat from last year's prescription for strep throat, with the thought that this sore throat is also strep throat
- A person who ingests double or triple the dose of over-the-counter Tylenol for a headache, thinking a higher dose of the medication will improve symptoms more quickly
- Failing to take the entire course of antibiotics

On the other hand, **medication or substance abuse** is a deliberate use of a drug for nonmedicinal reasons. Most often, it occurs because the person is trying to produce some desired effect. Prescription and over-the-counter medication misuse is the most common form of substance abuse by the older adult. While older adults constitute 13% of the U.S. population, they consume more than 30% of all prescription medications and 40% of over-the-counter medications.

To understand the potential for medication problems, consider the variety of medications prescribed to treat chronic health problems in older adults.

Table 3-6 Michigan Alcoholism Screening Test—Geriatric Version

In the past year:
When talking with friends, do you ever underestimate how much you actually drink?
Yes ☐   No ☐
After a few drinks, have you sometimes not eaten or been able to skip a meal because you didn't feel hungry?
Yes ☐   No ☐
Does having a few drinks help decrease your shakiness or tremors?
Yes ☐   No ☐
Does alcohol sometimes make it hard for you to remember parts of the day or night?
Yes ☐   No ☐
Do you usually take a drink to relax or calm your nerves?
Yes ☐   No ☐
Do you drink to take your mind off your problems?
Yes ☐   No ☐
Have you ever increased your drinking after experiencing a loss in your life?
Yes ☐   No ☐
Has a doctor or nurse ever said they were worried or concerned about your drinking?
Yes ☐   No ☐
Have you ever made rules to manage your drinking?
Yes ☐   No ☐
When you feel lonely, does having a drink help?
Yes ☐   No ☐

Scoring: If the person answered "yes" to two or more questions, encourage the patient to seek counseling. You may have to help, or even make, the first contact for help.

Source: © The Regents of the University of Michigan, 1991. Reproduced with permission from Frederic C. Blow.

Thirty percent of people 65 years and older take eight or more prescriptions on a daily basis. One can see the potential for misuse and abuse. Older women are less likely to abuse alcohol, but more apt to abuse or misuse prescription or over-the-counter medications.

The use of illegal or street drugs is minimal in the over 65 population—older Americans infrequently use illicit drugs (less than 0.1%).[13] However, the number of older drug abusers is likely to increase given the increasing numbers of older people in society.

If an older person is taken into custody related to prescription or illegal drug use, there are important considerations for law enforcement. The *effects* of medication misuse (particularly the clearance of medications from the body) will be increased in older people. For example, diazepam (Valium) can have an elimination half-life of 20–50 hours. Therefore, the older person must be "medically stable" prior to being incarcerated, even if only for a short time. During any period of incarceration, the older person should be monitored.

Intervention Strategies

By recognizing problem drinking and medication misuse in the older person, you as a law enforcement officer can take the appropriate first steps in referring the older person for treatment and counseling.

While it is safe to say that recognizing alcohol misuse can be easier than recognizing medication misuse in older people, there are several things that as a law enforcement officer you can do to ascertain the possibility of medication misuse. These things include:

- Ask the older person's family member or caretaker what medications the older person is taking. (**Figure 3-5** shows an example of a medication organizer.)
- Ascertain what medical conditions the older person has. An older person who has little or no medical problems but consumes many medications should arouse suspicion in the law enforcement officer.
- Learn if the older person is compliant with the medication regimen.
- Look at prescriptions to see if there are multiple prescribing doctors.
- Determine whether the older person's medical conditions (such as Alzheimer's or visual problems) prevent the person from consuming his or her medications correctly.

Figure 3-5 An example of a medication organizer.
Source: © Jim Barber/ShutterStock, Inc.

- Ask about alcohol consumption and use if the person is taking *any* medications. Certain medications do not mix with alcohol. The effect can be even more pronounced if the older person mixes certain medications with alcohol.

If you find that the answers to any of these questions lead you to a suspicion of medication misuse, there are things that you can do, such as:

- Contact the patient's primary care physician. Often, when the physician becomes aware of such problems, certain medications can be altered or discontinued.
- Speak with family members and solicit their help in assisting the older person in taking their medications (medication organizers, such as those that contain daily medications are extremely helpful. In some cases, drug manufacturers, the local hospital, or a civic organization, will provide these to local jurisdictions at no cost).
- If a severe medication reaction is suspected, EMS should be called to evaluate the person.

As a postscript to this section, we have discussed the misuse of medications in older people. Undermedication in older people can also cause significant problems. Sometimes, older people cannot afford to take the many medications that they must take. In these cases, the older person may reduce the dose, alter the dosing schedule, or simply not take the medication at all. As a law enforcement officer, you may encounter this circumstance. There may be a variety of local and state resources to assist the older person, such as prescription assistance. You may have to make the first call to obtain this assistance for the older person. In doing so, you will substantially improve the quality of the older person's life.

DEATH AND DYING

As a law enforcement officer, you experience death and dying as part of your job. Some deaths are violent; others are peaceful. Approximately three-fourths of all deaths in the United States occur in persons over age 65. **Table 3-7** lists the top 10 leading causes of death in the older population for 2007.

There are times when you will be called to assist EMS providers on the scene of a cardiac arrest or an already expired patient. There are several terms that you should be familiar with.

Hospice care is provided for those with terminal illnesses either in their own home or at a hospice facility. Hospice care allows for peace, comfort, and dignity when dying. In 2009, 83% of all persons receiving hospice were age 65 and older. Hospice care focuses on **palliative care**, which is care for persons whose disease is not responsive to curative treatment, and can include providing relief from pain and other distressing symptoms; neither hastening nor

Table 3-7 Top 10 Leading Causes of Death for Persons 65 and Older, 2007

Cause	Deaths
1. Heart disease	496,095
2. Malignant neoplasms (cancer)	389,730
3. Cerebrovascular (stroke)	115,961
4. Chronic obstructive pulmonary disease	109,562
5. Alzheimer's disease	73,797
6. Diabetes	51,528
7. Influenza and pneumonia	45,941
8. Nephritis	38,484
9. Trauma	38,292
10. Septicemia	26,362

Source: Data from National Vital Statistics, 2007.

prolonging death; offering a supportive system to help the family cope; and integrating psychological and spiritual aspects of care.

A **do not resuscitate (DNR) order** is written documentation giving permission to medical personnel not to attempt resuscitation even in the event of cardiac arrest. DNR orders vary widely from state to state, such as what care can be provided prior to the cessation of breathing and pulse. You can contact your local EMS agency or state EMS office to learn specifically how DNR applies in your state.

Ethical and legal issues regarding patient rights and expressed wishes also vary widely. There some universal terms, however. **Autonomy** is the right of an individual to make choices freely, in accordance with the individual's own goals and values. The attorney general in your state can provide clarification and training on what laws govern patient wishes with regard to death and dying in your state.

The ethical principle of autonomy is recognized legally in various ways. In every state, patients who are capable of thinking clearly (also known as having decision-making capacity) may give consent to receive or refuse proposed treatment. The **informed consent doctrine**, which was developed by the courts, allows a patient to decide against unwanted medical interventions. Even if an intervention would probably prolong a patient's life, the patient may refuse it. The right to refuse life-sustaining treatment is also protected under the U.S. Constitution and the constitutions of some states.

Many people want to make plans about their health care in case of future events. The means of expressing their decisions is called an **advance directive**. Every state has enacted a law allowing people to give directions about end-of-life care in advance of need—hence the term *advance directive*. One kind of advance directive names a future decision maker. This advance directive anticipates a future situation in which decisions about cardiopulmonary resuscitation (CPR) and other forms of life-sustaining treatment must be made, but the person is unable to make them at that time. The person uses the advance directive to name a decision maker of the patient's choosing. This type of document is variously called a **durable power of attorney** for health care, healthcare proxy, or a healthcare agent. The other kind of advance directive documents decisions about particular end-of-life treatments in particular situations. Depending on the law in each state, it can cover CPR and other forms of life-sustaining treatment in the event of a terminal condition, permanent unconsciousness, and fatal illness prior to the terminal phase. This type of document is called either a **living will** or an instructional directive.

Case Study 3

You are called to the home of an older woman by her neighbor. The neighbor reports that the older woman resides alone and has not been seen by anyone in about a week. As you knock on the door of the older woman's home, you notice that the mail has piled up in the mailbox. Mary greets you at the door. She is a 75-year-old woman who appears unsteady on her feet. She has tremors in her hands and appears malnourished. You begin to question Mary about her wellbeing, but observe that she has difficulty focusing on your questions.
What do you think Mary's problem is?
What are your interventional decisions?

SUMMARY

Often, older adults find themselves dealing with medical issues, physical limitation, and social loss. Psychological problems of this age group often involve depression, anxiety, and adjustment disorders. These conditions are found quite commonly, but they are by no means a normal part of the changes that occur with aging. Understanding these complex issues provides the law enforcement officer the tools that are needed to better serve the needs of older people. Remember, respect, compassion, and dignity are the hallmarks that older people need in a time of crisis.

CASE STUDY SUMMARIES

Case Study 1 Summary

Under the laws and protocols of most states, you should forego CPR measures. You would have good faith immunity for your actions. You should note the time, and initiate an inquiry as to the circumstances of the patient's passing.

Further, you should speak with the patient's physician to ensure that the physician will sign the death certificate. In most cases, if a patient has been under the care of a physician for a terminal or chronically debilitating medical condition, the physician will sign the death certificate, unless, in your opinion, some circumstance would make the death suspicious. If for some reason the physician will not sign the death certificate or you deem the circumstances of the death suspicious, the case should be referred to the medical examiner.

Case Study 2 Summary

The dispatcher was able to keep the now barricaded man on the telephone and establish a rapport with him. The subject recounted stories of World War II, of days gone past ("the good old days"), and of being frustrated with having to retire recently. When asked about suicidal ideations, the subject became irritated, but assured the dispatcher that he was not going to kill himself *now*. Given the current situation with the subject, and the subject stating he was not going to kill himself *now*, he was placed at a high risk for suicide. After several hours of conversation with the dispatcher, the subject agreed to lay down his weapon and come outside to police.

This case had a good ending, but illustrates an all too likely scenario that could occur anywhere. The case also illustrates some red flags that the subject identified and expressed through negotiations that should alert law enforcement that it was a serious situation involving an older person. The first red flag was the initial call: "Is suicide illegal?" asked the subject. The subject also sounded "intoxicated" and was identified to have had a handgun. Barricading oneself in one's home and threatening suicide is not seen as a rational act. In this case study, the subject had also been drinking. Alcohol lowered the subject's inhibitions and may have given him the courage to "go out in a blaze of glory" (remember, the subject was recounting days of World War II with the dispatcher). Additionally, the subject expressed his frustration with having to "recently retire"—a loss of a life role that could lead to depression. All of these factors place the older person at a serious risk of suicide. This is a subject who must be referred for medical and psychiatric evaluation and management.

Case Study 3 Summary

If Mary was 40 years old and you saw the same symptoms, you might immediately expect a substance abuse problem. However, in an older person, Mary's symptoms may or may not be related to alcohol or medication misuse. All too often, misuse of alcohol and medications may not be recognized. In Mary's case, further investigation is warranted. Does the environment suggest that Mary is unable to care for herself? Is there evidence of alcohol consumption? If Mary lives alone, is there family that can be contacted to obtain more information? Mary should be referred to the emergency department for evaluation and to rule out any medical reason for her symptoms. The emergency department physician or social worker should be made aware of any suspicion of alcohol or medication misuse, and Mary should be referred for appropriate counseling. If time permits, law enforcement officers who serve Mary's district can visit Mary periodically to ensure that things are going well.

ENDNOTES

1. National Center for Health Statistics. (2009). As summarized by the American Foundation for Suicide Prevention. *Facts and figures*. Retrieved from http://www.afsp.org/index.cfm?fuseaction=home.viewpage&page_id=050fea9f-b064-4092-b1135c3a70de1fda.
2. Centers for Disease Control and Prevention. (2010). *Suicide: Facts at a glance*. Atlanta, GA: Centers for Disease Control and Prevention. Available online at: http://www.cdc.gov/ViolencePrevention/pdf/Suicide_DataSheet-a.pdf.
3. Centers for Disease Control and Prevention. (2012). *National suicide statistics at a glance: Percentage of suicides by age group, sex, and mechanism, United States, 2005–2009*. Atlanta, GA: Centers for Disease Control and Prevention. Available online at: http://www.cdc.gov/ViolencePrevention/suicide/statistics/mechanism02.html.
4. Conwell, Y. (1994). Suicide in elderly patients. In L. S. Schneider, C. F. Reyonlds, III, B. D. Lebowitz, & A. J. Friedhoff (Eds.), *Diagnosis and treatment of depression in late life* (pp. 397–418). Washington, DC: American Psychiatric Press.
5. Cohen, D., Liorente, M., & Eisdorfer, C. (1998). Homicide-suicide in older persons. *The American Journal of Psychiatry*, 155(3), 390–396.
6. Institute on Aging. (2012). *Suicide & the elderly*. Retrieved from http://www.ioaging.org/aging/counseling_suicide_elderly.html.
7. Osgood, N. J., Brant, B. A., & Lipman, A. (1991). *Suicide among the elderly in long-term care facilities*. New York: Greenwood Press; pp. 95–98.
8. Slatkin, A. A. (2003, April). Suicide risk and hostage/barricade situations involving older persons. *FBI Law Enforcement Bulletin, 72*(4), 26–32. Available online at: http://www.fbi.gov/stats-services/publications/law-enforcement-bulletin/2003-pdfs/april03leb.pdf.
9. This section and the following case study are adapted from: Slatkin, A. A. (2003, April). Suicide risk and hostage/barricade situations involving older persons. *FBI Law Enforcement Bulletin, 72*(4), 26–32.
10. Ibid.
11. U.S. Department of Transportation, National Highway Traffic Safety Administration. (2008). *Traffic safety facts, 2008*. Retrieved April 11, 2012, from www-nrd.nhtsa.dot.gov/Pubs/811170.pdf.
12. American Association for Geriatric Psychiatry. (n.d.). *Aging and alcohol information sheet*. Retrieved from http://www.gmhfonline.org/gmhf/consumer/factsheets/alc_factsheet.html.
13. U.S. Department of Health and Human Services. (1999). *Mental health: A report of the Surgeon General*. Rockville, MD: U.S. Department of Health and Human Services, Substance Abuse and Mental Health Services Administration, National Institute of Mental Health.

RESOURCES

Alzheimer's Association (www.alz.org)—provides resources for law enforcement

American Foundation for Suicide Prevention (www.afsp.org)

American Association for Geriatric Psychiatry (www.aagponline.org/)

American Association of Retired Persons (www.aarp.org)—provides resources for older drivers

Association for Driver Rehabilitation Specialists (www.aded.net)

National Highway Traffic Safety Administration (www.nhtsa.gov)—provides resources to aid law enforcement, such as:

- *A Compendium of Law Enforcement Older Driver Programs*
- *Driving Safely While Aging Gracefully*
- *Safe Mobility for Older Drivers*
- *Driving When You Have Had a Stroke*
- *Driving When You Have Arthritis*
- *Driving When You Have Parkinson's Disease*
- *Driving When You have Sleep Apnea*
- *Driving When You Have Diabetes*
- *Driving When You Have Had Seizures*
- *Driving When You Have Cataracts*
- *Driving When You Have Glaucoma*
- *Driving When You Have Macular Degeneration*
- *Hey! Older Pedestrians Need More Time Than That to Cross a Street!*
- *Ice, Snow, and Slippery Sidewalks: For Many Seniors, Winter Is "Hip Season"*
- *Stepping Out—Mature Adults: Be Healthy, Walk Safely*
- *Walking as a Way of Life*
- *Zone Guide for Pedestrian Safety*

KEY TERMS

advance directive: Written documentation that specifies medical treatment for a competent person should the person become unable to make decisions

autonomy: The right of an individual to make choices freely, in accordance with the individual's own goals and values

depression: Persistent mood of sadness, despair, discouragement; depression may be a symptom of many different mental and physical disorders, or it may be a disorder on its own

do not resuscitate (DNR) order: Written documentation giving permission to medical personnel not to attempt resuscitation in the event of cardiac arrest

durable power of attorney: A type of advance directive that names a future decision maker and anticipates a future situation in which decisions about CPR and other forms of life-sustaining treatment must be made, but the person is unable at that time to make them; also called healthcare proxy or a healthcare agent

hospice care: In-home or hospice care facility services provided to patients with a terminal illness; services include supportive medical, social, and spiritual services to patients, and support for the patient's family

informed consent doctrine: Allows a person to decide against unwanted medical interventions

living will: A type of advance directive that documents decisions about particular end-of-life treatments in particular situations should the patient become incompetent; depending on the law in each state, it can cover CPR and other forms of life-sustaining treatment in the event of terminal condition, permanent unconsciousness, and fatal illness prior to the terminal phase; also called an instructional directive

medication misuse: Unintentional or willful use of a medication in a way that differs from the prescribed dose or intent

medication or substance abuse: Deliberate use of a drug for nonmedicinal uses

palliative care: Care of persons whose disease is not responsive to curative treatment. Such care can include providing relief from pain and other distressing symptoms; neither hastening nor prolonging death; offering a supportive system to help the family cope; and integrating psychological and spiritual aspects of care

Chapter Four

Communicating with Older People

LEARNING OBJECTIVES

1. Understand the process of communication.
2. Discuss and recognize communication challenges in older persons, including visual, hearing, speech, and disease processes that affect communication.
3. Describe the principles that should be employed when communicating with an older person.

Case Study 1

You respond to a call for a robbery that has just occurred. The location is a busy intersection in the downtown area. You arrive moments later to discover a few people standing around an older woman who is sitting on the bench at the bus stop. You learn from the bystanders that they heard the woman scream that a man has just robbed her of her purse.

You quickly ask the bystanders if any of them saw what happened. They all state that they did not; they simply heard the older woman scream. Your next step is to interview the older woman in an attempt to get suspect information.

Your first observation is that the older woman looks visibly upset. Standing over the bench, you begin your interview. As you attempt to obtain the older woman's name, age, what occurred, and a description of the suspect, the older woman repeatedly says, "I don't know . . . I'm so upset, I can't think."

How do you handle this situation?

COMMUNICATION AND THE OLDER ADULT

Every day, as a law enforcement officer, you communicate with many people—your partner, the dispatcher, and with the public. This **communication** is often hurried, and at times, wrought with emotion. Taking the time to think about how this communication takes place, and what makes for effective communication, will yield some interesting results. How do we interact with the public?—more specifically, how do we interact with the older people we come in contact with? Do we, as law enforcement officers, know how to communicate effectively with the senior citizens in the community? The following sections will identify the nature of communication with older people, communication disorders common in older people, and how, as law enforcement officers, we can communicate effectively with older people.

Communication is the basic life experience. It allows us to receive information that keeps us alive and healthy. For older people, the ability to communicate is crucial to life maintenance and personal satisfaction. Communication is necessary for the older person to live effectively in new or changing environments. For the healthy older person, it may be the crucial skill in negotiating the right to remain independent. For older people with disabilities, communication is important to maintain through rehabilitation in order to prevent further deterioration, isolation, and dependence.[1]

Communication is not just talking; it is also listening. Your first communication sets the tone with the older person—what you say and how you say it can mean success or failure.

Older people have a greater need for good human relations than younger adults. Older people need ties to reality, to family, and to friends to counterbalance the forces of aging. Enhancing communication with older people helps to

Figure 4-1 It is important to present yourself as competent, confident, and concerned.
Source: © Anthony Monterotti/ShutterStock, Inc.

maintain their integrity, preserve their wisdom, and enhance personal relations.[2] It is important, from the very beginning, that as a law enforcement professional, you present yourself as competent, confident, and concerned (**Figure 4-1**). Good communication skills will help you to gain more information to aid in your management of the situation. When the older person trusts you, it is easier for them to explain their problem and to answer your questions. No matter how difficult, law enforcement officers can find effective ways to enhance communication with older people, and thus make the experience a positive one.

Communication Tip—Communication includes both talking and listening.

There are several components involved in the communication process. These components are:

sender - message - channel - receiver

The sender is the person sending the message. The message is the verbal or nonverbal symbolic behavior—either written or oral. The channel is the acoustic, visual, or electronic medium through which the message is transmitted.

The receiver is the person listening. These components are constantly interacting, and can switch back and forth. Encoding, decoding, and interpreting messages are required in order for communication to take place. At a crime scene or other emergency, this flow of effective communication is easily disrupted.

TYPES OF COMMUNICATION SKILLS

Verbal and Nonverbal Communication

There are two types of communication—verbal and nonverbal. Your **nonverbal communication** is just as important as your **verbal communication**. Verbal communication includes your words and your volume, pitch, inflection, and tone. Nonverbal communication includes eye contact, hand gestures, body position, facial expressions, and touch. Touch can be important to the confused or distraught older person. Touch can often calm and reassure, and can increase attention and nonverbal communication in the confused older person. Take the older patient by the hand, or touch his or her on the arm. Be aware, however, that some patients prefer not to be touched. Cultural beliefs may prohibit touching as well. Some older female patients may feel uncomfortable when touched by a male. Law enforcement officials should respect a person's wish not to be touched.

It is important that verbal and nonverbal communication is congruent. Be sure that your words, facial expressions, and body language are consistent with each other. Older people can sense inconsistencies and insincerity, which will undermine the trust you are trying to establish.

Listening

Listening is a vital communication skill. Many older people will need time to process the questions that are being asked of them. Unless the need is urgent, take the time to listen patiently for the answers to your questions (see **Figure 4-2**). Additionally, listen to the way patients say their words. Effective listening will allow the law enforcement officer the opportunity to comfort and calm the person if the person's tone conveys fear or confusion.

> Attitude Tip—Be patient when interviewing older people; recognize physical, intellectual, and psychosocial barriers that slow or interfere with effective communication.

AGE-RELATED COMMUNICATION CHANGES

Communication disorders constitute the nation's number one handicapping disability. Studies indicate that more people suffer from hearing, speech, and language impairment than from heart disease, venereal

Figure 4-2 Older people may need time to process your questions and may speak slowly when responding.
Source: © Bob Daemmrich/PhotoEdit, Inc.

disease, paralysis, epilepsy, blindness, cerebral palsy, tuberculosis, muscular dystrophy, and multiple sclerosis combined. Conditions such as stroke, cancer, degenerative neurological diseases, and trauma can affect the older person's ability to communicate.[3] The aging process brings about changes in vision, hearing, taste, smell, and touch. Additionally, there are changes in communication abilities that accompany aging, dementia, and other diseases. Advanced age can make a person's voice tremulous, weak, hoarse, and higher or lower pitched than it was in middle age. Older people may say, "My voice tires." These symptoms may be bothersome, but they are considered a normal consequence of aging (barring the absence of any medical condition). In the sections that follow, those changes that primarily affect the interaction between the older person and the law enforcement officer are discussed.

Vision

Diseases of the eye, such as cataracts, glaucoma, **macular degeneration**, and visual problems secondary to stroke or diabetes become more common as one grows older. Fifteen percent of all adults over the age of 65 have serious visual impairments.

Any time you are called to the scene of an older person who is not wearing glasses, ask if he or she has glasses. If the person says yes, ask if he or she would like to put them on. If the person says yes, ask where the glasses are kept and if you can get them. Carefully help the person put the glasses on. If the older person is blind, tell him or her everything you are going to do. Do not assume that because the patient is blind, he or she is also deaf.

The law enforcement officer should be cognizant of visual changes when moving older people, making sure to support the older person to prevent him or her from falling.

Hearing Loss

Hearing loss is the most common communication disorder in the older population, and is the third most prevalent chronic condition in the older population. The prevalence of hearing loss is as follows:[4]

- Approximately 17% (36 million) of American adults report some degree of hearing loss.
- There is a strong relationship between age and reported hearing loss: 18% of American adults 45–64 years of age, 30% of adults 65–74 years of age, and 47% of adults over 75 years of age have a hearing impairment.

There are three basic types of hearing loss: conductive, sensorineural, and central auditory processing disorders.

Conductive hearing loss occurs when sound is not conducted efficiently through the outer and middle ears, including the ear canal, eardrum, and the tiny bones, or ossicles, of the middle ear. This type of hearing loss usually involves a reduction in sound level—the ability to hear faint sounds. This type of hearing loss can often be corrected with medicine or surgery. Absence or malformation of the pina, ear canal, or ossicles can cause this type of hearing loss as well. Other things that can cause conductive hearing loss include impacted cerumen, fluid in the ear associated with cold, allergies, ear infections, and poorly functioning eustachian tubes. Conductive hearing loss can occur in combination with sensorineural hearing loss as well.

Sensorineural hearing loss occurs when there is damage to the inner ear (cochlea) or to the nerve pathways from the inner ear to the brain. This type of hearing loss not only involves a reduction in sound level (the ability to hear faint sounds), but also affects speech understanding or ability to hear clearly. Causes include disease, birth injury, medications that are toxic to the auditory system, genetic syndromes, noise exposure, viruses, head trauma, tumors, and aging. Sensorineural hearing loss affects some 17 million Americans and is permanent.

A central auditory processing disorder occurs when auditory centers of the brain are affected by injury, disease, tumor, or heredity. These disorders do not (though they may) involve hearing loss. Central auditory processing involves sound localization and lateralization, auditory discrimination, auditory pattern recognition, the temporal aspects of sound, and the ability to deal with degraded and competing acoustic signals. Therefore, a deficiency in any of the above may constitute a central auditory processing disorder.

There are many causes of hearing loss in adults, such as **otosclerosis**, **Meniere's disease**, **ototoxic** medications, exposure to harmful levels of noise, acoustic neuroma, and trauma. Hearing loss as a result of aging is called

presbycusis. The hearing loss is progressive in nature, with the high frequencies affected first. While the process begins after age 20, it is often at ages 55 to 65 that the high frequencies in the speech range are affected. Thus, a lower pitch voice may be easier for older people to hear than a higher pitch voice.

Speech

Normal speech requires both energy and relaxation, which occurs in a delicate balance. Energy is required in skeletal muscles to support posture; in abdominal and breathing muscles to support loudness; and in the tongue, jaw, lips, and palate to support intelligibility. Relaxation is required in skeletal muscles to support pitch; in throat muscles to support clear tone; and in vocal tract muscles to support the best resonance. For many older people, it is difficult to produce signals that are loud enough, clear enough, and well spaced enough. Weakness, paralysis, poor hearing, or brain damage can destroy this balance.[5]

Dentures

While dentures may not be thought of in the realm of communication concerns, they do aid the person who wears them with communication. Without dentures, speech may be slurred or mumbled. Additionally, the patient may be embarrassed to talk.

Ask the person if he or she wears dentures. If the answer is yes, offer to get them. Dentures that are kept in a soaking solution need to be rinsed before inserting. Ask the older person if he or she can put the dentures in. If the person can insert the dentures, hand him or her the top plate first, just the way they would fit in the mouth (see **Figure 4-3**). After the top plate is inserted, hand the patient the bottom denture in the same manner. If the individual

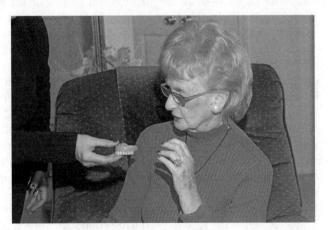

Figure 4-3 Hand dentures to a person the way the dentures would fit in the mouth, with the top plate first.
Source: Courtesy of John Valentini, Jr.

cannot insert the denture and desires that you do, insert the top plate first, holding it securely with your thumb. Then lay the bottom denture along the bottom ridge. Ask the person if the dentures are comfortable. Never allow older persons with dentures to lie on their backs unmonitored, as dentures could come loose and create an airway obstruction.

COMMUNICATION DISORDERS AFFECTING OLDER PEOPLE

Aphasia

Aphasia is an impairment of language, affecting the production or comprehension of speech and the ability to read or write. Aphasia is always due to injury to the brain, most commonly from a stroke. The range of aphasia can make communication with the person almost impossible, or it can be very mild. Aphasia may affect mainly a single aspect of language use, such as the ability to retrieve the names of objects, the ability to put words into sentences, or the ability to read. More commonly, multiple aspects of communication are impaired, while some channels remain accessible for a limited exchange of information. Approximately 1 million people in the United States are affected by aphasia. There are several varieties of aphasia:

- *Global aphasia*. This is the most severe form of aphasia. It describes persons who can produce few recognizable words and understand little or no spoken language. Global aphasic patients can neither read nor write. Global aphasia may be seen immediately after the person has suffered a stroke and may improve rapidly if the damage has not been too extensive. The person with global aphasia is the most difficult to communicate with—as comprehension and expression are impaired.
- *Broca's aphasia*. In this form of aphasia, speech output is severely reduced and is limited mainly to short utterances of less than four words. Vocabulary access is limited, and the formation of sounds is often laborious and clumsy for the patient. The person may be able to understand speech relatively well and be able to read, but be limited in writing. Broca's aphasia is often referred to as nonfluent aphasia because of the halting and effortful quality of speech.
- *Mixed nonfluent aphasia*. This term for aphasia is applied to persons who have sparse and effortful speech, resembling severe Broca's aphasia. However, unlike persons with Broca's aphasia, these people remain limited in their comprehension of speech and do not read or write beyond an elementary level.
- *Wernicke's aphasia*. With this type of aphasia, comprehension deficit is greater, while the ease of producing connected speech is not much affected. However, sentences do not hang together and irrelevant words intrude, producing a "word salad." This type of aphasia is referred to as fluent aphasia. Reading and writing are often severely impaired.

- *Anomic aphasia.* This term is applied to persons who are left with a persistent inability to supply the words for the things they want to talk about. In other words, they have an inability to name. Persons with anomic aphasia understand speech well, and in most cases, read adequately. Difficulty finding words is as evident in writing as in speech.

There are other forms of aphasia that do not fit into the above categories. Additionally, there are other isolated communication disorders that result from a stroke. For example, disorders of reading (alexia) or disorders of both reading and writing (alexia and agraphia).

Dementia

Dementia is a medical condition that does affect the person's ability to communicate. Language difficulties common in persons with dementia affect their ability to name things or say what they want to say. This is an early indication of the disease. Other characteristics of people with dementia include an appearance of frustration, withdrawal, suspiciousness, irritability, and restlessness—all of which affect the communication process. Those with dementia are no longer able to recognize close friends, family members, or themselves. Symptoms may get worse in the evening, a condition known as "sun-downing." Persons with dementia are often aware of their inability to perform as they once did. This is especially true in the early stages of the disease. Paranoia, delusions, or hallucinations often accompany dementia. Law enforcement officers may encounter one or all of these.

Those with dementia also become very concrete—that is, they can no longer think in abstractions. There is also a delayed reaction time in conversation. Those with dementia also forget what was just said to them, or what they were in the middle of saying. There are also recognition problems. The person with dementia may forget that you are a law enforcement officer. As the disease progresses, language difficulties become more severe.

Other Disorders Affecting Communication

Apraxia

Apraxia is a collective term used to describe impairment in carrying out purposeful movements. People with severe aphasia are usually limited in explaining themselves by pantomime or gesture, except for expressions of emotion. Commonly, persons with apraxia will show you something in their wallet, or lead you to show you something, but this is the extent of their nonverbal communication. These patients are unable to perform common expressive gestures on request (such as waving good-bye). This is referred to as limb apraxia. Apraxia may also primarily affect oral, nonspeech movements, such as pretending to blow out a candle. This is referred to as facial apraxia. This disorder may even extend to the ability to manipulate real objects.

Apraxia of speech is an impairment in the voluntary production of articulation and prosody (rhythm and timing) of speech. It is characterized by highly inconsistent errors.

Dysarthria

Dysarthria refers to a group of speech disorders resulting from weakness, slowness, or incoordination of the speech mechanism due to damage to any of a variety of points in the nervous system. Dysarthria may involve disorders to some or all of the basic speech processes: respiration phonation, resonance, articulation, and prosody. Dysarthria is a disorder of speech production, not language. Unlike apraxia of speech, the speech errors that occur in dysarthria are highly consistent from one occasion to the next.

Parkinson's Disease

Parkinson's disease is a chronic nervous disease characterized by a fine, slowly spreading tremor, muscle weakness and rigidity, and a peculiar gait. Forty percent of those with Parkinson's disease have dementia in later stages.

HEARING AIDS

A hearing aid is basically a device that makes sound louder. Hearing aids cannot restore hearing to normal. Just as glasses cannot cure vision problems, hearing aids cannot cure hearing problems. Hearing aids provide a benefit in that they improve hearing and listening ability, which ultimately improves the quality of life.

While there are different types of hearing aids, four basic components of a hearing aid can be identified. They are: the microphone, amplifier, receiver, and power supply. The microphone collects sound energy and converts that energy into a weak electronic current. The amplifier receives the electronic signal generated by the microphone and increases the amplitude. The receiver is like a miniature speaker. This component converts the amplified electrical signal into sound energy similar to that initially received by the microphone. It is this amplified signal which is then directed into the ear. The battery (power supply) is necessary to provide power to the amplifier.

When sound leaves the receiver, it is necessary to provide a means of directing the signal into the ear canal. This is accomplished through the use of a custom, fitted ear mold. An impression is taken of the outer ear and sent to a laboratory that will make a custom, fitted mold. Squealing that is often heard from a hearing aid is the result of feedback—sound escaping from the ear canal that is picked up by the microphone and further amplified.

Ask the older person if he or she has a hearing aid. Use hand gestures to signify putting a hearing aid in your ear. If the person says yes, ask where the hearing aid is, retrieve it, and assist the person in putting it in, if necessary.

Types of Hearing Aids

There are four different types of hearing aids (as shown in **Figure 4-4**):

- *In-the-canal and completely in-the-canal hearing aids.* These hearing aids are contained in a tiny case that fits partly or completely into the ear canal.
- *In-the-ear-hearing aid.* All parts of the hearing aid are contained in a shell that fits in the outer part of the ear. This type of hearing aid is generally larger than the canal-type hearing aids.
- *Behind-the-ear-hearing aid.* All parts of this hearing aid are contained in a small plastic case that rests behind the ear. The case is connected to an ear mold by a piece of clear tubing.
- *Conventional body-type hearing aid.* This type of hearing aid is an older style aid and is generally worn by people with profound hearing loss. It is generally worn on the chest, either in a shirt or coat pocket or in a harness. The microphone, amplifier, and battery are contained within the case of the hearing aid. A cord carries the electrical signal to the receiver that is attached to the ear mold placed in the external ear.

Many hearing aids have optional features that can be built in to assist in different communication situations. Some of these options are:

- *Directional microphone.* Some hearing aids have a switch to activate a directional microphone that responds to sound coming from a specific direction, as occurs in face-to-face conversation. A switch can be made from the normal nondirectional setting, which picks up sound almost equally from any direction, to focus on a sound coming from the front

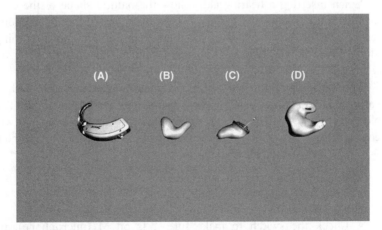

Figure 4-4 Different types of hearing aids. (A) Behind-the-ear type. (B) Conventional body type. (C) In-the-canal type. (D) In-the-ear type.
Source: Courtesy of John Valentini, Jr.

of the person. When the directional microphone is activated, sound coming from behind the person with the hearing is reduced.

- *Telephone switch.* Some hearing aids are made with an induction coil inside. A switch can be made from the normal microphone "on" setting to a "T" setting in order to hear better on the telephone. In the "T" setting, environmental sounds are eliminated, and the person can only pick up sounds from the telephone.

First Aid for Hearing Aids

Occasionally, the law enforcement officer may be asked to assist an older person with a hearing aid. You may be asked to assist the older patient with inserting his or her hearing aid. If so, the following generally apply to most hearing aids. Hearing aid users will often disconnect the batteries when not in use to prolong them (hearing aid batteries generally need to be changed every 5 to 7 days). If the back of the hearing aid is open, and the battery is inside, simply close the battery door. If the battery is not inside the hearing aid, you will have to insert it. Some hearing aids have a preset volume; others need to be turned on to set the volume. If the volume needs to be set, set in the midrange. This will prevent sudden loud noises. The person can then reset the volume as needed. The hearing aid with the red dot always goes in the right ear. One way to remember is red equals right.

> Communication Tip—The hearing aid with red dot always goes in the right ear. Remember, red equals right.

When inserting a hearing aid, follow the natural shape of the ear. If a whistling sound occurs, this could mean the hearing aid is not in far enough to create a seal, or the volume is up too loud. Reposition it, and try turning the volume down. If, after two tries, the hearing aid will not go in properly, do not try any further.

The following will assist you in becoming familiar with troubleshooting hearing aids. This is not meant to be a comprehensive list, nor should the law enforcement officer attempt to do something he or she is not familiar with. If necessary, assist the person with contacting his or her audiologist. If the hearing aid will not work at all:

- Be sure the hearing aid is turned on.
- Try a fresh battery.
- Check the tubing to make sure it is not twisted or bent.
- Check the switch to make sure it is on M (microphone), not T (telephone).

- Try a spare cord (for a body aid). The old cord may be broken or shorted.
- Check the ear mold to make sure it is not plugged with wax.

If sound from the hearing aid is weaker than usual:

- Try a fresh battery.
- Check the tubing for bends and the ear mold for wax or dirt.
- If the hearing aid has been exposed to extreme cold, it may not work until it is at room temperature.
- There may be excessive wax in the ear. The person should consult his or her physician.

If the hearing aid goes on and off or sounds scratchy:

- Work the switches and dials back and forth, as lint or dust will interfere with electrical contacts.
- On body hearing aids, try changing cords.

If the hearing aid whistles continuously:

- A new ear mold or new tubing may be needed. The patient should see his or her audiologist.

Additional things that can be done include:

- If excessive dirt or wax collects on the mold, it can be washed in warm water using mild soap. The mold must be removed from the hearing aid prior to washing. Wipe excess water from the mold, blow to clear any moisture from the tube, and allow the hearing aid to dry overnight.
- Discard any batteries that appear to be leaking. Clean the battery case.

Hearing aids must be handled with care. The following should never be done with hearing aids:

- Never attempt to remove wax from any opening of an in-the-ear hearing aid.
- Never expose a hearing aid to excessive heat.
- Never allow a hearing aid to become wet. Should a hearing aid become wet:
  - Remove the batteries at once.
  - Wipe the exterior of the case with a dry, absorbent cloth.
  - Place the hearing aid in a warm place. The low heat setting of a hair dryer can be used for drying.
- Never take a hearing aid apart to examine the insides. This may void warranties.
- Never use alcohol, acetone, or cleaning fluid on a hearing aid.

- Do not wash the ear mold in alcohol, acetone, cleaning fluid, or extremely hot water. The use of chemicals may dissolve the plastic material of the ear mold. Hot water may soften the plastic and allow the ear mold to change shape.

If the older person will be accompanying you, ensure that the person's hearing aid is transported with the person.

COMMUNICATING WITH OLDER PEOPLE

General Guidelines

- Identify yourself. Do not assume the older person knows who you are.
- Be cognizant of how you present yourself. Frustration and impatience can be portrayed through body language.
- Explain what you are going to do before you do it. Avoid using jargon or slang.
- For persons who are visually impaired, the need to explain things in detail is paramount. If assisting the person with transferring, keep one hand on the person and tell the person what you want them to do, and in which direction to turn.
- Show the older person respect. Never use the person's first name without his or her permission. Refer to the patient as Mr. or Mrs.
- Do not talk about the person in front of him or her. To do so gives the impression that the older person has no say in any decision making. This is easy to forget when the person is cognitively impaired or has difficulty communicating. If there is a caretaker or someone involved in the decision-making process for the patient, continue to talk *to the person* as well as to the person's caretaker or decision maker.
- Avoid complex grammar.
- Be a good listener. Law enforcement officers must listen with their ears in order to understand intellectually what the person is saying, but must also listen with the heart. In other words, listen empathetically. For the older person who is in distress or acutely ill, it is important to maintain a relaxed, friendly, and calm manner. Persons who are nonverbal may actually be expressing themselves by refusing to display their disabilities to someone they perceive as cold and uncaring. Dysarthric persons need your patience because they cannot form the sounds that go into a ready answer. Those with aphasia need your patience because they cannot express the words of an answer, and may experience poor language comprehension when they feel rushed and embarrassed. Tips on modifying your listening include the following.
  For the dysarthric person:
  - Expect poor articulation; therefore, read gestures and nonverbal clues.
  - Listen for the slow-motion core of intelligibility.

For the laryngectomee:
- Expect low pitched monotone.
- Listen for shortened phrases without melody.
- Listen also with your eyes—lipread cues.

For the aphasic person:
- Listen slowly—give the person time to grope for words and ideas.
- Listen acceptingly, without negative reactions.
- Expect telegraphic messages from the expressive aphasic.

The National Victim Center has identified several useful techniques for communicating with older adults in stress situations:[6]

- Do not assume that every older adult has a sensory or cognitive impairment. Be sensitive to every person's particular needs.
- If possible and if circumstances permit, choose an environment that is conducive to communication. Eliminate factors that interfere with effective listening, such as the television or radio, and minimize any distractions. This may involve moving the person to a quiet environment where one-on-one communication can take place. This will prove vital if the older person has been victimized and must recount or give details of the event.
- If the person's story appears rehearsed, be aware that the person could be experiencing abuse.
- If the older person appears fearful while relating facts, be sure to listen carefully. There could be a number of different reasons for the person's fears. Additionally, the older person in crisis may not readily volunteer information.
- Try to position the older person so that the light is not shining in his or her eyes.
- Sit or stand facing the older person at eye level, so that your eyes and mouth are clearly visible. Be sure to have the person's attention before speaking.
- Keep interactions short and simple.
- If multiple officers are on the scene, have one officer conduct the interview, rather than multiple officers asking different questions.
- Keep your voice and mannerisms calm.
- Do not shout. If necessary, speak slightly louder without shouting or yelling.
- Show a willingness to listen through effective nonverbal communication. Be attentive.
- Ask questions to clarify confusion, but ask only one question at a time. Wait for a response to one question before asking another.
- Allow time for hearing and comprehending.
- Be especially sensitive to the older person who is tired and not feeling well. Tired or ill people are less able to understand or remember what is asked or said.

- Observe for nonverbal clues that the person understood you. For example, are you receiving a blank stare?
- Be patient. Expect to repeat what you say often. If the older person does not understand, rephrase the question, rather than repeating the same words.
- Never interrupt. It discourages free speaking, and the interruption may cause the patient to forget what he or she was going to say.

Communicating with Hard of Hearing Older Persons

- Ask the patient if he or she has a hearing aid and would like to use it.
- Stand at a distance of 3 to 6 feet.
- Reduce background noise, such as a television or radio.
- Arrange to have light on your face, not behind you, if possible.
- Position yourself within the visual level of the listener.
- Speak at a natural rate, unless you see signs of incomprehension.
- Speak *slightly* louder than normal, but do not shout.
- Always face the hearing impaired patient, and let your facial expression reflect your meaning.
- Never speak from another room or out of the sight of a hearing impaired patient.
- Use short sentences.
- Rephrase misunderstood sentences.
- Remember that the hearing impaired person will not hear and understand as well when tired or sick.

Communicating with Aphasic Persons

- Talk to the person with aphasia as an adult and not as a child. Avoid talking down to the person.
- Avoid open-ended questions. Used focused questions instead.
- During conversation, minimize background noise.
- Make sure you have the person's attention before communicating.
- Praise all attempts to speak. Encourage the use of all modes of communication.
- Give the person time to talk, permitting a reasonable amount of time to respond. If the person takes too long to answer, ask the person to repeat the question to see if he or she comprehended it. Accept all communication attempts (speech, writing, gesture) rather than demanding speech. Avoid insisting that each word be produced perfectly.
- Keep your own communication simple, but adult. Simplify sentence structure and reduce your own rate of speech. Keep your voice at a normal volume and emphasize key words.
- Augment speech with gesture and visual aids whenever possible. Repeat a statement when necessary.

In the previous section, the major forms of aphasia were reviewed in order to give the law enforcement officer an understanding of the disease, and the various ways communication can be disrupted. While most family members or caretakers will be able to identify that the patient suffers from aphasia, they may not be able to identify the type. In order to make communication easier and less frustrating for those with aphasia, the following guidelines will aid in communication. Ask the family member or caretaker the following questions:

- Is the difficulty listening or talking?
- How does the person usually communicate?

If the difficulty is with listening, use an environmental "show me" approach. In other words, show persons what you want them to do. For example, if you want the person to raise his or her arm, raise your arm first. If the difficulty is with talking, use choice questions. Give the person the question. The law enforcement officer can either point or say the word if prompted.

Communicating with Persons with Dementia

When communicating with persons with dementia, the following will prove helpful:

- Use clear, concrete, familiar language.
- Convey only one idea at a time, speaking simply and not too fast.
- Do not use police jargon.
- Use short sentences. If the person does not understand, repeat exactly what was just said. This allows time for the person's brain to process the information. If the words are varied, this requires greater effort for the patient. If the person still cannot understand, repeat using different words.
- Accompany your words with gestures.
- If the person tries to answer, but loses his or her train of thought, repeat the last few words the person said as a reminder.
- Do not give lengthy explanations as to why something is being done, as the person may not understand.
- Use nouns instead of pronouns. The person with dementia may lose track of whom the pronouns are referring to. Don't say, "Your husband is here; may I ask *him* some questions about you?" Instead, say, "Your husband is here; may I ask your *husband* some questions about you?" Even better, refer to the husband by name: "Your husband, John is here; may I ask John some questions about you?"
- Avoid using the word "don't." Those with dementia sometimes cannot understand this commonly used contraction.

If the person with dementia cannot understand spoken language, written communication may be helpful. Toward the middle stages of the disease, however, those with dementia can read words, but do not understand their meaning. Persons with dementia may have difficulty understanding language, though at times they may understand. It is best for the law enforcement officer to assume that the person can understand.

You may be tempted to talk about the severely demented person as though he or she were not there, especially if you never expect to get an answer in return.

Try a bit harder to communicate with the person with dementia. The result will be an increase in the quality of the person's life, if only for a short time.

Communicating with Persons with Parkinson's Disease

To enhance communication with people with Parkinson's disease, below are tips to maintain and enhance communication:

- Choose an environment with reduced noise.
- Allow (and encourage) the person to speak slowly.
- Be face to face with the person. Look at the person as he or she is speaking. A well-lit room also enhances communication.
- Encourage the person to use short phrases. Have the person say one or two words or syllables per breath.
- Have the person choose a comfortable posture and position that provides support during long and stressful conversations.
- Fatigue significantly affects speaking ability. Plan for periods of vocal rest before planned conversations or telephone calls.
- If the person has difficulty being understood, the following technique may help:
  - If the person is able to write without difficulty, have the person write what he or she is trying to say.

Attitude Tip—Though the older person's fears and anxieties may not seem important to you, they are very real and important to the older person. By acknowledging concerns and making it clear—with your words and your actions—that you understand their importance, you will do much to calm and reassure.

Case Study 2

At 11:00 a.m., the manager calls you to his continuing care retirement complex. The manager states other residents informed him that Melvin, an 85-year-old resident who resides alone, was not seen at breakfast this morning. Additionally, there was no answer at Melvin's door. The manager informs you that Melvin has no immediate family and rarely leaves the complex. He is very socially active and never misses breakfast. The manager states that he has a master key and can gain access to Melvin's apartment.

(Continues)

Once at the apartment, you knock repeatedly on the door, but do not get an answer. With the master key, you enter Melvin's apartment. Once inside, you observe Melvin lying on the living room sofa. You call his name, but he does not answer. You gently touch Melvin's arm, at which time he awakes. You identify yourself as a sheriff. Melvin looks at you with confusion and does not answer. You repeat what you have just said. Melvin shakes his head as if he does not understand. You notice Melvin trying to adjust a hearing aid in his right ear.

What are your observations?

What is your course of action?

SUMMARY

There are many things that make communicating with the older person challenging. Keeping in mind the age-related changes in the older person, disease processes affecting communication, and the cultural values of older people, law enforcement professionals will be able to effectively and compassionately communicate with older persons. Communicating effectively with your older patient can make a difference.

CASE STUDY SUMMARIES

Case Study 1 Summary

Your first priority, of course, is victim safety. You must determine if the victim has suffered any injuries as a result of the robbery. In this case, the victim has not. As a law enforcement officer, you know that the sooner you can get suspect information, the better. In this case study, however, as you begin your interview, the older woman says, "I don't know . . . I'm so upset, I can't think." You do learn that the woman is 80 years old; her name is Ethel Telman, and she lives "across town." You are not able to gather any more information from Mrs. Telman.

Preserving evidence at a crime scene is vital police work. In this case, though, there is no physical evidence—the suspect made off with Mrs. Telman's purse and has left the area.

Having now learned about communicating with older people, particularly older people in crisis, you know that a potentially more productive interview can be done away from the scene. The most prudent thing to do is to transport Mrs. Telman to an environment that is more conducive to the interview—most preferably, in her home. The victim's home provides an atmosphere that is comfortable to her. This will enhance the communication (interview) process. Use all of the techniques learned in the chapter that apply to the victim as you conduct the interview. As you learn what items Mrs. Telman had in her purse (such as identification, keys, etc.), provide information on how these items can be replaced. Offer to contact any family, friends, or neighbors the victim may want notified. Make appropriate referrals to any victim advocacy groups that are appropriate. Finally, assure Mrs. Telman that you (or the sector/post car) will drive by the home with more frequency. This will help the victim to feel safe and show that law enforcement cares about the victim and the victim's safety.

Case Study 2 Summary

You encounter an 85-year-old male who appears confused. You notice the person attempting to make adjustment to a hearing aid. Based on the information you have learned, you know that this person is socially active within the retirement community and attends breakfast every morning. Your first priority should be to ensure that there is no life-threatening emergency where EMS would be needed. The person appears to be displaying purposeful movements by attempting to adjust his hearing aid. You attempt to assist him. Taking a piece of paper you write the words "batteries." The person reaches into the end table and takes out an envelope containing hearing aid batteries. The person then removes his hearing aid. You replace the batteries and hand him his hearing aid, at which time he places the hearing aid in his ear.

Once again, you identify yourself and explain why you are there. The person intelligibly states that he fell asleep last evening on the sofa and apparently did not hear anyone knocking at the door or realize what time it was.

No further intervention is necessary. What you do learn is that in most senior housing complexes, there is a vast communication network among the residents. Residents of these facilities usually form a close network, which includes checking on each other frequently.

ENDNOTES

1. Wilder, C. N., & Weinstein, B. E. (Eds.). (1984). *Aging and communication.* New York: The Haworth Press; p. 51.
2. Dreher, B. B. (1987). *Communication skills for working with elders.* New York: Springer; p. xi.
3. Ibid., p. 49.
4. National Institute on Deafness and Other Communication Disorders. (2010, June 16). *Quick statistics.* National Institutes of Health. Retrieved from http://www.nidcd.nih.gov/health/statistics/Pages/quick.aspx.
5. Dreher, p. 28.
6. National Victim Center. Excerpted from *Focus on the Future: A Systems Approach to Prosecution and Victim Assistance, A Training and Resource Manual,* Grant Number 92-MU-MU-K003, made possible by a grant from the U.S. Department of Justice, Office for Victims of Crime.

RESOURCES

Websites

American Speech-Language-Hearing Association (ASHA) (www.asha.org)

National Aphasia Association (www.aphasia.org)

National Institutes of Health, National Institute on Deafness and Other Communication Disorders (www.nidcd.nih.gov)

Books and Articles

Hoffman, S. A., & Platt, C. A. (2000). *Comforting the confused.* New York: Springer.

Janing, J. (1991). Reflections on aging: Communicating with the elderly. *Journal of Emergency Medical Services, 16*(6), pp. 34–36, 39–40, 43–44.

Shanks, S. J. (1983). *Nursing and the management of adult communication disorders.* San Diego, CA: College-Hill Press, Inc.

KEY TERMS

apraxia: An impairment in carrying out purposeful movements, which can also manifest as a speech impairment, with inability to produce speech with the correct rhythm and timing, as well as highly inconsistent errors

communication: The transmitting of information from a sender to receiver and verification that the receiver received and understood the information

dysarthria: A disorder of speech production, resulting from weakness, slowness, or incoordination of the speech mechanism due to damage to the nervous system; speech errors are highly consistent from one occasion to the next

listening: The act of receiving information; includes observation of more than just the words; also includes the volume, pitch, inflection, tone, and nonverbal aspects

macular degeneration: Deterioration of the central portion of the retina

Meniere's disease: A disease affecting the membranous inner ear characterized by deafness, dizziness (vertigo), and ringing in the ear (tinnitus)

nonverbal communication: Includes eye contact, hand gestures, body position, facial expression, and touch

otosclerosis: A disease involving the middle ear capsule, specifically affecting the movement of the stapes (one of the three tiny bones in the middle ear)

ototoxic: Any drug with the potential to cause toxic reactions to structures of the inner ear

Parkinson's disease: A chronic nervous disease characterized by a fine, slowly spreading tremor, muscle weakness and rigidity, and a peculiar gait

presbycusis: Hearing loss associated with aging

verbal communication: Includes words, volume, pitch, inflection, and tone

Chapter Five

The Victimization
of Older Adults

LEARNING OBJECTIVES

1. Understand the nature of older victims.
2. Understand the fear of crime among older people.
3. Understand financial exploitation among older people.
4. Understand older victims of sexual assault.
5. Understand homicide of older people.
6. Understand how to prepare the older victim/witness for testimony.
7. Understand crime prevention and older people.
8. Understand how to help older people who have been victimized.

Case Study 1

You are called to the home of an elderly female by a neighbor. The neighbor states that he has not seen the 76-year-old woman in 2 days and is concerned. The neighbor states that the woman is widowed and lives alone. When the neighbor approached the back door of the older woman's home, the glass on the door was shattered. You immediately call for backup. When the second unit arrives, you and the second officer enter the residence. Once inside, you make a search of the home. Upon entering the bedroom, you find the older woman dead, lying on her bed in a blood-spattered room. It appears that she suffered multiple stab wounds to her face, neck, and chest. Her nightclothes were pushed above her breasts and her legs were spread. She was nude except for the nightshirt.

Two months earlier, you recall hearing of an elderly homicide in roll call. The offender had entered the home of a 74-year-old woman. The offender attacked the woman, causing multiple facial fractures. Afterward, the perpetrator ripped off the woman's clothing, raped her vaginally, then anally, and assaulted her vaginally with an umbrella. The offender then cut the woman's throat.

What are your thoughts as you survey the crime scene?

INTRODUCTION

There is more crime victimization of older people today because there is more crime and there are more elderly people than ever before. The criminal victimization of older people can take many forms. Historically, violent crime against older people was a rare event; however, the growing number of older people in society will increase the victimization older people may face. Law enforcement officers must understand the types of victimization that older people encounter, how to solve these crimes, and what preventive measures can be undertaken to reduce victimization in older people.

OLDER VICTIMS

Crimes against older people tend to be more serious in nature than those against younger persons. Older people are more likely to be victimized by strangers in their own home and are less likely to defend themselves. When older people are victimized, they usually suffer greater physical, mental, and financial injuries than other age groups. Older victims are twice as likely to suffer serious physical injury and to require hospitalization than any other age group. Furthermore, the physiological process of aging brings with it a decreasing ability to heal after injury—both physically and mentally. Thus, older victims may never fully recover from the trauma of their victimization. Also, the trauma that older victims suffer is worsened by their financial difficulties.

Because many older people live on a low or fixed income, they often cannot afford the professional services and products that could help them in the aftermath of a crime.

It is understandable why older people are fearful of crime. Older people, in fact, face a number of additional worries and fears when victimized. First, they may doubt their ability to meet the expectations of law enforcement and worry that officers will think that they are incompetent. They may worry that a family member, upon learning of their victimization, will also think they are incompetent. Further, they may fear retaliation by the offender for reporting the crime. Finally, older people may experience feelings of guilt for allowing themselves to be victimized. Depending upon your approach as a law enforcement officer, you can do much to restore confidence in and maintain the dignity of the older victims you work with.[1]

Crime data for older persons is shown in **Table 5-1**.

Table 5-1 Crime Data for Older Persons in 2010

Persons Age 60 Years and Older	*Persons Age 65 Years and Older*
Accounted for 14% of fraud complaints and 13% of identity complaints to the Federal Trade Commission; compared with those aged 50–59, are reported to have the largest escalation in complaints over 10 years	Totaled 92,865 persons that were victims of violent crime
	Made up 4.5% (585) of all murder victims • 46.32% (271) were female (versus only 22.45% homicide victims for females of all ages)
5% reported emotional abuse (and was only conveyed to law enforcement .4% of the time)	Encountered 2.4 violent victimizations per 1,000 persons (compared with 10.9 for those aged 50–64)
1.6% reported physical abuse	
5.1% reported neglect	
5.2% reported financial exploitation by relatives	
Older Persons in General	
Had a 2.28 times increase in mortality rate if they reported mistreatment	
Of those abused 30 days before examination, 72% showed signs of bruising, and 89.6% were aware of where the bruises had come from • 56% of victims possessed 1 or more bruises that were at least 5 cm large (as opposed to 7% of older persons who did not report abuse)	

Source: Data from The National Center For Victims of Crime. (2011). *Elder victimization.* Retrieved from http://www.victimsofcrime.org/library/crime-information-and-statistics/elder-victimization.

Tips for Responding to Older Victims

The following are tips to aid the law enforcement officer when responding to an older person who has been victimized. They are offered at the beginning of this chapter, as they are helpful in all elder victimization cases.

- Be attentive to whether victims are tired or not feeling well.
- Allow victims to collect their thoughts before you begin your interview.
- Ask victims if they are having any trouble understanding you. Be sensitive to the possibility that they may have difficulty hearing or seeing, but do not assume such impairments. Ask the victim if they have any special needs, such as eyeglasses or hearing aids.
- Ask victims whether they would like you to contact a family member or friend.
- Be alert for signs of domestic violence or neglect, since a victim's relative could be the abuser.
- Give victims time to hear and understand your words during the interview.
- Ask questions one at a time, waiting for a response before proceeding to the next question. Avoid interrupting victims.
- Repeat key words and phrases. Ask open-ended questions to ensure you are being understood.
- Avoid unnecessary pressure. Be patient. Give victims frequent breaks during your interview.
- Protect the dignity of victims by including them in all decision-making conversations taking place in their presence.
- Provide enhanced lighting if victims are required to read. Ensure that all print in written materials is both large enough and dark enough for victims to read.
- Provide victims written information that summarizes the important points you communicated verbally so they can refer to this information later.
- Remember that elderly victims' recollections may surface slowly. Do not pressure them to recollect events or details; rather, ask them to contact you if they remember anything later.
- In all your comments and interactions with elderly victims, their families, and other professionals involved in the case, focus on the goals of restoring confidence to and maintaining the dignity of the elderly victims you work with.[2]

FEAR OF CRIME AMONG OLDER PEOPLE

Surveys often show that becoming the victim of a crime is of concern for most Americans. The fear of crime is not evenly distributed among the population. The fear of crime is greatest among older people. Several studies have indicated that the fear of crime is greater for older people than worries about health, money, or loneliness. The fear of victimization by older people may be explained in part by declines in physical strength and the senses, which yield increased feelings of vulnerability. These fears may be heightened because many older people live alone and are more likely to be isolated from the neighborhood and community groups.[3]

Case Study 2

A 74-year-old widow inherits money from her late husband, whom she relied upon to make all financial decisions. The widow's 40-year-old female neighbor, with whom the widow is acquainted, begins to provide companionship for the widow. Over the next several months, the neighbor begins to assist the widow with bill paying and other financial matters. The neighbor convinces the widow to sign over her stock, saying she can make it grow faster. The neighbor gradually isolates the widow, and then infantilizes the widow, making her feel dependent. She then gains complete control over the widow's finances.

Is this a case of financial abuse/exploitation?

FINANCIAL EXPLOITATION

Financial (or material) exploitation is the illegal or improper use of an elder's funds, property, or assets.

Types of Financial Exploitation

Telemarketing fraud, identity theft, living will scams, lottery scams, and home-improvement frauds are usually perpetrated by strangers. The types of financial exploitation described as follows depend on a relationship of trust between the exploiter and the victim.[4]

Changes in Patterns of Expenditures and Bank Withdrawals

Unlike younger people, older people generally maintain a stable pattern of income and expenditures. Mortgage (or rent), utilities, and property taxes require regular payments. Social security and pension checks are usually deposited directly into the older person's checking or savings account. When financial exploitation occurs, withdrawals (some often large) are seen in addition to fixed expense withdrawals. It is not uncommon for the older person's life savings to be withdrawn in a 3- to 6-month period. District attorneys' offices (and banks) employ forensic accountants. Working with a forensic accountant can save the detective or investigator valuable time when investigating these types of crimes.

There are instances, however, when large withdrawals are legitimate (such as modifications to the older person's home to accommodate physical limitations, or a deposit on a vacation home).

Large monetary gifts made by older people with capacity (i.e., who are of sound mind) can be legitimate (legal) and problematic in financial exploitation cases. There is a provision in the tax code that allows individuals to give a monetary gift of up to $13,000 per year as a tax-free gift (investigators should consult with the local district attorney's office as regulations that govern amounts may vary and have specific guidelines). When prosecuting individuals for financial exploitation, the person receiving the money can claim that he or she received it as a gift. Investigators must look at financial patterns between the victim and exploiter in sum in order to establish wrongdoing.

Money Missing from Joint Accounts

A very common form of financial exploitation is taking money from joint accounts of older people. A friend, relative, or homecare worker will have his or her name added to an older person's account. This gives the financial abuser the legal right to take money out of an account without notifying the account holder or asking the account holder's permission. It also gives the abuser the legal title to the account once the older person has passed away. There is very little that can be done to prosecute this type of exploitation unless it can be proven that the older person did not have the mental capacity to sign the document opening the joint account.

Forgery of Checks or Credit Card Purchases

This type of financial exploitation involves the forgery of checks or credit card purchases, in which persons with access to the older person's checkbook or credit cards use them for their own purposes. In cases of forgery, the bank must restore the funds to the depositor's account, as it is the bank's responsibility to verify the signature. Criminal charges can then be brought. It is much more difficult to charge in cases when the older person signs blank checks. In these cases, it is not forgery, and it is necessary to show criminal intent—that is, that the older person did not give permission for the person to fill in the check or that it was not a gift. Older people suffering from dementia often cannot remember the circumstances under which they signed the check.

Misuse of ATM or Debit Cards

Many exploiters access the accounts of homebound older people using ATM cards. Use of the card may have been authorized or simply not noticed. Detectives may be able to obtain footage from banks to verify the identity of a card user. Excessive ATM or debit card use is a red flag for exploitation, especially since many older people prefer traditional teller banking and do not use ATMs or debit cards.

Fraudulent Wills and Property Transfers

Older people can be coerced into signing wills or property transfers that they do not wish to sign or do not have the capacity to sign. Home health aides and other exploiters have gained control of property by proposing an exchange whereby they promise to care for the older person for the rest of his or her life, avoiding nursing home placement.

Theft of Money or Personal Property by a Home Health Aide

Sometimes home health aides take money or property from an older person in their care. Criminal charges may ensue, but even a conviction will not guarantee restitution. Other avenues to restoring the victim's money or personal property are crime victim boards and bonding companies. Home health agencies may insist that their employees be bonded, in which case the elderly victim may be able to recover money under the bond.

Theft of Money by Attorneys, Accountants, Stock Brokers, Court-Appointed Guardians, and Representative Payees for Social Security Benefits

Professionals and others with the legal responsibility to safeguard an older person's funds may exploit them. Allegations of theft should be investigated, even if the accuser may have cognitive impairment and even if the alleged exploiter is a member of a respected profession.

Misuse of a Power of Attorney

A power of attorney is a document in which one party (the principal) gives another party (the agent) the right to handle designated financial transactions. These transactions include banking, stock and bond sales, real estate transactions, and many other financial matters.

It is important for law enforcement officers to know that powers of attorney only cover financial matters and do not cover matters of person, such as medical treatment and placement in a nursing home. Perpetrators often believe that they can make all decisions for the older person. However, only certain decisions can be made on behalf of the older person. Further, the power of attorney may have been obtained by coercion or the older person may not have had the legal authority to sign the document due to a diminished mental capacity. A power of attorney must be established voluntarily by a person who has the mental capacity to understand what is being signed and the powers that are being conveyed. In all cases of a misuse of a power of attorney, the investigating officer will want to obtain a copy of the power of attorney document and have it examined by the district attorney.

If it can be proven that coercion was used, or that the older person was already losing mental capacity, when the power of attorney was signed, it is not a legal document. A law enforcement officer who suspects that capacity may have been lacking can pursue an investigation of the older person's capacity at the time the document was obtained, the circumstances under which it was obtained, and the financial transactions that occurred using the document. Capacity can be assessed by a medical expert. Sometimes the agent with a legitimate power of attorney will abuse that power. For example, if the agent uses the principal's assets for his or her own benefit, this could be larceny.

Signs of Financial Exploitation

There are signs of financial exploitation in both the victim and suspected abuser.[5]

In the Victim

- Deviations in financial habits (e.g., bank withdrawals, loans taken)
- Numerous unpaid bills
- Checks made out to cash
- Little money while awaiting next check
- Elder unaware of monthly income
- A disparity between assets and lifestyle
- Personal belongings or financial documents missing
- Lack of amenities (e.g., television, clothing) when elder can afford them
- Recent will when elder clearly incapable
- Unprecedented transfer of assets to other(s)

Signs in the Suspected Abuser

- Always makes bank deposits/withdrawals for the older person
- Uses elder's ATM cards
- Makes withdrawals from a dormant account
- Makes all investment decisions for the older person
- Receives frequent expensive gifts from the older person
- Asks only financial questions, not caring questions
- Refuses to spend money on the older person's care
- Asserts powers based on power of attorney, or power does not appear properly executed

Profile of the Financial Abuser

The perpetrator of financial abuse/exploitation is often an unemployed relative (child or grandchild) who is dependent on the elderly victim and may be addicted to drugs or alcohol, and/or emotionally disturbed. Other perpetrators of financial abuse include paid caretakers, friends, and fiduciaries. Perpetrators sometimes use emotional and physical abuse to intimidate and coerce an older person for financial exploitation.[6]

Capacity

Investigation and prosecution of exploitation cases often depend on an assessment of the victim's capacity to sign or consent to a financial document and opinions as to whether they were pressured to do so.

Capacity is the ability to perform a task. Capacity is not a single state. A person can be said to have or lack capacity in specific aspects. Mental capacity focuses on mental processes such as remembering, reasoning, and understanding the consequences of an action or choice. There are varying degrees of capacity. A person may be perfectly capable of a simpler task, but unable to perform a complex one. A person may be deemed to have capacity in one area but not in another.

As an example, for a will to be legal, an older person must have enough mental capacity to:[7]

1. Understand what a will is
2. Recollect the nature and extent of his or her property
3. Remember and understand his or her relationship to living descendants and others who will be affected by the will

The capacity to sign contracts means understanding what a contract is and understanding consequences of the contract. Sometimes, no formal document is signed, but a person consents to make purchases, accept services, and the like. For proper consent, an older person must:[8]

1. Understand the transaction
2. Have mental capacity to execute a contract
3. Act voluntarily, free from threats or force

Capacity involves complicated issues that the law enforcement officer may not easily be able to discern. It should be determined early in the investigation if a diminished capacity evaluation has been completed for the victim. If the victim has already been determined to have diminished capacity, the investigator will want to ascertain who has power of attorney over the victim. If no diminished capacity judgment exists for the victim, and it is believed that the victim may not have understood what he or she was signing or the nature of the alleged exploitation, an evaluation of capacity should be ordered. Capacity evaluations are performed by medical experts. The outcome of a capacity evaluation may determine the next steps and a course of action in the investigation.

Undue Influence

Undue influence is defined as the substitution of one person's will for the true desires of another. If an older person was pressured, undue influence may have been exerted. It is not a criminal charge, but a catch-all term connoting excessive pressure. Persons using undue influence use their role and power to exploit the trust, dependency, and fear of others. Older people with financial assets are vulnerable targets for undue influence. Undue influence is used as a means to financially exploit the elderly victim. The consequences (both of the material loss and of the personal loss of power) can be devastating for the victim. Financial exploitation often contributes strongly to early death. Factors that increase vulnerability to undue influence include:[9]

- Recent bereavement
- Physical disability
- Isolation from friends, family, and community supports/activities
- Lacking knowledge about one's own finances
- Cognitive impairment

The likely perpetrators of undue influence almost always begin with a close and trusting relationship with the victim, and can include:[10]

- Family members
- Caregivers of the physically or cognitively impaired
- Neighbors, friends, or con artists who befriend the elderly person with financial gain in mind
- Fiduciaries such as attorneys, accountants, trustees, or guardians

Perpetrators may take deliberate actions to gain control of the older person. They may isolate the victim from other people, convince the victim that no one else cares for him or her, or take steps to make or keep the victim dependent.

Structured Interview Questions for Financial Exploitation

When investigating financial exploitation of an elderly person, a structured interview using a set of predetermined questions can be helpful.[11]

For the Victim of Financial Exploitation

1. What is your name (including maiden name), and date of birth?
2. Do you have any close relatives? (Identify nature of relationship, names, addresses, and phone numbers of any relatives.) Who are some of your close friends? (Identify names, addresses, phone numbers, and length and nature of relationship.)
3. Are you close to any of your neighbors? (Identify names and addresses.)
4. Do you own your own home? How long? Who is on the title to the house?
5. Does anyone live with you? (Identify names and relationships.) Do they pay rent? Do they provide any services for you in exchange for staying there?
6. How long have you known [name suspect]? How did you meet [suspect]?
7. Does [suspect] provide any services for you? If so, describe. Who hired [suspect]?
8. How is [suspect] compensated for any services provided?

9. Did you ever give [suspect] any loans or gifts (monetary or otherwise)?
10. Does [suspect] owe you any money?
11. Do you owe [suspect] any money?
12. Who handles your finances? Who writes the checks? Who pays the bills? Who does your taxes?
13. What is your monthly income? (Record amount and sources of income.)
14. What are your monthly expenses? Describe some of them.
15. Do you have a will or trust? Does anyone have power of attorney for you?
16. Do you have an attorney? (Obtain name and phone number, if available.)
17. When is the last time you saw a doctor? Who is your doctor?
18. Does anyone other than [suspect] provide any services for you? If so, describe.
19. Have you ever given anyone permission to sign your name? Use your credit card? Have you placed that person's name on any of your banking accounts?
20. Is there anyone else who can do the things [suspect] currently does for you?
21. Have you signed any documents lately? If so, what were they?
22. What are the balances on your bank accounts? Credit card accounts?

For the Suspect of Financial Exploitation

1. How do you know Mr./Ms. [name alleged victim]?
2. What is your relationship to [name victim]?
3. Describe [victim]. Is he/she slow, forgetful, trusting, easily influenced?
4. How did you get to be the caretaker? Who hired you?
5. Are you the only caretaker?
6. How long have you been the caretaker?
7. Who lives here with [victim]?
8. How long have you lived here?
9. Do you pay rent, or do you receive room and board in exchange for services you perform for [victim]?
10. Are you [victim]'s guardian? If so, since when? Do you have power of attorney over [victim]? If so, since when?
11. Who, if anyone, assists you in caring for [victim]? What is his or her name? What does he or she do specifically?
12. What are your duties (e.g., medication/toilet assistance, cooking/cleaning services)?
13. What are you paid? How are you paid? How often are you paid?
14. Who is responsible for [victim]'s finances/bills? Who pays the bills? If you pay the bills, how long have you been doing so? Does anyone else help?
15. What are [victim]'s sources of income (e.g., Social Security, pension)? What is the total monthly amount of [victim]'s income?

16. Do you have access to [victim]'s savings or checking accounts? Money market accounts? Investments? Is your name on any of these accounts? If so, why?
17. Do you have access to [victim]'s credit/ATM/debit card? Have you ever had permission to use [victim]'s credit/ATM/debit card?
18. Have you ever had permission to sign [victim]'s name?
19. Who writes the checks (to pay [victim]'s expenses)?
20. Where do you bank? (Name all banks.) Where does [victim] bank? (Name all banks.)
21. How many accounts?
22. Who, if anyone, do you talk to before making a financial decision on behalf of [victim]?
23. When was the last time [victim] saw a doctor? Who is [victim]'s doctor?
24. Has [victim] had any injuries, past or present? Describe.
25. Has [victim] given you any gifts, money, or loans?
26. Do you have any promissory notes showing loans to you from [victim] or from [victim] to you?
27. Does [victim] owe you any money? Do you owe [victim] any money?
28. Does [victim] have any wills or trusts? Insurance policies? Who is the beneficiary? Who is the trustee? Successor trustee?
29. What are your sources of income? What are the total amounts per month? Any recent inheritances, unusual winnings?
30. Has [victim] signed any documents lately? If so, what were they?
31. What are the current balances on [victim]'s banking and credit card accounts?

OLDER VICTIMS OF SEXUAL ASSAULT

Sexual assault in older people is covered in Chapter 6, "Elder Abuse."

HOMICIDE OF OLDER PEOPLE

Empirical work on the incidence of homicide against older persons has been slow to develop, and is historically an understudied crime. This section presents relevant literature on the topic and is intended to provide an overview of elder homicide victims. Though some studies are dated, they represent the relevant body of literature. Research on elder homicide is lacking, thus making investigation of these cases difficult.

Older people are both vulnerable to attack and more likely to be injured as a consequence. Violent assaults account for up to 14% of elder trauma patients and result in death more frequently than in younger people. Comorbid illness also contributes to the greater mortality rate in the elderly.

In many cases, a physician is willing to sign a death certificate of an older deceased person who has no outward signs of trauma, without any investigation being conducted, particularly if the older person has multiple comorbidities.

In 2006, Collins and Presnell reported on a 20-year study of elder homicide. The results of this study are reported as follows.[12]

The study examined all cases of referred to the Forensic Section of the Department of Pathology and Laboratory Medicine at the Medical University of South Carolina from 1985–2004. Included in the study were all victims 65 years of age or older. Homicide cases were extracted and further analyzed. Variables examined included age, race, gender, cause of death, location of death, time of year, perpetrator, victim-perpetrator relationship, motive/scenario, toxicology, and sexual assault component.

Over the study period, 2,137 cases of elder deaths were investigated. Of these, 127 were classified as homicide. Of these homicide victims, 73 (58%) were male, 54 (42%) were female, 70 (55%) were African American, and 57 (45%) were white. The age range of the homicide victims was 65 to 94 years, with 12 victims age 85 years and older. The causes of death were gunshot wounds (31%), blunt force trauma (28%), stabbing (22%), asphyxia (13%), and other (6%). The category of other included neglect (4 cases), fire (2 cases), and chop injury (1 case). The majority of deaths, 83%, occurred in the elderly persons' residences, including care facilities/nursing homes. Of the residence locations, three were in a nursing home/care facility and five homicides occurred at the home, but outdoors. Other locations (17%) were a motel, car, woods, job site, club, and road. When season of the year was examined, there was not a significant difference among the 12 months (though a slight majority was in the fall and spring). The victim knew the perpetrator in slightly over 50% of the cases. Of the cases in which law enforcement officials were able to identify the perpetrator and document gender, 86% were male and 14% were female. For the cases in which the victim knew the perpetrator (acquaintance or relative), 83% of the perpetrators were male and 17% were female. Of acquaintances of the victim, 83% were male, usually a friend or roommate. Of the relatives, 83% were male, usually the husband, child, or grandchild. The three male victims residing in a nursing home/care facility were killed by acquaintances; the causes of death were blunt-force trauma, strangulation, and stabbing. Two acquaintance perpetrators were fellow male residents, and one acquaintance was a female employee.

The most common motive in these homicides was robbery (46%), followed by argument (26%) and other (11%). The other category included rape, arson, hunting accident, neglect, and police shooting. The motive was not specified or known in 17% of homicides. Toxicology was positive for ethanol in 17% of the cases. In cases where no analysis was performed (14%), the victims had been hospitalized, and no admission specimens were available.

In cases where a sexual assault examination was performed (13), six victims showed evidence of sexual assault. All six victims were female and the perpetrators were male. The perpetrators were acquaintances in two cases and strangers in four. The incident location of the six cases was the victim's home (but not a nursing homecare facility). The causes of death for the six cases were asphyxia (four cases), stabbing (one case), and blunt-force trauma (one case). Toxicology of the six victims was positive for ethanol in two cases.

The discussion section of the study cited the following information.

The most common cause of death in the study was gunshot wound. This prevalence is also true of all homicides, regardless of the victim's age. Blunt-force trauma was second, followed by stabbing and asphyxia. These four categories of elder homicide have been previously reported in other studies. The large majority of elder homicides occurred in the victim's home. In more than half of the cases, the victim knew the perpetrator. The perpetrator is most often male. With respect to nursing home deaths, far too many are not investigated or autopsied to draw significant conclusions.

Studies have examined motives in homicides for all ages of victims. Argument is one of the most common motives, as well as robbery. The most common motive in the study of elderly victims was robbery, especially in the home, followed by argument. Alcohol is often present in homicide victims, making alcohol a risk factor, increasing the chance of a person being a homicide victim. Only 17% of the elder homicide victims in the study tested positive for cocaine.

The sexual assault component was significant in the study, as the examination was performed in only slightly over 10% of cases and positive for a sexual assault component in half of these. Collins and Presnell[13] cite that one study reported that 3.8% of elder homicide victims were positive for sexual assault. Most elder sexual assaults occur at home when the victim is alone. The victims are usually female and the perpetrators are male. Usually, the victim knows the perpetrator, and the perpetrator is a user of alcohol. Some report a high percentage of nursing home incidents, and usually the assault is in bed. Many elder victims have cognitive impairment, a physical disability, or are under the influence of alcohol. The majority, up to 75%, sustain trauma, most of this anogenital. The elder female is prone to vaginal injury secondary to decreased estrogen, atrophy, vaginal dryness, and thinning wall. A significant amount of trauma can also be to the nongenital areas. Positive laboratory evidence (spermatozoa and prostatic acid phosphatase) can be recovered from both the living and deceased elder victims. Due to the barrier of decreased mental status, delayed reporting, defecation, urination, bathing, and/or fear of retribution, evidence is often lacking.

The highest percentage of homicides that occur during the commission of a felony befall people age 65 and older.[14] Similarly, Fox and Levin reported that older people are at greater risk than younger individuals of becoming victims of homicide during the course of a felony, such as robbery.[15]

Abrams et al. reported on the characteristics of older homicide victims (65 years and older) versus younger homicide victims (aged 18 to 64) in New York City from 1990–1998.[16] They reported that older homicide victims had lower population-based homicide rates overall and included an increased representation of women, non-Hispanic whites, and individuals who died from non-firearm injuries, such as cutting, beating, or strangling compared with nonelderly victims. The data also suggested that many older homicide victims were killed in their own homes or in locations other than on city streets. The study concludes by saying that improved accountability for the safety and wellbeing of older persons must involve a collaboration of adult protective services, medical and social services, and law enforcement. Increased support for, and supervision of, caregivers, and greater attention to home security will be required.

In 2010, an analysis of elder homicides in the cities of Chicago, Houston, and Miami for the years 1985–1994 was conducted.[17] The research indicated that, when compared to younger victims, older victims were significantly more likely to be female, to be killed by family members, and to be killed in the course of a robbery or other felony. The findings of the study indicated that, although the relative homicide victimization rate of elders was small in the three cities studied, it was still three to four times greater than the mean annualized rate for this age group nationally for the 10-year period of the analysis. Also, when compared to younger persons, there was a significantly larger proportion of elder homicide victims who were female and non-Hispanic white, as well as a larger than expected number for whom the offender was also non-Hispanic white and female. The study also found that elder victims were more frequently killed by middle-aged to older offenders. Among known victim-offender relationships, similar proportions of older and younger victims were killed by strangers, but twice the proportion of elder versus younger victims were killed by family members.

Among all elder homicide victims, over half of the incidents were motivated by robbery or another felony, compared to less than 20% of such incidents with younger victims. Yet, only 25% of elder homicide victims, compared to 65% of other homicides, were committed with guns. For elders across all three cities, 30% were killed with knives or other sharp objects, and 25% were killed with hands/feet or blunt objects. The findings also revealed that more than 80% of elder victims were killed indoors. The study also indicated that studies to date show that the characteristics of elder homicide are different from those for homicide of younger victims. That is, when compared to younger homicide victims, older persons are more likely to die, or sustain serious injuries, from violent attacks. Among homicide victims, there is also empirical evidence that elders are more likely than younger victims to be female, killed at home, by strangers, during the commission of another felony.[18]

One theory postulates five types of homicides committed against older people: [19]

1. *For-profit killings*: occurs when an offender kills an older or vulnerable adult for some form of profit
2. *Revenge killings*: occurs when offenders kill the older or vulnerable adult in order to get even with the victim or his or her family for some perceived injustice
3. *Eldercide*: entails the killing of older people simply out of prejudice against older persons
4. *Gerontophella*: refers to homicides that are committed in order to cover up an offender's sexual assault against the older victim
5. *Relief of burden killings*

Homicide in Long-Term Care Facilities[20]

Death of a resident in a long-term care facility is an expected event, and unlikely to trigger a death investigation. There are circumstances, however, where a death investigation is necessary and appropriate. When a death that could have been prevented has occurred, a death investigation is warranted.

Death investigation in a long-term care facility includes the following: examining the living arrangement of the deceased (signs of abuse or neglect may be detected upon inspection of the deceased's living area), inspecting the body for signs of abuse or neglect, and interviewing (staff and family of the deceased).

The American Bar Association Commission on Law and Aging has developed a document entitled *Elder Abuse Fatality Review Teams: A Replication Manual*.[21] The concept of a fatality review team involves bringing together a group of professionals to examine deaths that result from or relate to a certain cause in order to improve the thing or system that caused, contributed to, or failed to prevent the death and, thus, prevent similar deaths in the future. This means that the primary goal of an elder abuse fatality review team is the improvement of services to victims so that they receive the services and interventions they need.

Sexual Homicide of Older Females

While overall awareness of elder victimization has increased, there has been little attention focused on elderly females who have been the victim of sexual homicides and those who perpetrate such crimes. Law enforcement officials respond daily to violent criminal behavior; however, few have investigated the brutal sexual assault-homicide of an older female. The lack of frequency of cases and lack of knowledge regarding offender characteristics make these cases difficult for investigators. This section is intended to provide the investigator with insight into offender characteristics of those who perpetrate sexual homicide of older women.

Studies have demonstrated that older women, in certain ways, are inherently more vulnerable to crime than younger women. This is true because older women are more likely to live alone (due to increased risk of widowhood and longer life expectancy) and that vulnerability is related to physical size and strength (older women are less capable of fleeing or resisting a physical attack than younger persons).

The routine activities perspective offered in criminology is consistent with the notion of vulnerable victims. The interaction of available victims, motivated offenders, and the lack of guardianship may offer an understanding of how these incidents occur. Older women are more likely to lack the guardianship common to children and younger women with parents, boyfriends, and husbands. Thus, a motivated offender may view the older woman as more vulnerable. Predators assess a victim's vulnerability and accessibility in the course of their daily activities. Offenders of sexual homicide of older females are no different in their decision making.

What research exists on sexual assault of older females reveals that these victims are much more likely to be injured or killed compared to other victims of similar crimes. In 1988, a study[22] was conducted that focused specifically on those who rape older women. According to the study, when a rapist attacks an older woman, the rape or sexual assault is likely to be a particularly brutal act, largely motivated by rage or sadistic intent. The study also suggested that apparently motiveless violent attacks on older women may be cases of sexual assault.

Obtaining reliable statistics relative to sexual homicides of older females is difficult. Difficulties include the identification of the offense as a homicide without note of the subordinate offense of rape or sexual assault; the lack of necessary investigation to identify the sexual behavior; poor communication between investigators and other personnel relative to understanding the sexual nature of the offense; and classification errors in official data entries.

In 2002, Safarik et al. attempted to link offender characteristics to victim and crime scene attributes of those who perpetrate sexual homicide of older females.[23] The results of the survey revealed that although the victim population in the study was disproportionally white (86%), both African Americans (9%) and Hispanics (4%) were also victimized. Only one Asian victim was identified. Of the victims, 94% were killed in their own residences. The majority of victims lived in their neighborhoods for 10 years or more. More than 80% of the victims had no additional home security beyond locks normally found on doors and windows. Strangulation was found to be the most frequent cause of death (63%), followed by blunt force trauma (38%). Death by firearm (1%) was the least frequent.

The offender population in the study included 48 whites (44%), 46 African Americans (42%), 14 Hispanics (13%), and 1% being in the "other" category. There were no Asian offenders in the study. The offenders ranged in age from

15 to 58. African Americans offended interracially 77% of the time, Hispanics 80%, and whites only 4%. Of the offenders, 56% lived within six blocks of the victim, with nearly 30% living on the same block. Overall, 81% of the offenders traveled to the scene on foot. Ninety-nine percent of the offenders had criminal records, with burglary (59%) making up the highest proportion. However, property and violent offenses were found to be approximately equally represented among those with criminal histories. It should be noted that just 21% were found to have sex offenses in their criminal histories. Ninety-three percent of the offenders were unskilled, with nearly 70% unemployed. Of the offenders, 93% had 12 years or fewer of formal education, and 19% of the study offenders had 8 years or fewer. Regarding substance abuse, 93% of the offenders had a history of substance abuse. The drug abused most often was alcohol (85%), followed by marijuana (54%) and cocaine (44%).[24]

Of the offenders, 40% gained entrance through unlocked doors or windows, and 20% were freely admitted to the residence. Close to 40% used force on a door or window to gain entry. Study analysis of offender behavior at the crime scene indicated that 77% of the offenders brought nothing with them to the scene. When they did bring something, the items consisted of mostly weapons (10%) or tools (8%). Property was removed 72% of the time, mostly small, easily accessible items such as cash and jewelry. Offenders left the body of the victim uncovered 57% of the time. There were racial differences regarding covering the body, with white and Hispanic offenders being most likely to leave the victim uncovered (64%); African American offenders were more likely to cover the body (43%), and white offenders were least likely (21%). The approach used by 82% of the offenders was found to be a blitz attack.[25]

Offenders were found to have sexually assaulted their victims vaginally (65%) and anally (24%). African American offenders assaulted their victims both vaginally (71%) and anally (29%) more often than white offenders, who assaulted at 58% and 16%, respectively. Hispanic offenders assaulted anally 36% of the time, more often than either African American or white offenders. Overall, these offenders inserted foreign objects into the victim's body 22% of the time, with white offenders responsible for just more than half of those cases. Of note, offenders younger than 24 years of age perpetrated more than half of all foreign object insertions. Semen was identified in only 48% of the cases, with no differences noted for race or age. Sexual activity, without the presence of semen, was noted in the remaining 52% of cases. This sexual activity, in addition to vaginal, anal, and oral assault, included fondling the sexual areas of the body, foreign object insertion, and posing the victim to expose sexual areas, among others.[26]

Noteworthy is the fact that these crimes may be seen as having a financial motive. That is, in the process of committing the financial crime, the offender discovers the older victim and changes his primary motive, resulting in him not only sexually assaulting the victim but murdering the victim as well. However, from both a behavioral and experiential perspective, such a scenario stands in stark contrast to the findings in the study. The suggestion of a financially motivated crime gone awry is contradicted by the observation that the preponderance of the behavior was directed at the victim in furtherance of not only the sexual assault, but also the effort required to kill the victim. Not only was the majority of the interaction occurring with the victim, but also chronologically, it was occurring first. The removal of property occurred subsequent to the homicide. **Table 5-2** summarizes both crime scene and offender attributes regarding the offender of sexual homicide of older women.

Table 5-2 Attributes of the Older Sexual Homicide Offender

Attribute	Elderly Sexual Homicide Offender
Crime Scene Attributes	
Body disposition	Left at death scene Not transported Left in view Partially undressed or naked
Criminal sophistication	Criminally unsophisticated
Planning	Little or no planning, spontaneous offense
Evidence consciousness	Leaves evidence at the scene
Organization	Scene appears random and sloppy with no set plan for deterring detection
Protects identity	No measures taken to protect identity
Approach	Sudden violence to victim (blitz attack) to gain control
Sexual activity	Sexual activity at scene, usually postmortem
Weapon	Weapon used from scene and often left
Forensic evidence	Leaves forensic evidence
Cause of death	Most often death results from strangulation and blunt force trauma
Use of restraints	Minimal
Other activity	Property taken, financial gain
Level of force	Often excessive or brutal
Paraphilic behavior	Absence of paraphilic behavior
Motivation	Underlying theme of anger

(Continues)

Table 5-2 Attributes of the Older Sexual Homicide Offender (Continued)

Offender Attributes	
Work history	Poor work history
Skill level	Unskilled work
Employment	Unemployed
Criminal history	Arrest history diverse and generally antisocial Depending on age, history will reflect a multiplicity of crimes with no specific theme Criminal histories with both property and violent offenses Burglary or theft convictions
Intelligence	Lower intelligence Most have only some high school
Travel and search patterns	Lives or works near death scene Association with area Travels shorter distance to offend, half live within six blocks
Social skills	Socially incompetent
Substance abuse	Abuse of drugs and/or alcohol

Source: Adapted from Safarik, M. E., Jarvis, J. P., & Nussbaum, K. E. (2002). Sexual homicide of elder females, linking offender characteristics to victim and crime scene attributes. *Journal of Interpersonal Violence, 17*(5), 518.

Table 5-2 and the study described in this section are provided to offer law enforcement officials an insight into offender characteristics of those who perpetrate sexual homicide of older women. It should be noted that data for this crime are limited, and more extensive research is needed to sustain the findings.[27]

SUICIDE RISK AND HOSTAGE/BARRICADE SITUATIONS INVOLVING OLDER PEOPLE

Hostage/barricade situations pose particularly challenging situations for law enforcement officials. With the increasing numbers of older people in society, law enforcement officers must familiarize themselves with the potential dangers older people may pose to themselves and to others in the community.

The *FBI Law Enforcement Bulletin* (April 2003) in an article entitled "Suicide Risk and Hostage/Barricade Situations Involving Older Persons" offered these strategies when encountering a hostage/barricade situation involving an older person:

> Crisis negotiation strategies with older persons in hostage/barricade/ threats-of-suicide situations should take into account those developmental life span issues that concern and characterize older persons. Because of the

triple threat of substance abuse, depression, and suicide in older people, negotiators must consider these factors in planning a negotiation strategy.

A crisis played out as a hostage/barricade incident or suicide by cop constitutes a desperate act—an attempt at problem solving, however misdirected and unconstructive. It may be the desperate act of an otherwise adequate person struggling under the overwhelming stresses of old age or a continuation into old age of a lifelong pattern of dysfunction and bad judgment. In either case, a precipitating event has interacted with the person's age, ethnicity, depression, and substance abuse.

To deal with such situations, negotiators need to employ strategies designed to incorporate the effects of aging and the older individual's reactions to the aging process. First, negotiators should encourage older people involved in hostage/barricade situations to reminiscence through active listening. This can establish rapport with older persons, allowing them to ventilate pent-up emotion and to feel heard and, thereby, validated. It also enables negotiators to learn more about these individuals as their stories convey themes and underlying emotions that negotiators then can use to engage the subjects, hooks that they can exploit in negotiating with the older person. Recalled past events about which subjects may feel proud, from a time when they were younger, felt more adequate, and were more hopeful about the world and themselves can help negotiators find fruitful avenues to pursue while, at the same time, aid in bolstering subjects' wounded egos. Family memories, old times, athletic and academic achievements, courtship and marriage, military service, career and financial security, all before the vicissitudes of aging, retirement, and loss took their toll, are some of the likely reminiscences.

Second, and similarly, recalled past events about which subjects may feel ashamed or embarrassed over which they express deep regrets also can help negotiators find further areas to explore. This can include helping subjects see that unfinished business remains, such as reestablishing lost or estranged connections with others, making amends, finding meaning and purpose in their remaining lives, or anything that denotes a mission unfinished. Helping subjects picture themselves enacting their mission projects them into the future and on the other side of their present feelings and circumstances.

Finally, getting subjects to verbalize aloud their thoughts and feelings about death helps them feel validated and less frightened; paradoxically, they may value living more. Along with this, negotiators should point out to subjects that intoxication and depression color their world view and distort their judgment, just as they produce the effects and symptoms associated with each condition. Therefore, subjects should not make critical decisions while in that state.[28]

A note on reminiscing: Reminiscing is another mechanism for avoiding or minimizing a present that is painful or empty from losses. It is a recalling of time when one had more self-worth and greater capabilities, and when life was more rewarding and pleasant.

This section was offered to provide the law enforcement officer with the theory of negotiating with older people in hostage/barricade situations. It should be mentioned that hostage negotiation is a specialty within law enforcement. Whether to employ these strategies must be based on the risk/threat at hand. It is wise to consult with, and have access to, a geriatric psychiatrist (or a trained mental health professional who routinely works with, and counsels older people) for such incidents.

CULTURAL ISSUES

U.S. communities are becoming more diverse. Since no cultural/ethnic group is immune from elder abuse, it is likely that the victim and/or perpetrator in an elder abuse case may be from a culture different than your own. In order to effectively intervene in these situations, it is important to have an understanding of the cultural factors that might influence the victim or the victim's family.

Cultural factors may inhibit the reporting of elder abuse crimes or cooperation with the police if the crimes are reported:

- Cultural norms of perseverance, silent suffering, and quiet endurance are valued in many communities. These qualities are also associated with victimization. Consequently, elders may deny or minimize problems, or refuse to cooperate with authorities.
- Some cultures place great value on family interdependence and multigenerational households. They may fear the social consequences of bringing shame to the family.
- Some cultures believe that maintaining community or family honor is more important than the interests of the individuals and that the authorities should not be involved in what they consider "family matters." Laws and customs in some countries forbid intervention in family affairs without the permission of families.

Elders who are immigrants may also have fears in relation to police based on experiences in their country of origin. They may not know they have rights in the United States, regardless of their immigrant status. They may fear deportation if the police get involved. Empathy and reassurance can help to reduce these fears.

Good cross-cultural communication begins with respect. As with any older victim/witness, begin by addressing a person formally, using his or her last name.

Cultural beliefs often emerge during interviews:

- While a gentle touch on the shoulder may be comforting to some elderly victims, in some cultures this is considered an intrusion.
- In some cultures it is considered disrespectful to make eye contact with an authority figure such as a police officer, while in others it is rude not to make eye contact.

- Some victims may be reluctant to reveal injuries that are covered with clothing due to cultural customs of modesty or religious beliefs. Be careful not to interpret an unwillingness to show injuries as an indication that there are no injuries.

While culture does play a significant role in shaping a person's behavior, it should not be seen as an automatic predictor of how a given victim will respond. Each case is unique and should be assessed, keeping relevant aspects of culture in mind.

It is beyond the scope of this text to identify all of the specific cultural differences that exist among ethnic older people. The reader is encouraged to find out the ethnic older groups who may live in the community and learn specific cultural issues as they relate to crime and the perception of law enforcement. Community and religious leaders are an excellent source of information for this task.

Language

Many elders who live in insular ethnic communities do not speak English. In these situations, it is important to use an impartial interpreter. Avoid using a family member, friend, or neighbor to communicate with the victim or with the suspected offender. This is likely to bias the translation. The interpreter may be involved in the abusive situation, or may give an inaccurate translation due to his or her personal bias. The victim may also be reluctant to speak honestly in front of an acquaintance or family member.

PREPARING THE OLDER VICTIM/WITNESS FOR TESTIMONY

While this may not be a primary law enforcement function, law enforcement officers who have the knowledge and understanding of communicating with older people and how older people are affected by crime and victimization can offer valuable assistance to the state's attorney with trial preparation. Further, the investigator or officer may have been the older person's main contact prior to testimony at trial. A pattern of trust and understanding that has developed between the victim/witness and the investigator makes the law enforcement officer ideally suited for this task.

Prior to Testimony

Determine the impact of the crime upon the older victim or witness:

- Does the older victim need counseling or psychological support?
- Has the local or state supporting victim services unit been contacted? There is a victim/witness advocate assigned to every U.S. Attorney's Office; he or she can make referrals to other available resources.

- In situations regarding victims, have victim impact statements (VISs) been prepared? VISs can provide valuable information for case preparation. VISs should cover the physical, psychological, and financial impact of the crime upon the victim, and the impact upon the victim's family as well.

Help the older victim or witness understand the criminal justice system and his or her role:

- Victim/witness advocates should be able to provide the necessary information—including a tour of the courtroom showing the older victim/witness where key personnel will be located and explaining their roles.

Provide reassurance:

- Many older victims, especially those who lose money to con artists, tend to place varying degrees of blame upon themselves. They repeatedly ask themselves how they could have been so gullible and may imply that they "should have known better." As a result, some of these individuals lose so much of their self-confidence that they could make poor witnesses unless they receive help.
- Prosecutors and victim advocates should talk with and counsel older victims that the fault lies entirely with the con artists who prey on them and that these con artists are very clever criminals. Older victims should understand that very intelligent and professional people are scammed every day, and that they have done nothing wrong. Older victims should also not begin to believe that they have lost their ability to think logically and properly handle their affairs in the future.

Demonstrate your personal commitment. Many older victims and witnesses often come away from the process with feelings that they have been treated as furniture and simply used by the system instead of receiving assistance from it:

- Stress to older victims (and perhaps older witnesses as well) that you and your staff are personally, as well as professionally, committed to bringing truth to the trial process, and justice to them as individuals.
- Inform older victims and witnesses that you need their help to do what is right for them and society. To do this, determine their needs. For example, they may require compensation for expenses resulting from the crime (victims' assistance personnel can assist with this process); transportation to and from court; reassurance that the accused will not attempt to intimidate them.

Assess whether the older victim or witness shows signs of vision or hearing problems that could impact the way he or she will give testimony:

- If vision or hearing difficulties are present in the older victim or witness, prepare to use compensation techniques during testimony.

During Testimony (Information for the State's Attorney)

Evaluate the courtroom from the perspective of the vision and hearing environment.

Lighting

- Determine if the lighting in the courtroom is sufficient for an older eye. Older people usually need more light to see well, but the lighting should be evenly distributed throughout the room. Highly concentrated light causes a glare problem for older eyes.
- Consider differences in the lighting within the courtroom from the lighting conditions just outside the courtroom. Older eyes usually adjust slowly to differences in lighting conditions. Care in this area will avoid any chance that the older victim or witness will trip or appear hesitant when approaching the witness stand.

Sound

- Be prepared to compensate for the occurrence of background noise, which is especially disturbing to older people. Also, if a microphone is used, understand that its natural distortion will create an additional hearing problem for many older persons.

Techniques to Compensate for Vision Problems

- Use large lettering with a simple type style for materials that the older victim or witness will be required to read.
- Avoid problems with glare. Do not use glossy paper or metallic inks on charts.
- Do not combine the colors of blue and green on the same chart because these colors tend to fade to the older eye and are often difficult for older persons to distinguish. If colors are to be used, be aware that reds, oranges, and browns fade the least.

Techniques to Compensate for Hearing Problems

- Control the pace of your voice when addressing the older victim or witness. Speak slowly at about 120 to 130 words per minute. This will give you more time to improve your pronunciation and more time for the older victim or witness to concentrate on what you are saying.
- Control the volume and pitch of your voice. Talking louder to an older person will often be counterproductive, as loud sounds cannot be heard clearly by older ears. If possible, also slightly lower the pitch of your voice, as older persons often hear lower sounds more distinctly. When hearing begins to deteriorate, the higher pitched sounds are usually the most difficult to hear.
- Adjust for background noise. If excessive background noise develops, stop your questioning until this subsides.

- Face the older victim or witness whenever talking to or asking him or her questions. Many who do not hear well rely on lip reading to supplement their hearing.
- Allow a few extra seconds for the older victim or witness to mentally process your question. Some older people require a few extra seconds to think about what they have heard before they can formulate an answer. This will often be even more difficult in a courtroom situation. Do not allow the defense to appear to overcome the older victim or witness by asking him or her questions in quick succession.

Body Language and Voice Tone

Do not show impatience through body language or voice tone if the older victim or witness begins to experience difficulty. This would simply add to the witness or victim's problem of loss of self-confidence. Older victims and witnesses will often closely observe the prosecutor; your continuous demonstration of confidence will help to reassure him or her.

CRIME PREVENTION AND OLDER PEOPLE

As every law enforcement officer knows, three things must be present for a crime to happen:

1. Someone has a criminal intent
2. An available target
3. An opportunity

All protection strategies work by either making the target unavailable or by denying the criminal any opportunity or by making the risks so high that the would-be culprit backs off. [29]

Broad crime changes have occurred in recent years: there are more criminals than there used to be; today's criminals are more violent; and consumer frauds, scams, and corporate crimes are on the rise. We do know a lot more now about how criminals operate. Given this, we can target certain crime prevention strategies for older people. This section provides such strategies.

When embarking on crime prevention strategies with and for older people, employ help. That is, utilize local resources that are already established to assist older people. Some of these organizations include: local area agencies on aging, the local American Association for Retired Persons (AARP) chapter, senior centers, banks, and local religious organizations. If there are senior apartment buildings in your jurisdiction, contact the management staff and arrange to have a crime prevention seminar in the apartment building. Many have common rooms that are well suited for this. It is sometimes easier to promote such programs and have the buy in of the audience you are targeting when groups and organizations familiar to older people are sponsoring or supporting the effort.

Protecting Older People Through Crime Prevention[30]

Helping Older People Find a Safe Place to Live

Sometimes, older people are faced with the dilemma of where to live. As an example, older people who have lived in the same home for many years may no longer be able to physically, or financially, maintain the home. If the home is a multistory home, physical ailments may prevent them from remaining in the home. In some cases, the neighborhood where an older person may have resided is no longer safe. While locating adequate housing for citizens is not a primary police issue, the fear of crime is. Knowing where older communities (or senior apartment complexes) are, and being able to recommend such alternate housing, will help to allay fears of crime where they may live.

Crime Proofing the Home and Grounds

Conduct lectures or offer materials for seniors on how to crime proof one's home and grounds. Simple things such as locking doors and windows, having adequate outdoor lighting, landscaping which does not conceal windows, and alarm systems often require reminding and reinforcing.

Opening the Front Door

While this may seem obvious, it sometimes needs to be reinforced. Many older victims have been taken in by an offender wanting to use the telephone for some urgent need (car broken down, medical emergency). Also, offenders posing as utility workers only need a foot in the door to victimize the older person.

Telemarketing Scams

Telephone fraud occurs when an individual or organization uses the telephone to contact potential victims to steal money or property or to misrepresent the value of goods or services being offered or sold. Their offer may sound as simple as sending money to help the victims of the most recent fire or hurricane, paying money in advance to receive a valuable free prize, or asking the older person to catch a thief by giving them the credit card number, or as complex as offering the older person an investment opportunity in a new product or technology.

In 1996, the American Association of Retired Persons (AARP) published a survey in which they noted that the people who fell for telemarketing scams were not the isolated, old-fashioned, or confused people sometimes pictured as the typical victims. Instead, the victims were well off, well educated, active, community-involved, and alert older adults. Older people are the scam artist's favorite target because older people tend to be more polite and trusting. For some older people, a telephone call is welcome on a lonely day. Clever con artists rely on the older person's good manners and trust to gain confidence. Scam artists first call with a plausible sales pitch for a product, an investment opportunity, a travel package, or the good news that the victim has won a valuable prize.[31]

In 1995, the Federal Trade Commission (FTC) passed the following regulations. Legitimate telemarketers should be observing them; scammers will not. These regulations include the following:

- Telemarketers are prohibited from calling before 8:00 a.m. or after 9:00 p.m.
- They are prohibited from calling consumers who have told the telemarketer that they do not wish to be called.
- Telemarketers are required to disclose their identity; the purpose of the call; the nature of the goods or services being sold; the odds of winning prizes, if any, are offered; the fact that no purchase is necessary to participate; and if it is a prize promotion, the method by which the customer can enter without making a purchase.
- Telemarketers are required to disclose refund and cancellation policies and tell consumers if refunds and exchanges are not permitted. It is illegal for telemarketers to withdraw money from a person's checking account without the person's express, verifiable authorization.

The following is a list of common telephone scams:

- *Sweepstakes or prize scams.* The caller says the potential victim has won money or a valuable prize. In order to receive it, the victim must send money for shipping, taxes, or handling in advance.
- *Lottery scams.* The caller says the victim has a chance to buy a share in a ticket to the Irish Sweepstakes, Powerball, or other well known lotteries.
- *Sure-fire investments.* The caller has an investment opportunity that can't go wrong. The caller may state that there's no time to send information and request money. The caller may even call back several times and state that the value of the investment is increasing and request the victim to send more money to invest.
- *Something for nothing (or nothing for something).* The caller offers the victim the opportunity to get a valuable product at a very low price.
- *Fraudulent charities.* The caller asks for money for a popular cause or to help in a recent disaster. The caller may give the name of a charity that sounds very familiar, except it is not the one the victim thinks it is—its name just sounds the same.
- *Identity theft scams.* The caller asks the victim for personal information about the victim, the victim's family, or the victim's home. This information is then used to commit fraudulent acts, such as opening a charge account, establishing credit, changing the victim's long distance service, or creating a false identity for a thief.
- *Travel scams.* The caller offers a fantastic travel package for a low rate. The victim must provide his or her credit card number to the caller.

- *Paying duty or handling charges for an inheritance or prize.* The caller may claim that he or she is a U.S. Customs official and that there is an item being held at the border for the victim. The caller will ask for duty and taxes.
- *The living trust kit.* The caller tells the victim that the victim's beneficiaries can save a lot of money if the victim uses the caller's Living Trust Kit to help with estate planning.
- *Make "big money" working at home.* The caller promises the victim information on how to work at home and get rich. For a fee, the caller will give the victim the information needed to start making money.
- *Buy a franchise over the phone.* Franchises are a growing scammer enterprise; perhaps because there are so many opportunities in this field. The caller may want to sell the victim a starter kit, start-up supplies, a list of things that require up-front money, or the victim may have to purchase a large initial inventory.
- *Franchise pyramid schemes.* The caller may tell the victim that the victim can get a commission simply for recruiting additional distributors, without having to sell products.
- *Just before your spouse died.* The caller tells the victim that just before the victim's spouse died, the spouse placed an order and the caller needs to confirm the credit card number in order to send the product.
- *Recovery room scam.* The caller states that for a fee, he or she will recover money the victim lost in a previous scam or fraud.

Making older people aware of these (and other) telemarketing scams may prevent an older person from losing his or her life savings.

Protecting the Mail

Seniors should be reminded to pick up their mail as soon as possible after it is delivered. Leaving mail in the box for long periods of time provides an opportunity for identity theft. It also alerts a would-be burglar that no one is home, or in the case of an older person, that they may not be physically able to get to the mailbox, making them an easy target for robbery.

Home Improvement Scams

Many times, older people are solicited by a home improvement contractor who states that he or she is in the neighborhood and will offer a discount on certain work. Some even ask for the money prior to the work. The older person should be encouraged not to make the deal. Rather, he or she should get the contractor's information, check references, and contact his or her state's home improvement commission (or licensing bureau) or the better business bureau.

Protecting the Older Person's Money and Valuables

People enjoy having money and valuables—as do thieves. Encourage older persons to walk through their homes and think like a thief. That is, what could a burglar grab that is valuable and accessible? Rather than leave certain items in the home, including expensive jewelry that is not used regularly and large amounts of cash, suggest that the older person secure these items in a bank (or bank safety deposit box). Advise older persons that if they can think of common hiding places in the home, so can a thief. Discuss having adequate insurance coverage with older people in case a theft does occur.

Household Activities Precautions

It is an unfortunate reality that older people are seen as easy prey. Would-be burglars and thieves are watching. Encourage older people (especially if they live alone) to secure their home while they are in it. This may seem rudimentary enough. However, there are situations where an older person may be in the backyard working in the garden with the front door opened or unlocked. If the home is a multistory home, encourage the older person to secure all door and windows on floors that they are not occupying. Complacency allows opportunity.

Outside Activities

Older people enjoy outside activities, including recreational activities. Walking, jogging, running, and sports are now a part of many older people's daily activities. However, older people need a place to enjoy these activities where they feel safe. Communities can create "senior friendly" parks and other areas where older people can feel safe. Older people enjoy most of these activities in the morning and early afternoon. A law enforcement presence at one or more of the parks where older people gather will give the sense that they are safe, and that their local law enforcement cares about their safety. Mall walking has become very popular with older people. This activity takes place in the morning before the mall opens. This offers a safe and secure place for older people to exercise. If a mall in your area does not offer this, encourage the mall to do so. There will be benefits for both.

Living Alone

There are special risks for older people who live alone. The older person's home may be unoccupied for a greater period if the older person goes out frequently. With only one person living in the home, there is a lower level of activity, which may be apparent to outsiders. Because older people are considered vulnerable to criminals, an offender may see an older person living alone as easy prey. Burglary prevention methods become more important in this circumstance. Local population data, as well as local areas on aging, can identify older people in the community who are shut-ins. This information can be provided to law enforcement. While patrolling one's beat, periodic visits to older shut-ins can show that law enforcement is protecting this vulnerable group. It can also be an opportunity to identify any needs that the older person may have so that appropriate referrals can be made.

Vehicle Safety

Many older people still enjoy the privilege of driving. Reminding older people of basic safety measures will help them avoid complacency. Locking all doors and windows when exiting the vehicle; not leaving the car running when stopping for gas or at the convenience store; and placing packages in the trunk are a few examples. Remind older people to park as close as they can to the store or other destinations. If it is nightime, asking a store clerk or security guard to accompany them to their car is good practice. Finally, even if the older person drives only occasionally, keeping their car in good working order is important, as is not letting the gas tank fall below one-quarter full.

Purse Snatchers and Pickpockets

Being around a lot of people is a deterrent for most types of crime. However, some offenders, like purse snatchers and pickpockets, thrive on crowds. Pickpockets almost never physically harm their victims; but, purse snatchers will sometimes knock their victims down or break their arms to get the purse. There are some prevention strategies that older people can take to avoid being the victims of either. One of these is to avoid carrying a purse altogether. Instead, recommend that older persons carry a wallet inside their coat. If an older woman does choose to carry a purse, it is recommended that the purse have a long strap, and not a short handle. In this way, the strap can be placed over the shoulder, across the chest. The pocketbook should never be carried swinging freely from the hand or wrist. Additionally, the flap should be closed (or the button or buckle closed). It can also be recommended to carry only the cash or credit cards that will be need.

In order to assist law enforcement agencies in developing a crime prevention program, a model program plan is offered as follows:[32]

I. Problem identification: Identify the problem and define the task to be performed
   A. Data collection
      1. Determine the type or kind of data required (e.g., demographics of older people in the community).
      2. Collect available data from police incident reports, the Uniform Crime Report, and other available crime data. Data should be both local (for trending) and national (for comparison).
      3. Evaluate available data to determine additional data requirements.
      4. Collect additional data required.

    B. Data analysis
1. Organize the data collected.
2. Analyze the data in terms of the victim, offender, type of crime, time of crime, and location of crime, taking into consideration the location of the occurrence and its relation to the victim's and offender's residences, if deemed appropriate.

II. Available resources
    A. Identify those community agencies, organizations, and individuals who may be able to provide input.
    B. Identify those personnel within the law enforcement agency who would be valuable assets to the program.
    C. After consultation with these agencies, determine which individuals should be invited to participate in the program planning.

III. Program selection
    A. List all possible or feasible programs that are felt to have a potential impact on the problem as defined in the first step of this outline.
    B. Assess the program alternatives, considering all positive and negative factors of each.
    C. Based upon the assessment, select the most feasible alternative for implementation.

IV. Program implementation
    A. Design policy and establish those procedures required for the implementation of the chosen program.
    B. Assign responsibilities for implementing the program to the appropriate personnel.
    C. Implement the program as desired.

V. Program evaluation
    A. Determine, prior to program implantation, the method to be used to evaluate the program.
    B. Conduct the evaluation in accordance with the predetermined methodology.
    C. Based upon the evaluation, review the program as it now operates and make those changes as deemed necessary.

Triads

Triad is a national community policing initiative wherein law enforcement professionals, seniors, and community groups partner to meet the crime-safety needs of seniors.

Triad has two goals:

1. To reduce crime against the elderly
2. To reduce the unwarranted fear of crime that older people often experience

The process of forming a Triad should entail:

1. Signing a formal agreement to partner in which the leadership of community agencies and organizations agree to work together to keep older people safe.
2. A signing ceremony, in which the community is made aware of the initiative.
3. Establishing a SALT Council (Seniors and Law Enforcement Together) to carry out programs and activities.
4. Staffing and organizing the SALT Council by:
   • Identifying 10 to 20 representatives who are willing and able to attend meetings, conduct activities, and manage the council
   • Selecting council leadership
   • Adopting bylaws and/or other rules of order
5. Conduct a survey to ascertain older people's crime-safety needs.

Triad is a concept of partnership. It is not an acronym; rather, it represents a group of three: law enforcement, older people or organizations in the community representing the needs of older people, and community. The Triad agreement, or signing, is a conceptual agreement by community leaders to work together for, and with, older people.

The SALT Council is an included part of Triad. It is the operations arm, the functioning piece where the ideas, initiatives, and activities are put into action.

A local Triad, through its SALT Council, and based on National Association of Triads programs, conducts organized programs and activities to meet its objectives. Some examples are: Files of Life, wherein magnetic refrigerator cards are distributed to older people that capture information for use in case of emergencies; educational talks given to senior groups on crime prevention, scams and schemes, or personal safety; senior visitations or "adopt-a-senior"; and intergenerational programs, to name a few.

Forming a Triad in a community has many benefits, among them, it:

1. Opens communication between public safety personnel and older people
2. Allows older people to voice their concerns about crime and safety
3. Provides an avenue for active older volunteers to help others
4. Reduces isolation of older people, a contributing factor to the victimization of older people
5. Strengthens the ties amongst community groups
6. Builds a sense of community
7. Expands law enforcement personnel capabilities within the community

For more detailed information on forming a Triad, see the *Triad Program Manual*, available on The National Association of Triads website: http://www.nationaltriad.org/tools/NATI%20Manual-2012.pdf.

HELPING THE OLDER PERSON WHO HAS BEEN VICTIMIZED[33]

The Office for Victims of Crime states that there are three critical needs for all victims:

1. *Victims need to feel safe.* People usually feel helpless, vulnerable, and frightened by victimization. When working with victims, be sure to follow these guidelines:
   - Introduce yourself by name and title and briefly explain your role.
   - Ensure privacy during your interview. Assure confidentiality when possible.
   - Reassure victims of their safety. Pay attention to your own words, posture, mannerisms, and tone of voice. Use body language to show concern, such as nodding your head, using natural eye contact, placing yourself at the victim's level, keeping an open stance, and speaking in a calm, sympathetic voice. Tell victims that they are safe and that you are there for them.
   - Ask victims to tell you in just a sentence or two what happened, and ask if they have any physical injuries. Tend to medical needs first.
   - Offer to contact a family member, friend, victim advocate, or crisis counselor.
   - Ask simple questions to allow victims to make decisions, assert themselves, and regain control over their lives.
   - Ask victims if they have any special concerns or needs.
   - Develop a safety plan before leaving them. Pull together personal or professional support for the victim. Give the victim any written information concerning resources available to help, including contact information for local crisis intervention centers and support groups, the prosecutor's office, the victim/witness assistance office, and other nationwide services, including toll-free hotlines and websites.
   - Give them, in writing, your name and information on how to reach you. Encourage the victim to contact you if he or she has any questions or if you can be of further help.

2. *Victims need to express their emotions.* Victims need to express their emotions and tell their story after the trauma. They need to have their feeling accepted and have their story heard by a nonjudgmental listener. They may feel fear, self-blame, anger, shame, sadness, or denial, and most will say, "I don't believe this happened to me." Some may have a reaction formation and act the opposite of how they feel, such as laughter instead of crying. Some feel rage at the sudden, unpredictable, and uncontrollable threat to their safety or lives, and this rage can even be directed at the professionals who are trying to help them. When working with victims, be sure to follow these guidelines:
   - Listen. Show that you are actively listening to victims through your facial expressions, body language, and comments such as, "Take your

time; I'm listening," and, "We can take a break if you like. I'm in no hurry."
- Notice victims' body language to help you understand and respond to what they are feeling, as well as what they are saying.
- Assure victims that their emotional reactions are not uncommon. Sympathize with the victim by saying such things as, "You've been through something very frightening. I'm sorry."
- Counter self-blame by the victim by saying such things as, "You didn't do anything wrong. This not your fault."
- Ask open-ended questions.
- Avoid interrupting victims while they are telling their story.
- Repeat or rephrase what you think you heard the victim say for validation.

3. *Victims need to know what comes next after their victimization.* Victims usually have concerns about their role in the criminal investigation and legal proceedings. They may also be concerned about payment for health care or property damage. You can help relieve some of their anxiety by telling the victim what to expect in the aftermath of the crime and by preparing them for upcoming stressful events and changes in their lives. When working with victims, be sure to follow these guidelines:
   - Refer the victim to a victim's advocate who will assist the victim through the investigative and legal proceedings.
   - Tell victims about subsequent law enforcement interviews or other kinds of interviews they can expect.
   - Discuss the general nature of medical forensic examinations the victim will be asked to undergo (if known) and the importance of these examinations for the legal proceedings.
   - Counsel victims that lapses of concentration, memory losses, depression, and physical ailments are normal reactions for crime victims. Encourage them to reestablish their normal routines as quickly as possible to help speed their recovery.
   - Give victims a listing of resources that are available for help and information.
   - Ask victims whether they have any questions. Encourage victims to contact you if you can be of further assistance.

Specifically with older victims, law enforcement agencies should:

1. Assist older victims of reported crimes with obtaining services.
2. Provide follow-up contact with older victims of crime to ensure they are receiving needed services.
3. Establish agreements with local agencies to expedite services to older victims.
4. Seek out ways to provide assistance to older victims of unreported crimes.
5. Compile a manual of resources to publicize older victim assistance services.

Often, older people lose their social network, and thus, their support mechanism. This can be especially devastating in a time of victimization. It is important in this situation to make necessary referrals so the older victim is not left alone to cope with the victimization.

SUMMARY

Understanding the nature of victimization in older people and how the older person perceives crime will allow the law enforcement officer to effectively aid, counsel, and refer older crime victims for services. Using crime prevention strategies specifically designed for older people will heighten awareness among the older population and show an attitude of caring on the part of law enforcement. Helping to protect this vulnerable population from predators should be considered a hallmark of effective community policing.

CASE STUDY SUMMARIES

Case Study 1 Summary

As you survey the room where the 76-year-old woman was killed, you immediately notice the brutality of the crime. You also recall 2 two months earlier in roll call, the case of a 74-year-old woman who was brutally murdered and raped was discussed. Based upon the scene and the previous case, you determine that this is a sexual homicide of an older victim. Begin your investigative procedures as you would in other homicide cases. In this case, however, based upon your knowledge of offender characteristics, you can begin to look critically to narrow your search profile for a suspect.

Case Study 2 Summary

There are several issues that an investigator must determine in order to conclude if this is a case of financial abuse/exploitation. In the case, "the neighbor convinces the widow to sign over her stock, saying she can make it grow faster." How this transfer was made should be determined. The first step is to make a determination of capacity. If the widow did not have the capacity to understand the transfer or what documents were being signed, this could be a case of exploitation. Further, the neighbor "gradually isolates the widow then infantilizes the widow, making her feel dependent, and gains complete control over the widow's finances." Capacity should be determined for the widow. Like all forms of elder abuse/neglect, there may be multiple forms of abuse occurring at once. For example, in cases of physical abuse or neglect, there is usually psychological abuse occurring at the same time. In this case study, the neighbor is infantilizing the widow. This could be, and probably is, a form of psychological abuse. If the neighbor gains complete control over the widow's finances without the widow's consent, this would be a case of financial abuse/exploitation. Capacity, consent, and awareness are three key indicators in making a determination.

ENDNOTES

1. U.S. Department of Justice, Office of Justice Programs. (2000). *First response to victims of crime: A handbook for law enforcement officers on how to approach and help, II. Elderly victims.* Washington, DC: Author.
2. Office for Victims of Crime. (2010). *First response to victims of crime: A guidebook for law enforcement officers.* Washington, DC: Office of Justice Programs.
3. Weaver, G. S., Martin, C. D., & Petee, T. A. (2004). Culture, context, and homicide of the elderly. *Sociological Inquiry, 74*(1), 2–3.
4. New York City Elder Abuse Training Project. (2004). *Police curriculum on elder abuse.* New York: New York City Elder Abuse Training Project. Available online at: http://web.archive.org/web/20061229024852/http://www.nyc.gov/html/dfta/downloads/pdf/elderabuse_policecurriculum.pdf.
5. Ibid.
6. Ibid.
7. Ibid.
8. Ibid.
9. Ibid.
10. Ibid.
11. Ibid.
12. Used with permission from Collins, K. A., & Presnell, S. E. (2006). Elder homicide, a 20-year study. *American Journal of Forensic Medicine and Pathology, 27*(2), 183–187.
13. Ibid.
14. U.S. Department of Justice, Bureau of Justice Statistics. (2004). *Homicide trends in the United States.* Washington, DC: Author.
15. Fox, J. A., & Levin, J. (1991). Homicide against the elderly: A research note. *Criminology, 29*(2), 317–328.
16. Abrams, R. C., Leon, A. C., Tardiff, K., Marzuk, P. M., & Sutherland, K. (2007). "Gray murder": Characteristics of elderly compared with nonelderly homicide victims in New York City. *American Journal of Public Health, 97*(9), 1666–1670.
17. Titterington, V. B., & Reyes, N. C. (2010). Elder homicide in urban America: An exploratory analysis of Chicago, Houston, and Miami. *Southwest Journal of Criminal Justice, 6*(3), 228–249.
18. Ibid., p. 229.
19. Payne, B. K. (2005). *Crime and elder abuse, an integrated perspective.* Springfield, IL: Charles C. Thomas Publishers; p. 73.
20. *Quick reference to adult and older adult forensics: a guide for nurses and other health care professionals* by Brown, Kathleen M.; Muscari, Mary E. Copyright 2013. Reproduced with permission of SPRINGER PUBLISHING COMPANY, INC. in the format Republish in a textbook via Copyright Clearance Center.
21. Stiegel, L. A., American Bar Association Commission on Law & Aging. (2005). *Elder abuse fatality review teams: A replication manual.* Washington, DC: American Bar Association. Retrieved April 12, 2012, from http://www.americanbar.org/content/dam/aba/migrated/aging/PublicDocuments/fatality_rev_manual.authcheckdam.pdf.
22. Pollock, N. L. (1988). Sexual assault of older women. *Sexual Abuse, 1*(4), 523–532.

23. Used with permission from Safarik, M. E., Jarvis, J. P., & Nussbaum, K. E. (2002). Sexual homicide of elder females, linking offender characteristics to victim and crime scene attributes. *Journal of Interpersonal Violence, 17*(5), 500–525.

24. Ibid.

25. Ibid.

26. Ibid.

27. Ibid.

28. Used with permission from Slatkin, A. A. (2003). Suicide risk and hostage/barricade situations involving older persons. *FBI Law Enforcement Bulletin, 72*(4), 26–32.

29. Simmons, J. L. (1993). *67 ways to protect seniors from crime.* New York: Henry Holt and Company.

30. Ibid.

31. American Association of Retired Persons. (1996). *Telemarketing fraud and older Americans: An AARP survey.* Washington, DC: American Association of Retired Persons.

32. Modified from Goldstein, A. P., Hoyer, W. J., & Monti, P. J. (1979). *Police and the elderly.* New York: Pergamon Press; p. 44.

33. Brown, K. M., & Muscari, M. E. (2010). *Quick reference to adult and older adult forensics: A guide for nurses and other health care professionals.* New York: Springer; p. 95.

RESOURCES

National Association of Crime Victim Compensation Boards (www.nacvcb.org)

National Association of Triads (www.nationaltriad.org)

KEY TERMS

capacity: The ability to perform a task

undue influence: The substitution of one person's will for the true desires of another

Chapter Six

Elder Abuse

LEARNING OBJECTIVES

1. Define elder abuse and neglect and discuss their incidence.
2. Discuss the profiles of an at-risk elder and an abuser.
3. Determine the techniques used to assess elder abuse and neglect.
4. Demonstrate sensitivity to the abused older person.
5. Understand the link between animal cruelty and other forms of domestic abuse.
6. Discuss the initial investigative techniques used when encountering an elder abuse or neglect situation.

Case Study 1

You are called to a home where an 82-year-old man, Mr. Bartlett, lives with his 52-year-old son. The son receives his father's monthly pension check and handles all deposits and withdrawals. The son is also responsible for paying all of his father's bills, along with purchasing groceries, medications, and personal items for his father. A neighbor stops by one day and sees the father lying in bed. The bed sheets are soiled, and the 82-year-old man's pajamas are soiled as well. The neighbor asks the father where the son is. The old man replies that the son is at work, but that he has not seen his son in the last couple of evenings.

Your scene observation indeed reveals that the bed sheets and the 82-year-old man's pajamas are soiled. Further inspection of the potential victim reveals that bed sores are beginning to form on the elder man's thigh and buttocks. During your initial interview, Mr. Bartlett states that he and his son are under extreme financial difficulties. Mr. Bartlett states that his illnesses are getting worse. It seems, Mr. Bartlett states, that the worse his illnesses get, the less he sees his son.
What are your immediate priorities?
What are your thoughts regarding the son's obligations to his father?

ELDER ABUSE AND THE LAW ENFORCEMENT OFFICER

Elder abuse is a shocking revelation. Reports of physical, emotional, and financial elder abuse have risen significantly, increasing 150% nationwide since 1986.[1] The National Center on Elder Abuse in Washington, DC estimated that in 1997, 2.1 million people over age 60 were exploited or neglected. It has been suggested that elder abuse is suffered by 4–5% of all older persons. Elder abuse is insidious. It forces many older persons to live the end of their lives in fear and deprivation. Elder abuse can occur anywhere, at anytime. The phenomenon of elder abuse is being coined "the hidden iceberg," as estimates are that many more incidents of elder abuse take place than are reported.[2] According to the House Select Committee on Aging (1990), elder abuse is less likely than child abuse to be reported.[3] With the increasing number of elderly in society, new challenges will be created, and sadly, new problems. Elder abuse and neglect is one such problem. Elder abuse is a full-scale national problem. Like child abuse and domestic violence a decade ago, elder abuse is moving toward the front of the nation's social consciousness. Therefore, a variety of issues involved in identifying and managing elder abuse must be confronted.

Historically, elder abuse has been defined as a social problem rather than a criminal problem. Beginning in the 1980s, this changed when legislators across the United States developed elder abuse statutes, penalty enhancement statutes, and mandatory reporting laws. This, in effect, criminalized elder abuse. Along with this criminalization came the expectation that police would intensify their efforts in helping to prevent and intervene in elder abuse allegations.

As in other criminal victimization cases, your role as a law enforcement officer in elder abuse cases is to protect the victim, prevent and stop abuse and exploitation, enforce the law, arrest offenders, and provide appropriate referrals.[4] The first step in combating elder abuse and neglect is the education of law enforcement personnel in the identification of suspected cases. Additionally, as the first official representing the criminal justice system on the scene in suspected cases of elder abuse and neglect, your actions are crucial in the prosecution of these cases.

Attitude Tip—Acting in the victim's best interest is at the forefront of the law enforcement officer's responsibility. Nowhere is more important than in the face of elder abuse and neglect.

DEFINITIONS

Elder abuse is any form of mistreatment that results in harm or loss to an older person.[5] The following definitions are for the specific types of abuse and neglect:

- **Physical abuse**—the use of physical force that may result in bodily injury, physical pain, or impairment
  Examples include: direct physical harm, including shoving, pushing, hitting, shaking, hair-pulling, and unreasonable physical or chemical restraint.
- **Sexual abuse**—nonconsensual sexual contact of any kind with an elderly person
- **Psychological or emotional abuse**—infliction of anguish, pain, or distress through verbal or nonverbal acts
  Examples include: verbal assaults, threats, creating fear or isolation, and withholding emotional support.
- **Financial/material exploitation**—illegal or improper use of an elder's funds, property, or assets
- **Neglect**—failure to provide needed care, services, or supervision

  Two types of neglect have been identified:
  - **Active neglect**—deliberate withholding of companionship, medicine, food, exercise, and/or assistance to bathroom[6]
  - **Passive neglect**—being ignored, left alone, isolated, or forgotten; passive neglect can result from inadequate knowledge, laziness, or illness on the part of the care provider;[7] (see **Figure 6-1**)
    Examples include: failure to provide food, clothing, shelter, health and safety, or medical care

- **Self-neglect**—behaviors of an elderly person that threaten the elder's health or safety; self-neglect can result from the elderly person being in

Figure 6-1 Passive neglect occurs when the older person is ignored, left alone, isolated, or forgotten.
Source: © Yuri Arcurs/ShutterStock, Inc.

poor health, having mental decline, or lacking the financial resources to care for him- or herself

Examples include: being unable to provide for one's own needs, such as hygiene, food, and medications. The older persons most at risk for self-neglect are those living alone in the community.

- **Abandonment**—the desertion of an elderly person by an individual who has physical custody of the elder or by a person who has assumed responsibility for providing care to the elder[8]

These definitions are necessary to provide an understanding of the types of abuse and neglect. One of the problems with defining elder abuse and neglect is that there is no national, uniform set of definitions. Also, while the different types of abuse and neglect are defined separately to provide categorical understanding, more than one form of abuse can be, and often is, occurring at the same time—for example, physical abuse and psychological abuse being perpetrated upon a victim.

A simple way of understanding the manifestations of any type of abuse or neglect is to ascribe to the principle of *inadequate care*. If the care of the elderly person appears inadequate for whatever reason, suspect abuse or neglect.

Attitude Tip—The goal of elder abuse detection, investigation, and prosecution is to help the older victim live a life free from abuse, fear, and intimidation.

THEORIES OF ABUSE AND NEGLECT

There are many theories that attempt to explain abuse and neglect. An understanding of *why* abuse and neglect occur is worthy of a brief discussion. Among the most prominent theories are **social learning** or **transgenerational violence**, **stressed caregiver**, **isolation**, **dependency**, and **psychopathology of the abuser**.

The social learning or transgenerational theory maintains that violence is learned. It states that if children are abused, they will abuse their own children. If this theory is extended to elder abuse, the theory holds that these same children will abuse their parents. The stressed caregiver theory contends that when the caretaker reaches a certain stress level, abuse and neglect situations will occur. Isolation theory maintains that a diminishing social network is a major risk factor in elder abuse. The dependency theory maintains that frailty and medical illness set up the older person for abuse and neglect. Finally, the psychopathology of the abuser theory states that the abuser's problems (such as personality or substance abuse) lead to abuse and neglect.[9]

INCIDENCE

In 1998, the National Center on Elder Abuse reported the results of its National Elder Abuse Incidence Study.[10] The study posed the basic question: What is the incidence of domestic elder abuse and neglect in the United States today? Major findings of the study were that:

- The best national estimate is that a total of 551,011 elderly persons, aged 60 and older, experienced abuse, neglect, and/or self-neglect in domestic settings in 1996. Of this total, 115,110 (21%) were reported to and substantiated by Adult Protective Services (APS) agencies. One can conclude from these figures that almost four times as many new incidents of elder abuse, neglect, and/or self-neglect were unreported than those that were reported to and substantiated by APS agencies in 1996. The standard error suggests that nationwide as many as 787,027 elders or as few as 314,995 elders could have been abused, neglected, and/or self-neglecting in domestic settings in 1996.

Given the standard error, the importance of recognizing and reporting elder abuse and neglect cannot be overemphasized. Recognition and referral of elder abuse cases will have a profound impact on the lives of many older people, who would otherwise continue to be subjected to a life of abuse and neglect. Additionally, through the study, it was learned that:

- Female elders are abused at a higher rate than males, after accounting for their larger proportion in the aging population.
- Those age 80 and older are abused and neglected at two to three times their proportion of the elderly population.

- In almost 90% of the elder abuse and neglect incidents with a known perpetrator, the perpetrator is a family member, and two-thirds of the perpetrators are adult children or spouses.
- Victims of self-neglect are usually depressed, confused, or extremely frail.

The National Elder Abuse Incidence Study did not address abuse in institutional settings. While only about 5% of the nation's elderly reside in nursing facilities, those who do often suffer multiple chronic and debilitating illnesses. Additionally, many residents of nursing facilities have no relatives or close acquaintances who visit—leaving the elderly nursing home resident alone. Nursing home residents who receive no visitors have a higher likelihood of abuse and neglect, as there is no outside influence to watch over the residents' care.

Small-scale studies have been conducted in an attempt to examine the prevalence in institutions. One study conducted surveyed 577 staff members from 31 nursing facilities in order to determine the extent of physical and psychological abuse perpetrated by staff. [11] In the year preceding the study, 81% of staff reported seeing at least one incident of psychological abuse, and 36% witnessed physical abuse within the preceding year; 10% admitted to committing acts of physical abuse, and 40% admitted to committing at least one act of psychological abuse within the study period.

In July 2001, the United States House of Representatives released a study entitled "Abuse of Residents Is a Major Problem in U.S. Nursing Homes."[12] This study investigated the incidence of abuse in nursing homes in the United States by evaluating state inspections of nursing homes or complaint investigations from the period beginning January 1, 1999 through January 1, 2001. The study reported that for 5,283 nursing homes in the United States, nearly one out of every three was cited for an abuse violation during the study period.

The study also found that more than 2,500 of the abuse violations in the last 2 years of the study were serious enough to cause actual harm to residents or to place residents in immediate jeopardy of death or serious injury. Many of these abuse violations were discovered only after the filing of a formal complaint; the percentage of nursing homes with abuse is increasing—the percentage of nursing homes cited for abuse violations increased every year since 1996. The state inspection reports and citations reviewed in the investigation describe many instances of appalling physical, sexual, and verbal abuse of residents. The report concluded that abuse of nursing home residents is a widespread and significant problem.[13]

Besides the risk factors discussed in the theories of abuse, older people have an increased risk for abuse in nursing facilities that have a history of providing inadequate care, are understaffed, and provide poor training for their employees. Some nursing home residents who are the victims of abuse and neglect may not have a way to report the abuse, may not know how to report it, or may fear retaliation for reporting it. Others may be the victims of abuse by visiting family members.

The Nursing Home Reform Amendments of the Omnibus Budget Reconciliation Act (OBRA) of 1987 require that nursing facilities "promote and protect the rights of each patient." See **Table 6-1** for the general provisions of these rights.

Table 6-1 Rights of Nursing Home Residents

Quality of Life: The law requires nursing homes to "care for the residents in such a manner and in such an environment as will promote maintenance or enhancement of the quality of life of each resident." A new emphasis is placed on dignity, choice, and self-determination for nursing home residents.

Provision of Services and Activities: The law requires each nursing home to "provide services and activities to attain or maintain the highest practicable physical, mental, and psychological well-being of each resident in accordance with a written plan of care which . . . is initially prepared, with participation to the extent practicable of the resident or the resident's legal representative."

Participation in Facility Administration: The law makes "resident and advocacy participation" a criterion for assessing a facility's compliance with administration requirements.

Assuring Access to the Ombudsman Program: The law grants immediate access by ombudsmen to residents and reasonable access, in accordance with state law, to records. It requires facilities to inform residents how to contact an ombudsman to voice complaints or in the event of a transfer or discharge from the facility and requires state agencies to share inspection results with an ombudsman.

Specific nursing home residents' rights include:
Rights to Self-Determination: Nursing home residents have the right:
- To choose their personal physician
- To full information, in advance, and participation in planning and making any changes in their care and treatment
- To reside and receive services with reasonable accommodation by the facility of individual needs and preferences
- To voice grievances about the care and treatment they do or do not receive without discrimination or reprisal, and to receive prompt response from the facility
- To organize and participate in resident groups (and their families have the right to organize family groups) in the facility

Personal and Privacy Rights: Nursing home residents have the right:
- To participate in social, religious, and community activities as they choose
- To privacy in medical treatment, accommodations, personal visits, written and telephone conversations
- To confidentiality of personal and clinical residents

Rights Regarding Abuse and Restraints: Nursing home residents have the right:
- To be free from physical and mental abuse, corporal punishment, involuntary seclusion, or disciplinary use of restraints
- To be free of restraints used for the convenience of the staff rather than the well-being of the residents
- To have restraints used only under written physician's orders to treat a resident's medical symptoms and ensure the resident's safety and the safety of others

---

(Continues)

Table 6-1 Rights of Nursing Home Residents (Continued)

- To be given psychopharmacologic medication only as ordered by a physician as part of a written plan of care for a specific medical symptom, with annual review for appropriateness by an independent, external expert

Rights to Information: Nursing homes must:
- Upon request provide residents with the latest inspection results and any plan of correction submitted by the facility
- Notify residents in advance of any plans to change their rooms or roommate
- Inform residents of their rights upon admission and provide them with a written copy of the rights, including their rights regarding personal funds and their right to file a complaint with the state survey agency
- Inform residents in writing, at admission and throughout their stay, of the services available under the basic rate and of any extra charges for extra services, including, for Medicaid residents, a list of services covered by Medicaid, and for those for which there is an extra charge
- Prominently display and provide oral and written information for residents about how to apply for and use Medicaid benefits and how to receive a refund for previous private payments that Medicaid will pay retroactively

Rights to Visits: Nursing homes must:
- Permit immediate visits by a resident's personal physician and by representatives of the licensing agency and the ombudsman program
- Permit immediate visits by a resident's relatives, with the resident's consent
- Permit visits "subject to reasonable restriction" for others who visit with the resident's consent
- Permit an ombudsman to review resident's clinical records if a resident grants permission

Transfer and Discharge Rights: Nursing homes "must permit each resident to remain in the facility and must not transfer or discharge the resident unless":
- The transfer or discharge is necessary to meet the resident's welfare and the resident's welfare cannot be met by the facility
- Appropriate because the resident's health has improved such that the resident no longer needs nursing home care
- The health or safety of other residents is endangered
- The resident has failed, after reasonable notice, to pay an allowable facility charge for an item or service provided upon the resident's request
- The facility ceases to operate

Notice must be given to residents and their representatives before transfer:
- Timing: at least 30 days in advance, or as soon as possible if more immediate changes in health require more immediate transfer
- Content: reasons for transfer, the resident's right to appeal the transfer, and the name, address, and phone number of the ombudsman program and protection and advocacy programs for the mentally ill and developmentally disabled
- Returning to the Facility: the right to request that a resident's bed be held, including information about how many days Medicaid will pay for the bed to be held and the facility's bed-hold policies, and the right to return to the next available bed if Medicaid bed-holding coverage lapses
- Orientation: A facility must prepare and orient to ensure safe and orderly transfer or discharge from the facility

Protection of Personal Funds: Nursing homes must:
- Not require residents to deposit their personal funds with the facility

Table 6-1 Rights of Nursing Home Residents (Continued)

- If it accepts written responsibility for resident's funds:
  - Keep funds over $50 in an interest-bearing account, separate from the facility account
  - Keep other funds available in a separate account or petty cash fund
  - Keep a complete and separate accounting of each resident's funds, with a written record of all transactions, available for review by residents and their representatives
  - Notify Medicaid residents when their balance account comes within $200 of the Medicaid limit and the effect of this on their eligibility
  - Upon the resident's death, turn funds over to the resident's trustee
  - Purchase a surety bond to secure residents' funds in its keeping
  - Not charge a resident for any item or service covered by Medicaid, specifically including routine personal hygiene items and services

Protection Against Medicaid Discrimination: Nursing homes must:
- Establish and maintain identical policies and practices regarding transfer, discharge, and the provision of services required under Medicaid for all individuals regardless of source payment
- Not require residents to waive their rights to Medicaid, and must provide information about how to apply for Medicaid
- Not require a third party to guarantee payment as a condition of admission or continued stay
- Not "charge, solicit, accept, or receive" gifts, money, donations or "other consideration" as a precondition for admission or for continued stay for persons eligible for Medicare

Source: Data from Title 42 Code of Federal Regulations, Part 483.

PROFILES OF THE ABUSED

While elder abuse can occur anywhere, and at anytime, profiles of potential victims (i.e., those that are most at risk) can be drawn. Abused older people tend to be:[14]

- Women
- Over age 75
- Those with one or more chronic physical or mental impairment(s) which places them in a care-dependent position
- Those who live with their abusers
- Socially isolated
- Exhibit problematic behavior (e.g., incontinence, shouting in the middle of the night)

PROFILES OF THE ABUSER

As with the abused, profiles of abusers can be drawn. Abusers tend to:[15]

- Live with their victim—as most abusers are adult children and spouses
- Be over 50

- Be dependent on the victim for financial support
- Be poor at impulse control
- Be ill-prepared or reluctant to provide care
- Have a history of domestic violence
- Have drug or alcohol dependency problems

Also, more than 50% of abusers tend to commit more than one type of abuse.

RISK FACTORS

Older people who are at risk for abuse and neglect include those with chronic, progressive, disabling illnesses that impair function and create care needs that exceed or will exceed their caretakers' ability to meet them, such as:[16]

- Dementia
- Parkinson's disease
- Severe arthritis
- Severe cardiac disease
- Severe chronic obstructive pulmonary disease (COPD)
- Severe non-insulin dependent diabetes
- Recurrent strokes
- Those with progressive impairments who are without informal supports from family or neighbors, or whose caretakers manifest signs of burnout
- Those with a personal history of substance abuse or violent behavior, or who have a family member with a similar history
- Those who live with a family in which there is a history of child or spouse abuse
- Those with family members who are financially dependent on them
- Those residing in institutions that have a history of providing substandard care
- Those whose caretakers are under sudden increased stress due, for example, to loss of job, health, or spouse

If assigned to the same location for a period of time, or in a small community, many law enforcement officers know the people they serve. This can be helpful for identifying abuse in older people. Suspicion should be aroused if an older person repeatedly presents with injuries that are inconsistent with the history stated, has experienced recurring multiple injuries, or has symptoms that cannot be explained medically. When an older person is injured, any delay in accessing emergency medical care and/or law enforcement should be noted. Law enforcement officials should also take note of a caretaker who will not allow the patient to provide his or her own history, and frail or cognitively impaired older people who are alone. Careful questioning and detailed observations will help yield clues as to the presence of elder abuse and/or neglect.

Case Study 2

You are called to a location to check on the wellbeing of a subject. Upon your arrival, the caller who states that she is concerned for her 72-year-old neighbor, Mrs. Jefferson, greets you. The caller further states that she has not seen the elderly woman in a month since a nephew has moved in.

When you knock on Mrs. Jefferson's door, there is no answer. When you call out, you hear only a faint cry from the residence. Having probable cause, you force entry into the home. Upon entering, you find Mrs. Jefferson confined to a room on the first floor. Mrs. Jefferson appears weak and has bruises about both arms and to the left side of her face. The elder woman states that she is glad to see you, as she is afraid of her nephew.

What are your initial priorities?

How do you conduct this investigation?

OBSERVING FOR CLUES TO ELDER ABUSE

Elder abuse can be very subtle, and in a crisis or emergency setting, can often be overlooked. Each situation with an older person should be evaluated with a critical eye toward potential abuse/neglect situations. Awareness and a high index of suspicion are the most important elements when considering elder abuse. If the environment, care, and attitudes of those surrounding the older person are anything but adequate, *suspect that something may be wrong.*

The proper evaluation for mistreatment has four components:[17]

1. A detailed history from the older person
2. A corroborative history from the potential abuser
3. A comprehensive physical examination of the victim
4. Confirmatory testing and documentation

The law enforcement officer is able to perform the first two of these functions. A medical examination is needed to confirm the third function. Confirmatory testing, the fourth function, will have to be performed in the emergency department or hospital. Law enforcement officers also bring an advantage to the information gathering and investigative function of elder abuse cases: They are able to provide information regarding the victim's environment that would otherwise be unknown to social services and other healthcare providers, as the law enforcement officer is often on the scene initially.

Environmental Assessment

Many of the factors associated with putting elders at risk of abuse—alcohol/substance abuse by the caregiver, the presence of other family violence, ineffective coping strategies of the caregiver, and dependency between caregiver and

Figure 6-2 The older person's environment can provide clues to abuse and neglect.
Source: © Richard Levine/age fotostock.

victim—will, in most circumstances, be unknown to the law enforcement officer. Given these unknowns and the sometimes subtle nature of neglect, the assessment phase should begin with a scene survey (the victim's environment) (see **Figure 6-2**). Things to look for in the environmental assessment include:

- The physical condition of the victim's residence—is the exterior of the home in need of repair? Is the home secure?
- Hazardous conditions that may be present (e.g., poor wiring, rotten floors, unventilated gas heaters, broken window glass, or clutter that prevents adequate egress).
- Is the home too hot or too cold?
- Are the utilities (electricity, heat, water, toilet) working and adequate?
- Is there a fecal or urine odor in the home?
- Is food present in the home? Is it adequate and unspoiled?
- Are liquor bottles present (lying empty)?
- Is bedding soiled or urine soaked?
- If the older person has a disability, are appropriate assistive devices (such as walker or wheelchair) present?
- Are there restraints in the home?
- Does the older person have adequate access to a telephone (near the bed or other location where the older person spends time)?
- Are medications out of date, unmarked, or from many different doctors?
- Are smoke detectors present and working?
- If living with others, is the older person confined to one part of the home?
- If the person is residing in a nursing facility, does the care appear to be adequate to his or her needs?

Clinical Assessment

The clinical assessment portion of this chapter is provided to give the law enforcement officer an understanding of the physical indicators of abuse and neglect. Additionally, some law enforcement officers have basic medical training as a first responder or as an emergency medical technician. These assessment guidelines will aid those law enforcement officers with medical training and certification. Whenever an assessment or clinical evaluation is performed on any elderly person, there should always be a critical eye toward abuse and neglect.

There are, however, clinical syndromes and disease states that can mimic elder abuse and neglect. Some medications, for instance, cause changes in the older person's clotting and bleeding mechanisms that place some people at risk to bruise more easily. Environmental and social indicators, the interaction between victim and caregiver, and the physical assessment can yield important clues for the presence of elder abuse and neglect, but must be weighed together. Context is the key in making a determination. When a physical examination is performed on an older person, the person's dignity must be preserved.

Overall Hygiene

Look at the person's overall hygiene and consider the following: Is the older person's clothing clean and appropriate? Is the person dressed appropriately for the season? Are there cigarette burns on clothing? Are undergarments torn, soiled, or bloody? Does the older person have poor hygiene? Is there evidence of recent weight loss (this may have to be obtained by asking the person or caregiver) or malnutrition? Does the person lack assistive devices (glasses, hearing aid, dentures, walker, wheelchair) when it is obvious the older person requires them?

Head and Neck

When observing an older person with a head injury listed as a fall, observe for other associated injuries from the fall (such as to the extremities or trunk). A head injury ascribed to a fall with no other associated injuries may have come from an assault. Observe for the presence of facial bruises, lacerations, or abrasions; tooth fractures; ill-fitting dentures (secondary in some cases to weight loss); mandibular and maxillary (facial) fractures; poor dental hygiene; oral venereal legions; uvula ecchymosis (indicating possible forced oral copulation); and cigarette burns on the lips (this may signal either a neglect situation or a functional decline of the person).

Ophthalmologic assessment may indicate trauma (recent or chronic). Findings indicative of recent trauma include subconjunctival or vitreous hemorrhage. Examination of the eyes and periorbital area should be limited to pupillary assessment (pupil size and reactivity; extra-ocular movements if trained) and observing for signs of orbital fractures or the presence of subconjunctival bleeding. If the victim is deceased, are there signs of petechial hemorrhage?

When examining the nasal area, observe for signs of a deviated septum (a sign of repeated trauma). When examining the anterior/posterior neck, be observant for signs of circumscribed rope burns, handprints, or fingertip bruising (indicative of recent strangulation attempts or bondage). If strangulation is suspected, patency of the trachea and an adequate airway must be confirmed. Bruising of the tracheal rings can result in gradual swelling that can lead to hypoxia and death. In persons with arthritis, the risk of paralysis or death increases when atlantoaxial cervical subluxation worsens (this is a partial or incomplete dislocation of the atlas and the axis—the first and second cervical vertebrae). In an older person with severe osteoporosis, cervical fractures/spinal cord injuries may result.

Skin

Bilateral bruising on soft parts of the body (such as the inner arm or thigh) should be thought of as suspicious; as well as bruising that is clustered. The shape of skin legions may suggest a patterned mechanism of injury, such as a belt buckle or cigarette burn. Multiple bruises in various stages of healing strongly suggest abuse.

Decubitus ulcers that are present and how they are cared for may be a clue of neglect. A decubitus ulcer is ischemic necrosis and ulceration of tissue overlying a bony prominence (such as sacrum, heels, trochanter, lateral malleoli, ischial areas) that has been subjected to prolonged pressure against an object, such as a bed or wheelchair.

Urine burns may be suggestive that a person has been allowed to remain unchanged for long periods of time. Additionally, **excoriations** or chaffing may also suggest poor attention to continence (bladder control). **Infestations** may also be present. Assess skin turgor for signs of dehydration. Other pertinent integumentary findings relevant to elder abuse include traumatic **alopecia** (as opposed to hair loss suggestive of alopecia of normal aging); ecchymoses; burns; lacerations; skin disorders such as rash, impetigo, or eczema; and undiagnosed and untreated fractures. Stocking or glove injuries may suggest an immersion burn.

Thorax and Abdomen

Blunt trauma to the thorax and abdomen may result in rib fractures and a **pneumothorax** or **hemothorax**. Serious abdominal trauma can lead to such life-threatening conditions as splenic rupture and intra-abdominal hemorrhage. Grey Turner's sign and Cullen's sign are suggestive of extravasation of intra-abdominal hemolyzed blood to the flank and periumbilical region, respectively. These forms of ecchymosis may not be immediately apparent. Context is the key to discovery. Bruising about the abdomen ascribed to a fall without other associated trauma to the older person should be viewed as suspect.

Musculoskeletal

The presence of abrasions around the wrist or ankles may indicate the presence of restraints. Differentiating among lower extremity abrasions, erosions, and ulcerations from burns, scratches, lacerations, stasis dermatitis, and plantar ulcerations is difficult. It will then be the responsibility of the emergency department staff to investigate further. The emergency department staff may be able to access additional information through the patient's medical records or private provider.

Neurological

A neurological examination in the elderly person may prove difficult due to preexisting neurological conditions. The person's level of orientation upon presenting to law enforcement should be weighed against the person's normal level of orientation. However, this may be difficult to determine unless someone well known to the older person is present who can provide information regarding subtle cognitive changes. Focal neurologic signs and symptoms may be the result of spinal cord injury or head trauma with development of concussion or subdural/epidural hematoma. Note the person's orientation to person, place, and time and his or her recollection of the present circumstances. More appropriate mental status examinations and neurologic testing can be performed at the hospital.

Genitourinary

Vaginal or rectal bleeding in the elderly requires the differential diagnosis of sexual abuse or malignancy. Injuries to either the vagina or rectum should be treated accordingly. If sexual abuse is suspected, the preservation of evidence should be performed, as with all other sexual assault victims.

Social Assessment

Soliciting a social assessment from an older person or caregiver is usually not conducted by the law enforcement officer. However, when considering cases of elder abuse and neglect, a social assessment will prove valuable when taken in context with other information. Some of the most important social assessment indicators are activities of daily living (ADLs). Recall that ADLs include self-care activities that people must accomplish to survive without help, such as eating, dressing, bathing, transferring, and toileting. Persons who are unable to perform these activities usually require a caregiver. If, during your observations, you find that an older person is unable to perform one or several of these functions, ask the following:

- Are these activities being provided for the older person? If so, by whom?
- Are there any delays in obtaining food, medication, or toileting? The older person may complain of this, or the environment may be suggestive of this. There may not be food in the home.
- In an institutional setting, is the person able to feed him- or herself? If not, is food still sitting in the food tray? Has the person been lying in his or her own urine or feces for long periods of time?

There have been few studies that have analyzed how older persons perceive abusive acts. Emotional suffering is one of the most important clues pointing to psychological abuse, but one that is very difficult for law enforcement officers to assess. Examples of psychological abuse include harassment, intimidation, manipulation, belittling, and isolation. Victim responses and the observed interaction between the older person and the family/caregiver may yield clues as to the presence of abuse or neglect.

Undermedication of the older person could be a sign that a family member/caregiver is stealing the older person's medication, or the caregiver is not providing the medication. Overmedication can also be a sign of abuse. People are sometimes sedated for the caregiver's comfort.

SEXUAL ASSAULT IN THE ELDERLY

Sexual assault in the elderly deserves some discussion. Sexual crimes against the elderly have not been described in the literature with any frequency. There are some things about this crime that the law enforcement officer must know.

One thing that the law enforcement officer must keep in mind when responding to sexual crimes against the elderly is intergenerational differences. Most elderly women were raised in a time when sexual matters were not discussed. Being the victim of a sexual crime will be emotionally devastating for the older person, and is often seen as a loss of dignity. Additionally, elder crime victims may not wish to discuss the crime with law enforcement or medical personnel. The older victim may also be reluctant to submit to a pelvic exam. Many older victims are sexually assaulted in their own homes, and by those known to the victim—in some cases the perpetrator is a family member. Behaviors common in older sexual assault victims include withdrawal, fear, depression, anger, insomnia, increased interest in sexual matters, or increased sexual or aggressive behavior.

Three types of individuals have been identified who perpetrate rape against elderly victims. The first are **gerophiles**—sexual predators who target older people. These individuals often seek jobs in nursing homes. A second group is sexually aggressive older men, who themselves reside in nursing homes. The last group is strangers or people who are known to the victim who rape non-institutionalized elderly women.

Older sexual assault victims with any degree of cognitive impairment are unable to consent to sex. These victims are unable to defend themselves, and often delay reporting a rape. The majority of victims are female and are highly dependent. Dementia is a factor in many of these crimes, and limits the ability of the victim to stop the abuse and report the crime.

Age-related changes in older women make them more prone to injury after a sexual assault. Vaginal linings are not as elastic as those of younger women due to hormonal changes; this proclivity toward increased sexual trauma may cause bleeding, pain, infections, or tears that may never fully heal. Brittle bones such as the pelvis and hips can be more easily broken or crushed by friction and the weight of the rapist.[18] Victims of sexual abuse may present with oral venereal legions. Additionally, bruising of the uvula and bruising of the palate and the junction of the hard palate may indicate forced oral copulation. Bleeding and bruising of the anogenital area as well as difficulty in sitting and walking may also indicate sexual abuse. A 2005 study[19] of forensic markers in 125 older female sexual abuse cases reported that the offender's hand was the primary mechanism of physical injury to the nongenital area of the older victim's body, and the offender's hands, fingers, mouth, penis, or foreign object caused injury to the genital area. Over half of the older victims had at least one part of their body injured, and nearly half had signs of vaginal injury.[20] If investigating sexual assault in a nursing home facility, inquire about any new cases of sexually transmitted diseases or clustered cases of urinary tract infections.[21]

There are challenges that may be presented to the law enforcement officer when responding to this type of crime. For example, interviewing older people with cognitive impairment or those with dementia may be difficult. The older rape victim may resist an examination of the pelvic area, or physical limitations such as lower extremity contractures may make an examination difficult.[22]

INTERVIEWING

Interviewing older people requires more time than interviewing younger people (see **Figure 6-3**). The situation and the urgency will determine the time that can be spent on the interview, but try not to rush through the interview.

Figure 6-3 Interviewing older victims requires more time, and must be done with compassion and respect.
Source: © Tom Carter/age fotostock.

Additionally, some aging persons tend to integrate past events with the present. When interviewing the elderly person, observe for the following:

- Does the older person appear fearful of a family member?
- Does the person appear reluctant to respond when questioned?
- Does the older person appear depressed? Recall that the symptoms of depression include:
  - Dissatisfaction, restlessness, malaise
  - Sleep disturbance
  - Poor concentration; slowed thoughts
  - Change in appetite or weight
  - Loss of interest in usual activities
  - Psychomotor agitation or retardation
  - Suicidal ideations, recurrent thoughts of death
  - Sense of worthlessness, self-reproach, excessive guilt
  - Loss of energy

  (Note: Symptoms of depression are present at least 2 weeks with no other major psychiatric or organic disorder present and are not due to bereavement.)
- Do the older person and caregiver provide conflicting accounts of the situation?
- Does the caregiver seem indifferent or hostile toward the older person?
- Does the caregiver "hover" around, not allowing the law enforcement officer privacy with the older person?
- Does the caregiver seek to prevent the older person from interacting with the law enforcement officer?
- Does the caregiver seem concerned about the problem at hand, but not with the person's overall health?
- Does the caregiver answer for the older person even when that person can provide verbal history?
- Does the older person look to the caregiver before answering?
- Does the older person sound like he or she is reciting a "script" to explain injuries?
- Does the caregiver refer to the older person as accident prone? Remember, injuries that do not fit medically or differ from the stated history should arouse suspicion.

Asking About Abuse and Neglect

The following questions may elicit a history of elder abuse from an older person. If abuse or neglect is suspected, ask the person directly:

- Are you afraid of anyone at home?
- Has anyone ever made you do things you didn't want to do?
- Are you in fear of your caregiver?

- Have you ever been threatened or scolded by your caregiver?
- Has anyone ever touched you without your consent?
- Has anyone at home ever hurt, beaten, or struck you?
- Has anyone ever taken anything that was yours without asking?
- Have you ever signed any documents you didn't understand?
- Have you ever been left alone?
- Have you ever been restrained?
- Has anyone ever failed to help you take care of yourself when you needed help?

If the suspected perpetrator is on the scene (as it may be a family member or the older person's care provider), ask these questions of the victim alone. If the victim is to be transported to the emergency department by emergency medical services (EMS), you may have to wait until the victim has been removed to the ambulance. It is essential to document (in quotes) the victim's response. These are difficult questions to ask; it may be best to save them for the end of the interview. If the perpetrator is a family member, the older victim may be reluctant to identify them as the abuser.

Interviewing Suspected Abusers

At times in suspected cases of abuse or neglect, it may be necessary to interview family members or the older person's caretaker. The abused or neglected older person must always be the law enforcement officer's first responsibility. The following basic principles are offered for the law enforcement officer when these interviews become necessary:

- Advise the suspected abuser of their rights, if appropriate, at the time of the initial interview.
- Do not be accusatory, as this will put the person on the defensive and limit the amount of information that will be offered.
- Interview the suspected abuser alone, as this may reveal discrepancies between the victim's account and the suspected abuser's account of the situation.
- Focus initially on the present situation, and then move to more broad questions regarding the victim's general condition. For example:
  - What happened to the person today?
  - What is the older person's medical history?
  - What kind of care does the person require?
  - Who provides this care?
  - Is there anything else I should know about the person (victim)?
- If the suspected abuser is cooperative and calm during the interview, and a strong index of suspicion is present, more direct questions may be asked, such as:
  - Can you tell me how the person received those bruises (or lacerations, abrasions, etc.)?

- The older person appears undernourished. Can you tell me how he got that way?
- Have you ever threatened or struck the person?

When interviewing a suspected abuser, pay attention to the following:

- Does the suspected abuser offer an implausible explanation for the older person's injuries?
- Is the suspected abuser uncooperative or disinterested?
- Does the suspected abuser appear dominant and overly protective?

If the suspected abuser admits to abuse or neglect during the interview, ask him or her to specify the abusive or neglectful event(s). Record exactly (in quotes) what the abuser states. While the suspected abuser may be arrested for his or her admission (and ultimately convicted), the victim is not removed permanently from his or her residence or caregiver in all cases of documented abuse or neglect. Often, family counseling and effective coping strategies/resources will allow family and victim–caregiver relationships to improve. In these cases, adult protective services will monitor the victim and abuser for a period of time.

INVESTIGATING ELDER ABUSE CRIMES

Law enforcement officers may be called to investigate allegations of elder abuse and neglect by adult protective services, a concerned neighbor, EMS providers who are on the scene with an elderly patient, or by an emergency department physician. No matter who initiates the call for law enforcement, you will be the first link in the criminal justice system, involving perhaps one of many who will assist in the investigation of a crime involving elder abuse and neglect. Individuals involved may include adult protective services, ombudsmen, members of state nursing home regulatory agencies, and healthcare professionals.

As the first responding law enforcement officer on the scene of a suspected case of elder abuse and neglect, the actions you take, and your initial investigation, will have a profound impact on the case, obtaining a conviction, and ultimately of helping the older person to be free from an abusive or neglectful situation.

Law enforcement officers rarely, if ever, witness abuse or neglect in progress. Instead, the law enforcement officer must rely on the indicators and forensic markers of abuse and neglect. Unfortunately, very little data exists regarding forensic indicators. This section compiles what is known in order to aid the law enforcement officer in detecting clues to abuse and neglect cases. An understanding of age-related changes versus indicators of abuse and neglect is important when investigating these crimes.

Forensic Indicators of Abuse and Neglect

Abrasions and Lacerations

An abrasion is a superficial injury involving the outer layer of the skin (see **Figure 6-4**). A laceration is full-thickness splitting of the skin (see **Figure 6-5**).

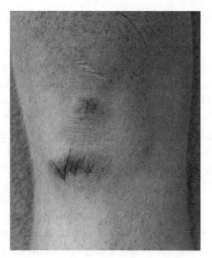

Figure 6-4 Abrasion.
Source: © Jones & Bartlett Learning. Photographed by Kimberly Potvin.

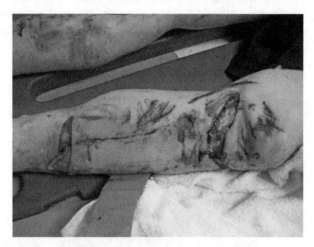

Figure 6-5 Laceration.
Source: Courtesy of Rhonda Beck.

When evaluating an abrasion, identification of the mode of injury is the most important factor.[23] The victim should be evaluated for an abrasion or multiple abrasions. Abrasions often heal with scarring.[24] The victim or care provider may be able to provide information. Suspicion should be aroused for an implausible explanation of how the lacerations or abrasions were caused. Evaluate for multiple lacerations as well. Lacerations found on the palms of the hand or on the underside of the forearm may indicate that the victim was defending him- or herself from being stabbed.

Bruises

A bruise is the result of blunt force trauma with concomitant rupture of small blood vessels under the skin[25] (see **Figure 6-6**). The eyelids, neck, and scrotum are very susceptible to bruising.[26] The pattern of a bruise may suggest its cause. Look for bruising that is in the shape of familiar objects (such as a belt buckle). Bruises will also retain the shape of fingers or knuckles. Parallel marks, called **tramline** bruising, indicate injury from a stick.[27] The evaluation of bruising in older people must be taken in context. Blood thinning medications taken by older people (e.g., warfarin, clopidogrel) can cause bruising to occur more easily (from nonassault-related causes). Additionally, older people are more prone to fall-related injuries that may cause bruising. The care provider or perpetrator may ascribe injuries to the victim being "prone to falls." However, the most common locations for nonaccidental bruising are the face and neck, chest wall, abdomen, and buttocks.[28] Bruising on the palms and soles may indicate abuse, as these areas are not usually injured.[29] Multiple bruises, and bruises in various stages of healing, may indicate abuse. Medical research and data indicate that bruising can be dated by its color. However, the dating of bruises is very problematic, and is dependent upon many factors that vary from person to person, such as age, overall health, and medications. It is best to simply describe the location and size of bruises that are found on the victim's body.

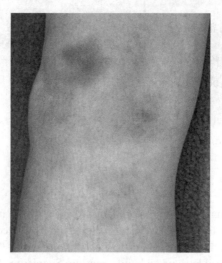

Figure 6-6 Bruising.
Source: © Jones & Bartlett Learning. Photographed by Kimberly Potvin.

Burns

The age group at greatest risk for experiencing a burn injury is the over 75 population. Unlike other age groups, this population is most commonly burned by space heaters, cookers, and flammable liquids. Burns to older people should be evaluated as to their cause. For example, immersion burns may be the result of a caregiver placing the older person in water that is too hot. Cigarette burns can result from a self-neglecting situation or from an intentional burn inflicted by someone else.

Financial Exploitation and Fraud

Financial and material exploitation, as previously defined, is the illegal or improper use of an older person's funds, property, or assets. This can include credit card and telemarketing fraud, predatory lending, and theft or exploitation.

Fractures

A fracture is a broken bone. Unfortunately, there is little data on fracture resolution in older people.[30] Fractures in older people often result from falls. As a result, falls alone may not be the sole indicator of abuse or neglect. However, there are certain fracture locations that should arouse suspicion and warrant further investigation as to their origin. Fractured, subluxed, or avulsed teeth or fractures of the zygomatic arch or the mandible and maxilla may indicate abuse.[31] Research also indicates that fractures of the head, spine, and trunk are more likely to be assault injuries than limb fractures, sprains or strains, or musculoskeletal injuries.[32] Additionally, a spiral fracture of a long bone with no history of gross injury is diagnostic of abuse, as are fractures with a rotational component. Fractures in nonalcoholics at sites other than the hip, wrist, or vertebrae should raise suspicion of abuse.[33]

Hygiene

Old age alone does not bring about changes in one's hygiene. There may be many factors that contribute to improper hygiene in the older person. Some older people, for example, may to choose to live an eccentric lifestyle, while others may be limited in their ability to maintain proper hygiene by decreased mobility, eyesight, or underlying disease processes. In the face of neglect, the law enforcement officer should attempt to determine if there is someone responsible for the older person's care. If so, an investigation is warranted as to why proper hygiene is not being maintained for the older person.

Malnutrition and Dehydration

There is no uniform definition of malnutrition. Generally, malnutrition describes a person who is very thin (low weight) or losing weight or has a low muscle or fat mass, is eating poorly, or has abnormal blood markers of nutritional status.

Malnutrition can be a result of caregiver neglect. An example of this is in institutional settings where the staff to patient ratio is inadequate to assist residents who require assistance with eating. Additionally, inappropriate prescribing of certain medications (e.g., anticholinergic drugs, psychotropic drugs, as well as other medications that impair mentation or appetite) may lead to malnutrition.[34]

Dehydration is defined as an inadequate level of water in the body. The loss of fluid from the body can lead to a variety of clinical manifestations in older people, including death. In neglect cases, dehydration can occur if food or liquid is withheld from the older person. In cases of neglect from malnutrition and dehydration, medical experts should be called upon early in the investigation. The older victim may be hospitalized as well. The medical investigator will need to review medical records of the victim in order to document (or show lack of documentation) weight loss, fluid intake/output, and appropriately prescribed medications.

Medication Use and Misuse

While older people represent only 12% of the U.S. population, they consume the greatest proportion of medications. Old age itself is not an independent risk factor for drug-related adverse advents, but the number of medications used may significantly increase the risk of drug-related complications. Regarding abuse and neglect, there are many causes related to medication use and misuse. For example, drug interactions (drug-drug interactions, drug-nutrient interactions, drug-disease interactions, and drug-herb interactions) may result from a practitioner failing to understanding specific precautions in older people. Further, a caregiver can be guilty of intentional neglect by failure to administer an older patient's medications. Conversely, the caregiver who administers a psychotropic medication to quiet an older person or control the person's behavior can be guilty of abuse. Additionally, older patients who suffer any form of confusion or dementia who are dependent upon a caregiver for medication assistance may over- or undermedicate themselves if the caregiver does not regulate medication administration. This situation will be extremely difficult for the law enforcement officer to discern.

During any investigation of possible abuse or neglect, determine what medical conditions the victim suffers from, and what, if any, medications the older person is prescribed—including dosages. A healthcare professional and medical investigator will have to determine (through blood sampling) therapeutic levels and appropriate prescribing dosages.

Pressure Ulcers

A pressure ulcer is a sore, initially of the skin, due to prolonged pressure, usually in a person who is lying down, and possibly at any site, but most commonly over bony prominences. The combination of pressure, shearing forces, friction, and moisture lead to the death of tissue due to lack of blood supply. It is often difficult to distinguish pressure ulcers that result from illness from those that result from neglect. Pressure ulcers should be prevented from occurring initially. In the presence of pressure ulcers, the questions that must be asked are: Were the ulcers preventable, and how were they being cared for?

Restraints

Restraints can be a way of controlling the behavior of an older person. However, older people do have rights regarding abuse and restraints. The Nursing Home Reform Amendments of OBRA 1987 (described fully earlier) state that nursing home residents have the right to

> be free from . . . disciplinary use of restraints . . . be free of restraints used for the convenience of staff rather than the well-being of the residents . . . have restraints used only under written physician's orders to treat a resident's medical symptoms and ensure the resident's safety and the safety of others.[35]

The only acceptable use of restraints is to prevent the older person from harming him- or herself or other people. This applies to the use of chemical restraints (medications) as well. The use of both physical and chemical restraints must be used only under physician's order.

With regard to restraints and abuse, abuse occurs whenever the older person is restrained in a noncritical manner.[36] Additionally, physical restraints should not be so tight as to restrict movement completely, or to cause injury to the skin and underlying tissues.

Sexual Abuse

Proceed as you would in other sexual assault crimes, keeping in mind those issues identified in the "Sexual Assault in the Elderly" section described earlier in this chapter.

Skin Tears

Skin tears are common in some older people due to the loss of elastin and collagen. Skin tears in areas other than the arms or legs, or multiple skin tears, should arouse suspicion.

Elder Abuse Investigation in Long-Term Care Facilities

The National Institute of Justice provides specific characteristics within four categories of markers that can be used to determine whether elder mistreatment is occurring or has occurred. These include:

1. Physical condition and quality of care
   - Documented but untreated injuries
   - Undocumented injuries and fractures
   - Multiple, untreated, or undocumented pressure sores

- Medical orders not followed
- Poor oral care, poor hygiene, and lack of cleanliness of residents (e.g., unchanged adult diapers, untrimmed finger- and toenails)
- Malnourished residents who have no documentation for low weight
- Bruising on nonambulatory residents; bruising in unusual locations
- Family statements and facts concerning poor care
- Level of care for residents with nonattentive family members

2. Facility characteristics
   - Unchanged linens
   - Strong odors (urine, feces)
   - Trashcans that have not been emptied
   - Food issues (cafeteria smells at all hours; food left on trays)
   - Past problems
3. Inconsistencies between:
   - Medical records, statements made by staff members, or what is viewed by the investigator
   - Statements given by different groups
   - The reported time of death and condition of the body
4. Staff behaviors
   - Staff members who follow the investigator too closely
   - Lack of knowledge or concern about a resident
   - Evasiveness, unintended and purposeful, verbal and nonverbal
   - Facility's unwillingness to release medical records

Conclusion

The investigation of elder abuse and neglect cases can be challenging. However, understanding the causes, and knowing the forensic markers of abuse and neglect will aid invaluably in the investigation process.

Older people who suffer injuries, where the law enforcement officer suspects abuse, or where there are indicators of neglect, should also be medically evaluated. Evaluation by a healthcare practitioner and confirmatory testing (x-rays, lab tests) are necessary for the wellbeing of the older victim, and become part of the investigation. If possible, injuries should be photographed. The scene (or environment) the older victim is in should also be photographed. They will provide valuable assistance in the investigation. Context is the key to discovery in elder abuse and neglect cases.

When investigating these cases, the law enforcement officer must gather together the victim's complete medical history (to exclude a pathological basis) and a complete list of the victim's medications—to include prescriptions, over-the-counter medications, and herbal medicines (to determine therapeutic levels and to rule out overdose).

The investigation of elder abuse and neglect cases should be made by a multidisciplinary team, which should include law enforcement, the district attorney's office, adult protective services, the medical examiner's office, forensic pathologists, state ombudsmen, and members of the healthcare community involved in the care of older people (geriatricians).

PUTTING IT ALL TOGETHER

As stated earlier, context is the key to discovery in elder abuse and neglect cases. You must weigh your findings from environmental and social observations, the patient's physical condition, as well as observing the interaction between the older person and the caregiver. For example, does the caretaker dominate the situation or show a marked lack of concern? Or, does the caretaker blame the older person for his or her condition? Evaluate the caregiver for presence of drug or alcohol intoxication. If the caretaker is absent, does the older person present as someone who should be left alone? Does the elderly person speak of the caregiver in a negative way? Assess the older person's affect and nonverbal behavior. Is the older person fearful or overly quiet?

Abuse should be suspected whenever the older person presents with multiple injuries in various stages of healing. Neglect should be suspected whenever a dependent person (who has adequate resources and a caretaker) presents with deficiencies in hygiene, nutrition, and medical needs. If one type of abuse is present, look for other types. Frequently an elder is the victim of more than one type of abuse or neglect. Are there previous reports of similar injuries (if the person is known to law enforcement or EMS)? Does the older person express fear of any intervention? This may signal abuse. If, after you have made your assessment and conducted victim and caregiver interviews, your intuition tells you all is not well between the older person and the caregiver, it probably isn't.

Evidence of abuse can be determined, in part, by a physical examination. Evidence of neglect can be determined, in part, by the failure of the caretaker to:

- Assist with personal hygiene, or with the provision of food, clothing, or shelter
- Provide medical care for physical and mental health needs
- Protect from health and safety hazards
- Prevent malnutrition

Psychological abuse indicators (on the part of the victim) include:

- Ambivalence
- Deference
- Passivity
- Fear of caregiver or law enforcement
- Fearfulness expressed in the eyes (in some cultures it is considered rude to look a person directly in the eye—be careful not to confuse deference with fear)
- Withdrawal

- Helplessness
- Resignation
- Depression
- Hopelessness

Evidence Collection[37]

Law enforcement officers should investigate an elder abuse case as if it was a homicide. Treat the victim's home as a crime scene. Prosecutors must try to prove the charges without the victim's testimony (or, if the victim does testify, to try to corroborate the victim's testimony as much as possible). The best time to obtain evidence is in the beginning of the investigation.

Photographs

Photographs should be taken of:

- *The victim.* Photographs of the victim are taken to show general physical condition and hygiene, and to be able to identify the victim.
- *The victim's injuries.* Photograph all of the victim's injuries that may have resulted from the abuse and/or neglect. Try to obtain at least one photograph of the injuries that also shows the victim's face.
- *The defendant's injuries.* This is important if the suspected abuser claims self-defense. Identify what the abuser was wearing, including footwear if the victim was kicked. If this is the case, collect the footwear as evidence.
- *All blood-stained items.*
- *All property damage.*
- *Messages/numbers on pagers/cell phones.*
- *The home of the victim.* To show living conditions of the home. Include the location where the victim sleeps and of the refrigerator (if lack of adequate food).
- *Any property taken into custody.* Photograph any property taken into custody where it was found prior to seizing it.

Seizing Evidence

Evidence to be seized in elder abuse cases may include:

- *Weapons.* Weapons include any item that was used to injure or threaten the victim.
- *Containers of assaultive and/or flammable liquids* (if used on the victim).
- *Drugs and/or drug paraphernalia* (if used by the abuser as a motive to perpetrate the abuse or neglect). Photograph these items where they are found prior to collecting them.
- *Alcoholic beverages/empty bottles, cans, or other containers.* These items are important if used by the abuser in theft or neglect cases.

- *Items used to restrain, gag, or torture the victim.*
- *Letters with envelopes.* These can be used if sent by the abuser.
- *Victim's diary.* This will be useful if the victim documented the abuse.
- *Answering machine or voicemail.* May contain threats made by the abuser.
- *Clothing, sheets, blankets or other items with blood stains, feces/urine, or items that are torn.* These items should be placed in a paper bag.
- *Financial documents.* These will be necessary in financial abuse cases.

Remember, search warrants will be necessary for some evidence seizures.

Eyewitnesses

Eyewitnesses should be interviewed in these cases, but also interviewed regarding their association with the victim. This is important, as eyewitnesses may be able to assess the victim's wellbeing (or general deterioration) prior to the current event. Eyewitnesses may also be able to describe the relationship between the victim and abuser.

"Excited Utterances by the Victim"

Document all excited utterances by the victim. Include the victim's demeanor when these utterances are made. Obtain the initial 911 call if made by the victim.

Abuser's Statements

All statements made by the suspected abuser should be documented. This is especially true if the suspected abuser claims that the victim's injuries were ascribed to a fall and later concluded by a physician to be inconsistent with a fall. Attempt to obtain a statement from the suspected abuser, but do not forget to read the suspected abuser his or her Miranda rights.

Obtaining any previous addresses of the suspected abuser may prove helpful if there are previous convictions of abuse and/or neglect.

Expert Medical Opinion

Investigators should attempt to obtain a release from the victim in order that the physician who evaluated and treated the victim can be consulted and the victim's medical records obtained.

Medications/Medical Information

Obtaining past medical records for the victim may show a pattern of injuries or the victim being treated for the same injury. Obtain (or document) all medications prescribed to the victim and whether the victim is compliant with these medications. This is particularly important if the victim has a caretaker who is responsible for providing medications to the victim.

INTERVENTION DECISIONS

Law enforcement officers will face a variety of situations with regard to the possibility of abuse and neglect. Each has to be evaluated on its own merit. Some basic guidelines can help decide when it is necessary to intervene.

As a law enforcement officer, you are governed by several principles, two of which are your *police power* and the principle of *parens patriae*. Police power assumes the right and responsibility of government to make and enforce laws necessary for health, safety, welfare, and morals of the public. Police power allows the government to: protect people from bodily harm; protect people from loss or damage to property or financial interests; protect people from mental or emotional harm; and protect people from nuisances and annoyances by others. The principle of *parens patriae* means "the state as parent" and grants the state parental control over individuals who cannot manage for themselves. It allows the government to: maintain and preserve the personal property and assets of persons who are unable to care for their own property through guardianship and conservatorship; treat mental disorders through involuntary commitment for treatment; prevent self-inflicted bodily harm such as suicide attempts; and provide custodial care for persons who suffer from untreatable conditions and cannot care for themselves, such as placement of persons with developmental disabilities in group homes.[38]

In addition to established legal principles, there are also ethical principles involved in elder abuse cases. Ethical principles address conduct that is not covered by law or about which the law is unclear. Ethics involves the application of values that are considered good, responsible, and necessary for achieving a high quality of life.[39]

When immediate, life-threatening problems exist as the result of an abuse or neglect situation, EMS should be requested to immediately address the health crisis. Further follow up can be conducted after the victim is stabilized in the emergency department.

If the older person's condition is stable but he or she is in a physically unsafe environment due to lack of heat, water, or food or the caregiver's actions, see if the elder will accept transportation to an emergency department via EMS. Many hospitals will set aside "safe beds" where victims such as this can be transported and housed when immediate removal is necessary until more suitable living arrangements can be made. If not, determine whether he or she is receptive to assistance from local adult protective services. If the older person is receptive to assistance, notify the appropriate agency. If a caretaker seems to be the problem, determine what, if any, legal action can immediately be taken. There may be circumstances where referral to adult protective services may be necessary, and the only action that can immediately be undertaken.

Even if the suspected abuser is a family member, the existence of a family relationship does not change the law enforcement officer's responsibility to enforce the law and arrest suspected abusers. Further, if the suspected abuser presents a danger to him- or herself or others, an involuntary petition for mental health assessment may have to be sworn out by the officer.[40]

Some older persons choose to remain in an abusive or neglectful situation, despite offers of assistance, and/or where a lack of criminal evidence exists. If the older person is competent, there is often little that can be done since, unlike the cases involving children, competent adults' rights must be honored. A report should still be initiated and documented, and the case referred to adult protective services.

DOCUMENTATION

In addition to evidence collection, documentation is crucial. Detailed descriptions of the victim's environment, injuries (size, color, shape, location), social assessment, and interactions between the victim and the caretaker must be described. A sketch sheet is very useful. Specifically, document the following:

- Physical environment in which the victim is living.
- Injuries (type, location, size, shape).
- Complete past medical history.
- Social history.
- The name of the victim's physician and any health insurance the victim may have.
- Victim's current prescribed medications. Attempt to determine if the victim is taking these medications. This will be important later in determining whether therapeutic levels are present.
- Name of the victim's caretaker.
- Any statements made by the victim and/or caregiver. These statements must be written in quotes. If specific questions are asked relative to elder abuse, document the question that was asked as well as the response.
- Observations between the victim and the caregiver.
- If EMS was called to the location, document the EMS run number and the hospital where the victim was transported.
- Where does the victim's income come from, and who controls this income and the expenditures?
- Who has daily contact with the victim, and is the victim involved in any community activities?
- Does anyone have power of attorney or guardianship over the victim?
- If competent, what does the victim want?

Case Study 3

You are called to a home where a woman reports that her neighbor threw a dead dog into a trash dumpster. Animal control is summoned as well to remove the dead animal. The complainant states that the woman who threw the animal into the dumpster

(Continues)

is the daughter of an 84-year-old woman and that the daughter is also the elderly woman's caretaker. You decide to investigate the residence where the woman and her elderly mother reside. When you knock on the door, you hear only faint moaning coming from inside. Having probable cause, you force entry into the residence.

Once inside, you discover the 84-year-old woman lying on a sofa, appearing emaciated and disoriented. The home is covered in trash and dog feces, parts of the ceiling have caved in, and the walls are covered in mildew. You request EMS to the scene to transport the elderly woman to the emergency department. Your investigation reveals that the daughter often left her elderly mother alone for long periods at a time.

What are your thoughts about this case?

THE CRAWFORD DECISION[41]

The U.S. Supreme Court, on March 8, 2004, handed down a decision in the case *Crawford v. Washington*. The case was not an elder abuse case, but the decision impacted procedures for investigating and processing an elder abuse criminal case. Not only were police officers affected, but also professionals from other disciplines who investigate and gather potential testimonial material. These professionals include prosecutors, detectives, adult protective services workers, and social workers.

The Crawford decision makes it more difficult to use taped interviews of the victim or certain other testimonial material gathered when the defendant or his representative did not have the opportunity to cross-examine the maker of the statement ("declarant"). The decision was based on the Sixth Amendment to the U.S. Constitution, which guarantees that "in all criminal prosecutions, the accused shall enjoy the right . . . to be confronted with the witnesses against him."

Generally, hearsay, an out-of-court statement offered for the truth of the matter asserted, is not permitted as evidence in court. However, as many as 26 exceptions to the hearsay rule have been honored. Prosecutors could sometimes introduce recorded statements into evidence, and some states had statutes facilitating this practice. Those state laws may now be unconstitutional.

In one extreme scenario, an elderly victim identified the perpetrator in a videotaped statement shortly after the crime. The suspect fled, but was apprehended a few years later. The victim has died, but his taped statement cannot be used because the defendant could not cross-examine the witness.

Case law pursuant to Crawford is growing. Hundreds of appeals focusing on "confrontation" were decided in the first 6 months following the decision. Lawyers in your district attorney's office can advise you whether case law suggests changes in protocol for police.

Crawford applies in criminal cases when the witness is unavailable to testify, the statement is "testimonial," and the defense has not had an opportunity to cross-examine the witness.

Videotaped statements of an elderly victim may not be admissible in court. They have been ruled hearsay.

There are two ways to avoid this procedural obstacle and help your prosecutors get convictions. First, treat potential witnesses in a supportive manner so that more of them will be available and willing to testify at trial. Second, note that many traditional exceptions to the hearsay rule are still valid:

- "Excited utterances" are still admissible. They are not affected by Crawford.
- Dying declarations are still admissible in homicide and civil cases.
- "Business record rule:" Where records are regularly kept, such as interview notes by caseworkers at Adult Protective Services or an area agency on aging, these records may be admissible. Caution: If courts perceive social workers as agents of the police or as "government agents" gathering material for future use at trial, then they may not honor the business record exception. Instead, they will require the social worker to appear and be cross-examined.
- Formal police interviews will be considered "testimonial," including joint interviews with social workers or others. However, courts have admitted offhand remarks to police officers who had not solicited them.
- Forfeiture rule: If the defendant causes the elder to be unavailable for trial, then earlier videotaped statements may be admissible.
- Medical notes and diagnoses by doctors and nurses are usually admissible under a hearsay exception.
- Courts have ruled both ways on admissibility of 911 tapes. The rulings usually hinge on whether the call was an immediate call for help ("excited utterance") or was made to trigger a criminal justice response.

Note that in any case, statements are likely to be admitted if the law enforcement officer can produce the maker of the statement ("declarant") to be cross-examined at a trial or hearing.

Crawford strengthens the rights of defendants, posing an apparent loophole in some cases. By continuing to listen for usable evidence (e.g., excited utterances) and by working with prosecutors and collecting the work done by others (e.g., social workers and doctors), the law enforcement officer can still help bring offenders to accountability.

ELDER ABUSE, DOMESTIC VIOLENCE, AND ANIMAL CRUELTY

In a discussion of elder abuse, this chapter would be remiss if it did not discuss the association between animal cruelty, domestic violence, child abuse, and elder abuse. Many times, the law enforcement officer is called to a reported case of animal neglect or cruelty. The following brief discussion will shed light on the link between animal cruelty and other forms of abuse.

Since 2000, social service and law enforcement agencies have begun to examine cruelty to animals as a serious *human* problem closely linked to domestic violence, child abuse, elder abuse, and violent crimes.[42] Case histories of serial killers and mass murderers revealed an early history of abusing animals. Additionally, research has revealed a strong animal cruelty–family violence connection.

Perpetrators of domestic violence often use the family pet to silence, coerce, and further intimidate other vulnerable family members. In many cases, pets are harmed or killed by the abuser. Several studies conducted using interviews of domestic violence victims reported that victims were reluctant to leave the home or the relationship for fear that the abuser would harm the family pet.[43]

Child abusers often abuse animals to exert their power and control over children, animals, and other vulnerable family members. In some cases, abusers will force children to engage in sexual acts with animals or demand that they hurt or kill a favorite pet, to coerce them into keeping the family secret. Even the threat of animal abuse will intimidate children into maintaining silence about ongoing family violence or other criminal behavior. Unfortunately, many abused children may become animal abusers. These children begin abusing animals for a variety of reasons. These reasons include imitating the violence they have seen or experienced, using the pet as a victim; believing that animals lives are expendable, having seen a parent kill a pet; or they may kill their pets in an effort to control what they see as the inevitable end for the pet. These children are at risk for future aggressive and antisocial behavior as well.[44]

For many older people, a pet represents a source of companionship as well as a support system. Perpetrators of elder abuse may manipulate this relationship to intimidate or threaten the older victim, or out of retaliation. Frequently, as in cases of elder abuse and neglect, the perpetrator is a child or grandchild.

The Role of Law Enforcement

Animal cruelty is a crime, but the law enforcement officer, when called to an incident of animal neglect or cruelty, must look beyond just the cruelty perpetrated upon the animal. Recognizing that there exists a relationship between animal cruelty and other forms of domestic abuse warrants further investigation. Animal abuse is often one symptom of a dysfunctional or abusive family. There exists an opportunity to perhaps intervene on behalf of other vulnerable family members when investigating a report of animal cruelty. Law enforcement agencies should develop relationships with animal activist organizations, veterinarians, animal control agencies, and mental health organizations in order that cases of animal abuse can lead to cross-reporting to law enforcement so that other possible forms of family violence may be identified. Additionally, multi-agency training can be initiated regarding the link between animal cruelty and other forms of family violence.

SUMMARY

The crime of elder abuse and neglect is a multifaceted societal problem. Unlike other cases, elder abuse and neglect cases involve the coordination of key organizations and individuals. These organizations and individuals include adult protective services, case management services, district attorneys, state attorney generals, mental health organizations, departments of aging (local and state), state nursing home licensing agencies, emergency medical services, the banking community, and healthcare organizations (e.g., local hospitals and outreach health screening services).

Law enforcement agencies should have written protocols in place that address the response to elder abuse and neglect cases. The development of such protocols should be a collaborative effort involving these organizations and individuals. Such protocols should reflect local, regional, and state laws and policies governing elder abuse cases.

Additionally, local municipalities should form a consortium of key organizations so that each is aware of the others' roles in elder abuse investigation, prosecution, and prevention. This consortium should meet quarterly at a minimum to discuss progress and problem areas. This will lead to a coordinated effort in elder abuse awareness, prosecution, and prevention. Elder abuse awareness programs should be incorporated into continuing education and in-service training programs. This too will help open lines of communication and help make identification, investigation, and prosecution more effective. Feedback should also be provided to law enforcement officers on cases that are reported or where charges are filed.

The law enforcement officer's role in these crimes is crucial. Identification, investigation, and prosecution of the offender will help older victims live the end of their lives free of fear and deprivation.

CASE STUDY SUMMARIES

Case Study 1 Summary

There are several issues involved in this case. Your immediate issue is the health of Mr. Bartlett. EMS should be called to the scene, as this is someone who should be transported to the emergency department for evaluation. You note the pressure ulcers beginning to form on the victim. If left untreated, these ulcers will continue to become worse, and eventually become infected. Also, by calling EMS to the scene, medical documentation of the victim can be initiated early (and in the victim's surroundings, as the soiled bed linens will contribute to the pressure ulcers becoming infected).

You also have a potential witness in the neighbor. The neighbor may attest to the relationship between the victim and his son. Additionally, the neighbor may be able to relate when she last saw the victim and the victim's overall appearance at that time.

You major concern, though, is the care that the son is providing to the victim. You know that the son assumes responsibility for the victim's finances, shopping, medicines, and acquiring personal items for the victim. Mr. Bartlett stated that he and his son were suffering financial difficulties, and that the victim has not seen his son the last several evenings. Part of your scene assessment should be a comparison of the conditions of the father's bedroom with respect to the remainder of the home. You will, of course, need to interview the son. Photographs should also be obtained of any injuries to the victim and of the victim's living conditions.

There are several possible outcomes to this case. One is that the son is spending the father's money on other things, and simply neglecting his father's care. In this case, the son can be charged with neglect. The other scenario is that the son may be trying his best, perhaps working a second job at night for additional income. In this scenario, there may be the opportunity for monetary and other support services to aid in the father's care. This is a case that should be referred to adult protective services. The state's attorney will also need to review the victim and son's financial records. In the later scenario, the victim may be returned to the residence under the son's care if support services can be obtained. The son may be referred to a caregivers support program and the victim's care may be monitored for a period of time.

Case Study 2 Summary

Your first concern is with the health and safety of Mrs. Jefferson. If she appears weak and suffers from bruising, EMS should be called to the scene, and the victim transported to the emergency department for evaluation. Additionally, a healthcare practitioner can document bruising and any other injuries or signs of neglect. You will want to determine why Mrs. Jefferson is afraid of her nephew. Ask directly if the nephew perpetrated the bruises. Additionally, does the nephew have access to the victim's bank account or finances? If so, the victim (or you) must contact the bank or other financial institution to inform them that a criminal investigation is being conducted, and gain financial statements for evaluation. You will, of course, want to interview the nephew. Adult protective services should also be notified. The victim's injuries and living conditions should be photographed. Follow up will be made by adult protective services with the victim's physician in order to determine prior health condition and the existence of previous injuries.

Case Study 3 Summary

There is a link between animal cruelty and elder abuse and other forms of domestic violence. Understanding this link will help law enforcement officers to be aware and to dig deeper when confronted with cases of animal cruelty. In this case, the dead dog was only the tip of the iceberg. Some studies also reveal that people are more prone to report cases of animal cruelty than abuse in humans.

Knowing the link between animal cruelty and domestic violence does provide an opportunity to take these reports and conduct further investigation. You may, in fact, put an end to several types of abuse—both to animals and humans.

ENDNOTES

1. National Center on Elder Abuse. (1997, November). *Elder abuse informational series no. 2.* Washington, DC: Author. Retrieved April 12, 2012, from http://www.ncea.aoa.gov/Main_Site/pdf/basics/fact2.pdf.
2. National Center on Elder Abuse. (1998). National elder abuse incident study. Retrieved April 12, 2012, from http://aoa.gov/AoA_Programs/Elder_Rights/Elder_Abuse/docs/ABuseReport_Full.pdf.
3. U.S. Congress House Select Committee on Aging. (1990). *Elder abuse: A decade of shame and inaction.* Committee Print No. 101-752, 101st Congress, 2nd session. Washington, DC: Government Printing Office.
4. Nerenberg, L. (1993). *Improving the police response to domestic elder abuse: Instructor training manual.* Washington, DC: Police Executive Research Forum; p. III-6.
5. National Committee for the Prevention of Elder Abuse. (2008). *Physical abuse.* Retrieved from http://www.preventelderabuse.org/elderabuse/physical.html.
6. Fulmer, T. M., & O'Malley, T. A. (1987). *Inadequate care of the elderly: A healthcare perspective on abuse and neglect.* New York: Springer; pp.17–18.
7. Ibid.
8. This is the source for all definitions unless otherwise noted: National Center on Elder Abuse. (1997). *Elder abuse informational series no. 1.* Washington, DC: Author. Retrieved April 12, 2012, from http://www.ncea.aoa.gov/Main_Site/pdf/basics/fact1.pdf.
9. Lachs, M. S., & Fulmer, T. (1993). Recognizing elder abuse and neglect. *Clinics in Geriatric Medicine, 9*(3), 665–675.
10. National Center on Elder Abuse. (1998). National elder abuse incident study. Retrieved April 12, 2012, from http://aoa.gov/AoA_Programs/Elder_Rights/Elder_Abuse/docs/ABuseReport_Full.pdf.
11. Pillemer, K. A., & Moore, D. W. (1989). Abuse of patients in nursing homes: Findings from a survey of staff. *The Gerontologist, 29*(3), 314–320.
12. U.S. House of Representatives. (2001, July). Abuse of residents is a major problem in U.S. Nursing Homes. Retrieved April 12, 2012, from http://www.hospicepatients.org/ilaswan/nursinghomesabuse.pdf.
13. Ibid.
14. National Center for Victim's of Crime. (n.d.). *Focus on the future: A systems approach to prosecution and victim assistance, a training and resource manual.* Washington, DC: U.S. Department of Justice, Office for Victims of Crime.
15. Ibid.
16. Fulmer, T. M., & O'Malley, T. A. (1987). *Inadequate care of the elderly: A healthcare perspective on abuse and neglect.* New York: Springer; pp. 29–30.
17. Anetzberger, G. J., Lachs, M. S., O'Brien, J. G., O'Brien, S., Pillemer, K. A., & Tomita, S. K. (1993). Elder mistreatment: A call for help. *Patient Care, 27*(11), 93–130.
18. Illinois State TRIAD. (1998). *Responding to elder crime victims.* Springfield, IL: Author; p. 6.
19. Burgess, A. W., Hanrahan, N. P., & Baker, T. (2005). Forensic markers in elder female sexual abuse cases. *Clinics in Geriatric Medicine, 21*(2), 399–412.

20. Brown, K. M., & Muscari, M. E. (2010). *Quick reference to adult and older adult forensics, a guide for nurses and other health care professionals.* New York: Springer; p. 192.
21. National Research Council. (2003). *Elder mistreatment: Abuse, neglect, and exploitation in an aging America.* Washington, DC: The National Academies Press; p. 359.
22. Burgess, A. W., Dowdell, E. B., & Brown, K. (2000). Sexual assault: Clinical issues. *Journal of Emergency Nursing, 26,* 516–518.
23. National Research Council. (2003). *Elder mistreatment: Abuse, neglect, and exploitation in an aging America.* Washington, DC: The National Academies Press; p. 344.
24. Ibid., p. 345.
25. Ibid., p. 345.
26. Ibid., p. 346.
27. Ibid., p. 346.
28. Ibid., p. 346.
29. Ibid., p. 347.
30. Ibid., p. 347.
31. Ibid., p. 348.
32. Ibid., p. 348.
33. Ibid., p. 348.
34. Ibid., p. 350.
35. The Nursing Home Reform Amendments of OBRA 1987. *Volume 42, Code of Federal Regulations, Part 483.*
36. National Research Council. (2003). *Elder mistreatment: Abuse, neglect, and exploitation in an aging America.* Washington, DC: The National Academies Press; p. 348.
37. New York City Elder Abuse Training Project. (2004). *Police curriculum on elder abuse.* New York, NY: New York City Elder Abuse Training Project.
38. Nerenberg, L. (1993). *Improving the police response to domestic elder abuse: Instructor training manual.* Washington, DC: Police Executive Research Forum; p. V5-6.
39. Ibid. p. V-7.
40. Ibid. p. III-12.
41. New York City Elder Abuse Training Project. (2004). *Police curriculum on elder abuse.* New York, NY: New York City Elder Abuse Training Project.
42. Ponder, C., & Lockwood, R. (2000). *Cruelty to animals and family violence, Training key #526.* Alexandria, VA: International Association of Chiefs of Police; p. 1.
43. Ibid., p. 2.
44. Ibid., p. 3.

RESOURCES

Website

Humane Society of the United States (www.hsus.org)

Books and Articles

American Medical Association. (1992). *Diagnostic and treatment guidelines on elder abuse and neglect.* Chicago, IL: Author.

Baumhover, L. A., & Beal, S. C. (1996). *Abuse, neglect, and exploitation of older persons.* Baltimore, MD: Health Professions Press.

Capezuti, E., Brush, B., & Lawson, W. T. (1997, July). Reporting elder mistreatment. *Journal of Gerontological Nursing, 23*(7), 24–32.

Conlin, M. M. (1995). Silent suffering: A case study of elder abuse and neglect. *Journal of the American Geriatrics Society, 43*(11), 1303–1308.

Costa, A. J. (1993). Elder abuse. *Primary Care, 20*(2), 375–389.

Gallo, J. J., Reichel, W., & Anderson, L. M. (1995). *Handbook of geriatric assessment.* Gaithersburg, MD: Aspen Publishers.

Janing, J. (1991, June). Reflections on aging: Communicating with elderly patients. *Journal of Emergency Medical Services, 16*(6), 34–44.

Jones, J. S., Walker, G., & Krohmer, J. R. (1995). To report or not to report: Emergency services response to elder abuse. *Prehospital and Disaster Medicine, 10*(2), 96–100.

Lachs, M. S., & Pillemer, K. (1995). Abuse and neglect of elderly persons. *The New England Journal of Medicine, 332*(7), 437–443.

Marshall, C, E., Benton, D., & Brazier, J. M. (2000). Elder abuse: Using clinical tools to identify clues of mistreatment. *Geriatrics, 55*(2), 42–53.

Missouri Department of Social Services, Division of Aging. (1981, Summer). Indicators of Abuse, Neglect, and Exploitation of the Elderly.

National Aphasia Association. (1988). *Communicating with people who have aphasia.* New York: Author.

National Institute of Justice. (2008). Potential markers of elder mistreatment. Retrieved April 12, 2012, from http://www.nij.gov/nij/topics/crime/elder-abuse/potential-markers.htm.

Paris, B. E., Meier, D. E., Goldstein, T., Weiss, M., & Fein, E. D. (1995). Elder abuse and neglect: How to recognize warning signs and intervene. *Geriatrics, 50*(4), 47–51.

Quinn, M. J., & Tomita, S. K. (1997). *Elder abuse and neglect.* New York: Springer.

Pritchard, J. (Ed.). (1999). *Elder abuse work: Best practices in Britain and Canada.* Philadelphia: Jessica Kingsley Publishers.

KEY TERMS

abandonment: As it relates to elder abuse, a situation in which an older person is left at the emergency department by a family member or caretaker

active neglect: The refusal or failure to fulfill a caretaking obligation; a conscious or intentional attempt to inflict physical or emotional stress; examples include abandonment and denial of food or health-related services

alopecia: Hair loss, especially from the head, suggestive of normal aging (as opposed to traumatic alopecia, indicative of abuse)

dependency theory: A theory that attempts to explain the cause of elder abuse; maintains that frailty and medical illness set up the older person for abuse and neglect

elder abuse: An all inclusive term representing all types of mistreatment toward older adults; can be an act of commission (abuse) or omission (neglect), intentional or unintentional, and of one or more types: physical, psychological (or emotional), sexual, or financial, resulting in unnecessary suffering, injury, pain, loss or violation of human rights, and decreased quality of life

excoriation: Abrasion of the epidermis or of the coating of any organ by trauma, chemicals, burns, or other causes

financial/material exploitation: Illegal or improper use of an older person's funds, property, or assets; examples include cashing checks without permission, forging signatures, misusing money or possessions, forcing or deceiving into signing legal documents, and improper use of guardianship or power of attorney

gerophile: A sexual predator who targets older people

hemothorax: A collection of blood in the pleural cavity

infestation: The harboring of animal parasites; common infestations in the setting of abuse and neglect are "bed bugs" (*Cimex lectularius*); can cause hemorrhages in the skin, or wheals

isolation theory: A theory that attempts to explain the cause of elder abuse; maintains that the older person's diminishing social network is a major risk factor in elder abuse

neglect: Refusal or failure on the part of the caregiver to provide life necessities, such as food, water, clothing, shelter, personal hygiene, medicine, comfort, and personal safety

passive neglect: An unintentional refusal or failure to fulfill a caretaking obligation, which results in physical or emotional distress to the older person; examples include abandonment and the nonprovision of food and health services that are the result of the caretaker's lack of knowledge, laziness, infirmity, or addiction to drugs or alcohol

physical abuse: Force resulting in bodily injury, that is, from hitting, slapping, burning, unwarranted administration of drugs and physical restraints, force feeding, or physical punishment

pneumothorax: A partial or complete accumulation of air in the pleural spaces

psychological or emotional abuse: Infliction of anguish, emotional pain, or distress; includes verbal assaults, threats, intimidation, harassment, and forced social isolation

psychopathology of the abuser theory: A theory that attempts to explain the cause of elder abuse; maintains that the abuser's problems (such as personality disorders or substance abuse) can lead to the abuse or neglect

self-neglect: Behaviors on the part of the older person that threaten his or her own health or safety; generally manifests itself in refusal or failure to provide self with adequate food, shelter, or personal safety

sexual abuse: Nonconsensual sexual contact of any kind, including with a person incapable of giving consent; includes, but is not limited to, unwanted touching, sexual assault, or battery such as rape, sodomy, coerced nudity, and sexually explicit photographing

social learning theory: A theory that attempts to explain the cause of elder abuse; maintains that violence is learned—if a person was abused as a child, that person will abuse his or her parents; also called transgenerational theory

stressed caregiver theory: A theory that attempts to explain the cause of elder abuse; maintains that when the caretaker reaches a certain stress level, abuse and neglect will occur

tramline: A bruise appearing as a pale linear central area lined on either side by linear bruising

transgenerational theory: *See* social learning theory

urine burn: Reddening of the skin that occurs around the inner thighs and buttocks when the older person is allowed repeatedly to lie for prolonged periods of time in his or her own urine

Chapter Seven

The Elder as Perpetrator

LEARNING OBJECTIVES

1. Understand crimes committed by older people.
2. Understand the special considerations when arresting older perpetrators.
3. Understand the special needs of older arrestees.
4. Understand ways to prevent elder crime.

Case Study 1

You are dispatched to a local convenience store for a shoplifting report. Your dispatcher advises you that store security has a subject in custody. Upon your arrival, a security officer advises you that he has apprehended a subject who shoplifted several medicinal items and that store management wishes to press charges.

When you enter the office, you encounter the suspect—a frail 76-year-old female who is ambulating with the assistance of a walker. When you question the suspect, you learn that she has attempted to shoplift several over-the-counter medications valued at $21.09. Remorseful, the suspect advises you that she cannot afford these items, but requires them for her medical conditions.

How will this offender be handled?

Is this case different from any other larceny?

INTRODUCTION

A discussion of social gerontology in law enforcement would be remiss if the older person as perpetrator were not addressed. It should be noted that older people are less likely to be arrested for every crime, including felonies. Arrest rates are skewed to the lower age groups (25–29 and 30–34, respectively). Older people do not contribute in a major way to the nation's crime rate. Even if the incidence of crime among older people remains relatively low, the population growth of older people requires the attention of law enforcement. This chapter presents a profile of older perpetrators, the reasons older people commit crimes, special circumstances regarding arrest, housing older arrestees, and preventing elderly crime.

Criminologists study crime. Gerontologists study the social aspects of aging. Until recently, the study of the older person as the perpetrator has not been explored to any great extent. Accordingly, law enforcement agencies have received little education regarding the issues surrounding the older person as the perpetrator. Additionally, elder crime is difficult to explain because criminal behavior is atypical for this age group. There are two phenomena at work that are changing this. First, changing demographics show that older people are present in society as never before. Therefore, the number of older perpetrators will rise, even if crime rates remain relatively stable. Second, the housing of older prisoners (even if temporarily) presents unique issues and challenges for law enforcement agencies.

A nonissue in criminology for many years, elder crime gained attention in the 1970s largely because of the increased population of older people in the United States. During this period, scholars predicted older people would increasingly turn to crime and a "geriatric crime wave" would ensue. However, in the 1980s, scholars began to question earlier assessments of elder crime. While elder crime itself is on the increase, it should not be considered a

Table 7-1 Estimated Percent of U.S. Residents Age 65 and Older Arrested for All Offenses for 2009

	Estimated U.S. Resident Population		Persons Arrested	
Age group	Number	Percentage	Number	Percentage
Total	307,006,550	100.0	10,741,157	100.0
65 years and older	39,570,590	12.9	81,695	0.8

Source: Data From U.S. Department of Justice, Federal Bureau of Investigation, *Crime in the United States, 2009.*

geriatric crime wave. **Table 7-1** shows the estimated percentage of U.S. residents age 65 and older arrested for all offenses in 2009.

More than 30 years of literature regarding older perpetrators was reviewed for this chapter. Rather than enter into a discussion of the sociological perspective of the older perpetrator, this chapter provides the law enforcement officer with the knowledge and practical considerations needed when encountering older perpetrators, challenges and considerations of housing older arrestees, and how community-oriented policing can identify potential older perpetrators.

Case Study 2

You are called to an assisted living facility along with EMS. You arrive first on scene and encounter the facility director awaiting you at the entrance. The director advises you that a 74-year-old woman in the day room is acting aggressively and threatening the residents and the staff. The director states the staff is unable to speak to the woman or control her aggressive behavior.

Once in the day room, you encounter the woman, Beatrice Hicks, sitting in the corner. As you attempt to speak with Mrs. Hicks, she begins to scream profanities at you and swing her cane. The center director states that Mrs. Hicks cannot remain in the facility while displaying this type of behavior. As you again attempt to communicate with Mrs. Hicks, she rises from her chair, swinging her cane at you and says she is going to her room. As she attempts to leave the day room, she strikes a staff member with her cane.

How do you handle this situation?

CRIMES COMMITTED BY OLDER PEOPLE

Recent data reveal that larceny (with sharp increases in shoplifting) is the most frequent offense for which the older person is arrested. After larceny, older people are more likely to be arrested for assault, followed by murder, robbery, auto theft, and rape. Crime data analyzed from 1964–1982 revealed that arrests for property crimes committed by older people more than doubled, and that driving while intoxicated (DWI) arrests had risen precipitously.[1] Gun use is associated with violence among most criminal populations. Elderly individuals are frailer than their younger counterparts and therefore less likely to be able to kill or severely injure a victim without the use of a weapon.[2] **Table 7-2** shows arrests by offense for people age 65 years and older in 2009.

Shoplifting

Shoplifting is the most common offense for which older people are arrested. Older shoplifters have some unusual characteristics that are quite different from teenage shoplifters and others who are more professional. These traits include:

1. On average, not only do older shoplifters have clean records, but they also come from middle and upper-middle classes.
2. The most commonly shoplifted items are cosmetics and sport clothing. Necessary drugs or vitamin supplements are not high on the list, nor are bread and butter the most common foods stolen. Instead, older people steal more esoteric foods, such as imported cheeses, cocktail oysters, and the like. Note that there are two kinds of shoplifters: **boosters** and **snitches**. A booster is a thief who steals for resale, concentrating on higher priced goods for resale. The snitch is an amateur, stealing for his or her own use. Most shoplifters fall into the snitch category, regardless of age.
3. The major motive in older shoplifting is not real economic hardship, but that it provides the perpetrators with discretionary money when they are living close to the subsistence line from retirement income or social security. Sheer economic necessity might, however, become a major motive in older shoplifting, especially if the economy continues to deteriorate in the same fashion as it has in recent years.
4. Another motive in older shoplifting seems to be attention-seeking. A number of older people living in retirement homes distant from their children have discovered that they may get attention by being arrested.
5. It has been postulated that retired persons and juveniles share many characteristic lifestyles and tend to engage in similar criminal conduct.
6. Another theory being offered is that some older people feel that they have been "ripped off" by commercial concerns all their lives and shoplifting is a final chance to get even.[3]

Organized Crime, Professional Crime, and White Collar Crime

It has been asserted that older perpetrators play an important and often dominant role in three major crime types that are different from ordinary crime: organized crime, professional crime, and white collar crime. Control of organized crime is clearly in the hands of older "family" heads, with "godfathers" being by definition older (the godfather himself is likely to be a grandfather). Professional crime (e.g., confidence games, shoplifting, pickpocketing, large jewelry thefts, bank robberies, illicit auto rings) is predominantly done by

Table 7-2 Arrests by Offense for Age 65 Years and Older for 2009

Offense Charged	65 Years and Older
Murder and nonnegligent manslaughter	114
Forcible rape	145
Robbery	104
Aggravated assault	3,037
Burglary	427
Larceny-theft	6,787
Motor vehicle theft	97
Arson	78
Violent crime[*]	3,400
Percentage	0.7
Property crime[†]	7,389
Percentage	0.5
Other assaults	7,829
Forgery and counterfeiting	266
Fraud	1,561
Embezzlement	85
Stolen property—buying, receiving, possessing	226
Vandalism	776
Weapons—carrying, possessing, etc.	865
Prostitution and commercialized vice	472
Sex offenses (except forcible rape and prostitution)	1,566
Drug abuse violations	3,246
Gambling	211
Offenses against family and children	428
Driving under the influence	14,166
Liquor laws	1,896
Drunkenness	4,233
Disorderly conduct	3,456
Vagrancy	303
All other offenses (except traffic)	29,584
Suspicion	7

[*]Violent crimes are offenses of murder and nonnegligent manslaughter, forcible rape, robbery, and aggravated assault.
[†]Property crimes are offenses of burglary, larceny-theft, motor vehicle theft, and arson.
Source: Data from U.S. Department of Justice, Federal Bureau of Investigation, *Crime in the United States, 2009.*

older people. The assertion is that for the professional, crime is a lifetime career. White collar crime involves violations of law and trust by persons in the course of their occupations—generally business, politics, or the professions. White collar crimes range from embezzlement to corporate price fixing, and from accepting or offering a bribe to systematic tax evasion. By definition, white collar crime is not perpetrated by the young. It takes age and maturity to get to a position to commit white collar offenses.[4]

Alcohol- and Drug-Related Offenses

Alcohol plays both a direct and indirect role in the offenses committed by older people and figures prominently in the overall picture of older criminality. The direct role is demonstrated by the high percentage of arrests for public drunkenness, disorderly conduct, and driving under the influence of alcohol. The indirect criminogenic role of alcohol comes from its being a triggering factor and a disinhibitor in crimes of violence against the person (particularly homicide), sexual offenses, and certain property offenses such as shoplifting.

Older people use and abuse prescription (including prescription narcotics) and over-the-counter medications rather than use (or sell) illicit drugs. The use and misuse of prescription medications does increase visits to physicians by older people, but does not bring attention to law enforcement officials. This is an area that is under-researched in criminology and gerontology disciplines.[5]

The Disreputable Elder

While cautiously placed in the offender chapter, the disreputable older person is one who society views as a deviant. This type of crime committed by old people includes public drunkenness, disorderly conduct, simple assault, and vagrancy. These are older people who reside in "skid row" (though the term is disappearing). Many cities still have areas that house vagrants, wanderers, seasonal laborers, chronic inebriates, and old men retired from manual employment and living on meager pensions or savings, as well as steadily employed men without family or community affiliations. In many of these areas, older men make up a disproportionate percentage of the population. A majority of this population has never been married or has disrupted marriages. Another form of the disreputable elder is an elder residing in a single-room occupancy hotel. This group of older people is referred to as the "unseen elderly." Because of their location, both groups are surrounded by deviance: drugs, prostitution, theft, and violence. In spite of their efforts, the older person becomes the target of robberies, beatings, burglaries, and other forms of violence. Older people in these situations are as much victims as deviants.[6]

Assault and Aggravated Assault

There is a definite and dramatic decrease in index offenses as age increases. When compared with other age groups, the contribution of older people is small concerning violence. As with other age groups, assault is the most common violent offense committed by older offenders. Quite commonly, these assaults occur in retirement communities where older people live in close proximity to one another, or in domestic settings.

Robbery

Robbery is one of the least frequent offenses for which older people are arrested. Older men who commit robbery most frequently use firearms. This is because robbery committed without a firearm requires the perpetrator to use strength and speed, neither of which is characteristic in old age. It has been postulated that it is criminals who have grown old rather than persons who become criminals in old age that are the older armed perpetrators committing crimes like robbing banks or stores.

Sex Offenses

Among all offenses committed by older men, sex offenses have received the greatest attention. There is general agreement that various forms of child molestation are the major sex offenses committed by older people. In general, older sex offenders do not use overt violence. Physical force is not used to bring the victim into subjection. A significant number of older inmates are incarcerated for committing sexual offenses such as rape, pedophilia, and exhibitionism. Crime statistics show that those over age 50 accounted for 10% of all sexual offenses, including rape. It has been reported that the older sex offender differs from the younger sex offender in many ways. While pedophiles are typically older men, rapists are generally more likely to be young, violent offenders. In some cases, child sex offenders over the age of 60 were discovered to have some organic brain disorders. Declines in mental and physical functioning associated with aging are likely to be experienced more frequently and have been postulated as potential triggers for sexual offending. Sexual offenses committed by older offenders frequently involve child victims. The offender often knows the victim, who is, more than likely, a stepdaughter or even a grandchild living in close proximity.[7]

Older Homicide Offenders

The major hypotheses regarding older homicide offenders are:

1. *The homicide offender rate for older people will remain relatively stable across jurisdictions (states), whereas the overall homicide offender rate will fluctuate sharply.* It is likely that older homicide offenders will not be "carriers" of a subculture of violence or be influenced as greatly by broader sociological conditions as people in younger age categories are.
2. *Homicides by older people will be disproportionately "domestic" in terms of the victim–offender relationship.* Conflicts involving older people are

more likely to be domestic and less likely to be outcomes of committing other felonies, and that older offenders will be disproportionally involved in domestic homicides. It is noteworthy that older people are far less likely to be involved in homicides against strangers than are younger people.

3. *Homicides by older people will be disproportionally intraracial.* Most interracial homicides are incidental to robberies and burglaries, and since it is unlikely that older people will be involved in these types of crimes, it is hypothesized that their homicides are likely to be disproportionally intraracial.

4. *There are no sharp differences for older offenders in circumstances or motive by sex and race of offender.* Although data indicate no sharp differences in the circumstance or motive categories for various subgroups (sex and race) or older versus younger offenders, there is strong evidence that the relative frequency of homicides by these subgroups does vary sharply. It would appear that while the patterns of older versus younger homicides do not vary with respect to victim–offender relationships, when subgroups (by sex and race) are considered, the relative frequency/rates of older versus younger offenders do vary sharply. In short, the older and younger offenders are homogeneous (with respect to sex and race sub-groups) with respect to patterns of offenses, but heterogeneous with respect to relative frequency/rates. Thus, although sex and race do not appear to affect patterns of homicides, they do affect relative frequency.

5. *Homicides by older people will be predominately incidents involving one victim and a single offender.* Most multiple-offender homicides involve some type of felony-related activity, such as drug deals, robberies, burglaries, and other crimes. Because older people are not as likely to be engaged in these types of activities, older offenders will seldom be involved in multiple-offender slayings. Older offenders are more likely to be involved in homicide events with only one victim and offender than younger offenders.

6. *Older offenders are less likely to kill someone of their own age.* It appears that middle-aged persons (those 25–34 and 35–44) are more likely to kill those of their own age than the old. By contrast, those 60–64 and 65–74 (the "younger elderly") were less likely to kill someone of their own age. However, the very old (those age 74 and over) do not fit the pattern for the younger elderly, in that a third of those over 74 kill someone of their own age category.

7. *Older offenders will be more likely to use firearms than offenders in other age groups.* Because older people lose muscle mass and therefore are not as strong as younger people, older offenders are less likely to approach a younger person with a knife, stick, or other blunt object as a weapon. Older offenders are more likely to use a gun as a weapon of choice than younger offenders.

8. *Monthly patterns of homicides by older offenders are similar to those of other age groups.* Little or no differences are found for older offenders versus younger offenders regarding month of the year in which homicides are committed.[8]

A study conducted in 2007 examined homicides committed in Chicago over a 31-year period (1965–1995).[9] Cases involving perpetrators over age 60 were compared with younger perpetrators. The study concluded the following with respect to the offenders over age 60:

- Older perpetrators were more likely to follow homicide with suicide.
- Victims of older perpetrators were more likely to be related to the offender by being a spouse, and less likely to be a stranger or gang member (the proportion of victims aged 60 and older was significantly higher for older perpetrators).
- Older men were most likely to kill females.
- Older perpetrators were less likely to have multiple victims.
- Interracial killings were not the norm for older perpetrators.

Drawing from a review of the literature, the following is offered for empirical investigations:

1. The older offender–victim homicide relationship will involve a significantly greater proportion of spouse/family homicides than will nonelderly offender–victim homicides.
2. A significantly greater proportion of older homicides than younger homicides will occur in the home.
3. A significantly greater proportion of older versus younger homicides will be intraracial in nature.
4. There will be a significantly higher proportion of older male than older female homicide offenders.
5. The ratio of male–female older homicide offenders will be significantly lower than the ratio of male–female nonelderly offenders.
6. Older homicide offender–victim relationships will be significantly higher within their same age category than will younger offender–victim relationships.
7. The victims of older homicide offenders will be significantly less involved in alcohol consumption at the time of the incident than will be the victims of younger homicide offenders.[10]

A TYPOLOGY OF GERIATRIC OFFENDERS

Older people are the most heterogeneous of all cohorts. This also applies to older offenders. Their only common denominator is their old age. To put into perspective criminality in older age, the following tentative typology is offered.

The Inveterate Aging Offender

This type of offender is a persistent or chronic offender. These offenders begin their life of crime in adolescence or youth. Most persistent offenders cease their criminal activity by age 40, yet some continue into old age. The offenders may spend short or long intervals incarcerated. The inveterate aging offender should not be confused with the aging incarcerated offender. The latter type is usually a middle-aged person who receives a life sentence or a very long sentence for a serious crime, is not released on parole, and spends his or her senior years in a penitentiary. Several subtypes of the inveterate aging offender may be identified.

The Professional Criminal

What differentiates the professional criminal from the habitual criminal is the sophisticated forms of crime in which the former engages and the petty forms to which the later seems committed.

The Chronic Drunkenness Offender

The old, chronic drunkenness offender is a subtype frequently found in the skid row of every major city in North America.

The Habitual Criminal/Chronic Petty Offender

This offender is the persistent petty thief or false pretense offender who is often quite old and who has failed to make a satisfactory adjustment to life generally. Most commonly male, he has few ties; holds a job for a short period only; tends to have no roots; lives from day to day in cheap hotels, lodging houses, or on the streets; and tends to be a drain on social services whether in prison or not. He has been in and out of prison most of his life, and appears to be better adjusted to prison life than to life outside of prison.

The Organized Crime Head

Many of the individuals identified by police as mafia dons in the United States are older individuals, with some even being septuagenarians.

The Inveterate Psychopath

The psychopathic criminal has been described as one who is not psychotic (insane), but who indulges in irrational, antisocial behavior, probably resulting from hidden unconscious neurotic conflicts that constitute the driving force underlying the criminal conduct. Psychopaths are some of the most malignant and recidivistic offenders. Psychopaths feel little or no guilt and are unable to form lasting bonds. Among the old persistent offenders in prisons and penitentiaries, a good number fit the diagnostic label of a psychopath. A long, persistent career of offending is actually an important criterion in the diagnosis of a psychopath.

The Chronic, Nonviolent Sex Offender

The truly pedophilic sex offender, who is exclusively attracted to prepubertal children, can persist in his sexual activities with nondiscerning or seemingly "consenting" children long after his libido has weakened or subsided. Most of these offenders exhibit no other antisocial attitudes and are law-abiding, conforming citizens except for their sexual sphere. Because of this and because of the type of victims they select, they can go on with their deviant sexual activities for many years without being detected. Since their sexual preference or fixation does not change over time, their offenses persist, whether detected or not, until late in life.

The Relapsing Older Offender

Some older offenders, long thought to have been rehabilitated, suddenly relapse into crime after a very long period of successful adjustment and after having stayed away from crime for 2, 3, or 4 decades. The relapse into crime occurs after they have reached the age of 50 or 60, and is usually triggered by some life crisis or by some problems or changes brought about by old age. A distinction may be made between two subgroups: the monomorphic and the polymorphic.

The Monomorphic

The monomorphic is an older offender, who, after a long period of remission, re-offends in the same way, committing the same offense (or category of offense) as when he or she was a young person.

The Polymorphic

The polymorphic is an older offender whose later criminal activities are of a different type than the ones committed during youth.

The Older First-Time Offender

This older offender is the most atypical, and probably the most problematic of all older offenders. It is the person whose first offense is committed in old age. These offenders have no prior history of delinquency or criminality. The following subtypes offer theories of why people commit their first offense late in life:

1. Older first offenders who exhibit psychiatric and behavioral changes leading to loss of memory, impairment of judgment, loss of inhibitions, breakdown of the inner mechanisms of control, or to the sudden release of primitive instinctual urges, morbid jealousy, morbid irrationality, suspicion, and mistrust.
2. Older first offenders suffering from dementia.
3. Older first offenders whose criminality can be traced directly to alcohol abuse or chronic alcoholism. This subtype includes the use of some drug (illicit or prescription).
4. Older first offenders suffering from specific personality changes associated with, or resulting from, old age.

5. Older first offenders whose criminality can be related directly to the influence of the environment. Some older individuals with offending-free history start committing crime, mostly minor offenses, after a fundamental environmental change, such as placement in a nursing home or senior citizen residential setting.[11]

NURSING FACILITIES

Nature and Scope of the Problem

The traditional view of nursing facilities is that the residents of such facilities are infirmed, bed-bound, and predominantly the oldest of the old. Nursing facilities serve a variety of clients with a variety of health-related problems. Long-term care facilities also provide rehabilitation services. A proportion of nursing home patients are often victims of serious accidents, sufferers of communicable diseases, or gunshot and violent crime victims, and any can suffer from psychiatric problems. Others may be paraplegics confined to wheelchairs. Thus, given the variety of services that nursing facilities provide, residents and clients can range in age from 18 years old and beyond.

The care that younger clients receive in nursing facilities is governed under the same standards that care for older patients is governed under. Nursing facilities are regulated under state standards. If the facility is receiving any federal funds (through Medicare), federal regulations may apply as well. Medicaid reimbursement for all clients is governed by state standards as well.

Some of the crimes that the law enforcement officer may encounter in the nursing facility include:

- Possession, use, and distribution of controlled dangerous substances
- Sexual offenses and aggressive sexual behavior
- Possession and use of deadly weapons
- Assaults and threats on staff and other patients
- Bringing prostitutes into the nursing facility
- Leaving the premises on authorized leaves and engaging in criminal acts in the surrounding community

Responding to Calls for Service

There are several types of calls for service that the law enforcement officer will respond to: those that require law enforcement intervention, civil matters, and violations of facility rules.

If called to a nursing facility to investigate a criminal complaint, the same right is extended the law enforcement officer as if the law enforcement officer is summoned to a private residence. That is, if permitted access to the facility by a qualified representative of the facility, any reasonable inquiry may be made. Further, if there is probable cause to effect a warrantless arrest, this arrest can be made regardless of whether the suspect is a staff member, patient, or visitor.

There is one special note of concern for nursing facilities and those who reside in them. A frequent complaint regarding younger residents of nursing facilities is the possession (and sometimes sale) of controlled dangerous substances. The law enforcement official should be aware that a nursing home patient's room can legally be considered his residence and that searches for drugs or property should be accompanied by a search warrant based on probable case and not merely on hearsay or speculation by nursing home staff.

In circumstances where there is not sufficient probable cause to make an arrest, there should be an investigation. This will include:

- Identifying potential witnesses
- Recovering physical evidence
- Securing and processing crime scenes
- Interviewing staff, visitors, and patients

If your agency has a specialized unit that handles issues of elder crimes, these officers should be brought into any investigation as early as possible. If specialized officers are not needed, they may serve as advisors on cases in facilities where the responding officer is not familiar.

When called to a nursing facility where it is clear that the case is a civil complaint, the law enforcement officer must still show consideration, gather facts, and offer advice. Remember, for some residents, the nursing facility is considered *home*, and even minor civil infractions can be considered disastrous, particularly for those who have no outside influences to call upon. You, the law enforcement officer, may be the only one the resident may have to call upon.

Occasionally, you may be called to a facility for infractions that are neither criminal nor civil, but involve infractions by residents of the facility's rules and codes of conduct. Nursing facilities have a process that must be adhered to when addressing such matters. The facility cannot arbitrarily remove patients for infractions. Patients residing in such facilities have a Nursing Home Residents' Bill of Rights. Further, state regulations may be in place that govern the sanctioning or removal of residents for infractions of the facility's rules. Law enforcement officers are encouraged to become familiar with the laws that govern nursing facilities in your state.

Accordingly, if an arrest of a staff member is made for abuse of a resident, narcotics violation, or other crime, you should notify the state agency that licenses and regulates the facility. In this way, the regulatory agency is able to trend problems within the facility. Also, if the perpetrator who is a staff member is licensed in any way, the perpetrator's state licensing agency should be notified as well. Only in this way can the perpetrator's history of abuse be tracked by a licensing agency. The concern here is that the perpetrator may seek employment in another nursing facility if there is not a loss of license. Employees working in nursing facilities who hold a state license or certification include certified nursing assistants (CNAs), geriatric nursing assistants (GNAs), licensed practical nurses (LPNs), registered nurses (RNs), nurse practitioners (NPs), physician assistants (PAs), and physicians (MDs). Unfortunately, there is no inter-state mechanism in place to track the licenses of certified healthcare providers seeking employment in nursing facilities.

Most nursing facilities have a resident and/or family council. If there is a nursing facility within your precinct or post, find out which type of council your nursing facility has. Become involved by attending meetings and discussing relevant issues. This also demonstrates that the police and law enforcement officers are concerned about the residents' safety and wellbeing, and that there is a police presence in the facility. This will have a deterring effect on anyone who wishes to prey upon the elderly and infirmed. It is good public relations as well.[12]

SPECIAL CONSIDERATIONS FOR ARRESTING OLDER PERPETRATORS

There will be times when the law enforcement officer must take an older person into custody. As stated earlier, the aged are the most heterogeneous of all cohorts; that is, not everyone ages the same. There are many above the age of 85 who are mentally and physically fit and continue with very productive lifestyles. Conversely, there are those who are 65 who are frail and infirmed.

This section offers the law enforcement officer considerations to take when arresting the older, frail, or infirmed perpetrator. However, age and frailty are not exclusionary factors for harm. An older person who is armed or has the means to harm a law enforcement officer is just as dangerous as a younger perpetrator. Always follow local policies and practices when arresting older perpetrators. Additionally, the approach, interview, and investigation should be conducted in the manner prescribed by your agency's policies and procedures. You may have to alter the questioning or interrogation depending upon the older person's mental status.

One age-related change that may be a factor in arresting older people is the lack of mobility in the upper extremities. There are some older people who, because of arthritis and other infirmities, cannot place their hands over their head or behind their back. Similarly, frail skin can become problematic when handcuffs are place upon the person. Consider in these cases allowing the older person to be handcuffed in front and placing handcuffs over clothing so as not to cause skin tears, as shown in **Figure 7-1**.

Older persons who are not mobile present less of a problem. If the older person uses any type of assistive device (cane, walker), you must assure that it is transported with the arrestee and made available for use at the holding facility.

Figure 7-1 Increasingly, law enforcement officers will encounter older perpetrators.
Source: © Peter Baxter/ShutterStock, Inc.

Perpetrators in wheelchairs present unique challenges. Some wheelchairs are traditional in that the person in the chair rolls the chair along by its wheels. These chairs are usually lightweight and can be folded (see **Figure 7-2**). Other wheelchairs are battery powered and can be operated by users with a control on one of the arms of the chair. This type of chair is extremely heavy and cannot be folded readily (see **Figure 7-3**). When encountering perpetrators in this type of chair, the law enforcement officer will have to take control of the

Figure 7-2 Traditional wheelchair with patient seated.
Source: © wavebreakmedia ltd/ShutterStock, Inc.

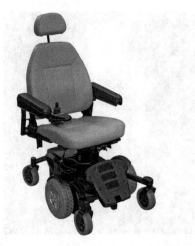

Figure 7-3 Battery powered wheelchairs are extremely heavy and cannot be folded readily.
Source: © daseaford/ShutterStock, Inc.

chair's operating device. The ideal place for the law enforcement officer to position himself is at the control side of the chair. Avoid standing in front of a battery-operated wheelchair, as the operator can engage the chair. If struck by this type of chair, its weight can fracture an ankle. The traditional method of placing the hands behind the back for handcuffing will not work with these perpetrators. A best practice is to handcuff the arrestee's arms to the sides of the wheelchair. Caution must be taken, however, as some wheelchairs have removable sides. Arms should be secured to the frame of the wheelchair.

Transporting arrestees in wheelchairs will require extra personnel. The arrestee will have to be uncuffed and lifted from the wheelchair into the police car. If utilizing a van-type transport vehicle, the arrestee can be transported in the wheelchair. However, if transporting the arrestee in the wheelchair, the chair must be secured in the vehicle. Vans can be outfitted with commercial wheelchair locking devices. An alternative would be to contract with a commercial wheelchair service. Commercial ambulance vendors often operate wheelchair vans. Commercial wheelchair vans are adequately equipped and possess wheelchair lifts. Personnel will also be knowledgeable in the transport of this type of client. In either case, the law enforcement officer must ensure that the wheelchair is transported with the arrestee. Remember, persons in wheelchairs are already limited in their mobility. Failure to transport the wheelchair will further deprive the arrestee of any mobility and may result in a deprivation of rights issue.

Rarely, older persons who have intravenous (IV) feeding tubes and IV medications in place must be taken into custody. Many of these patients are bedbound. Precinct holding facilities are not equipped to handle this type of detainee, as these prisoners require nursing care. Local law enforcement agencies may have to request holding these prisoners at detention centers, state prisons, or hospitals with prison wings who have the capability to care for this inmate population. Transportation by traditional means will not be impossible. Law enforcement agencies may have to secure an agreement with the local emergency medical services system, or commercial ambulance service for ambulance transport of these arrestees. Paramedics will be able to monitor the sometimes complex health problems of this detainee population while in transport. Agreements should be in place before the situation arises.

USE OF NONLETHAL DETERRENTS ON OLDER PERPETRATORS

Pepper Spray

Pepper spray is an effective neutralizing agent. However, in some persons, it can trigger an exacerbation of preexisting breathing problems. This is true in older people—particularly those with chronic obstructive pulmonary disorders (asthma, emphysema, and bronchitis). While the law enforcement officer will not know if the older person who has been neutralized will have such disorders, those who have been neutralized must be observed. A good practice for any older person who has been neutralized with pepper spray is to have these individuals immediately evaluated by EMS. In this way, the EMS provider will be able to assess for breathing problems and ascertain if the person has any breathing problems that may trigger an untoward event.

TASERS

A neuromuscular incapacitation (NMI) device, or electromuscular incapacitation (EMI) device, commonly known as a TASER, is a laser-sighted device that uses a cartridge to project a pair of prongs or darts on steel wires up to a distance of approximately 20 feet. The prongs or darts become imbedded into the skin and deliver 50,000 volts of electricity over the thin steel wires, with the effect of overriding a subject's motor and sensory nervous systems. In other words, it causes the muscles to contract uncontrollably, temporarily incapacitating a subject. The controlled energy is delivered over 5 seconds. The cycle can be interrupted by the user and repeated if necessary.

The TASER is intended to provide officers with a less lethal option to help them overcome a subject's combative intent, physical resistance, and/or assaultive behavior; subdue persons bent on harming themselves or others; and to provide self-defense.

There are multiple cases of TASER use on persons in their 70s. Questions and controversies have arisen with TASER use in older people. These questions and controversies mainly center on the inducement of ventricular fibrillation (a lethal heart rhythm) and pacemaker disruption in older people when tased.

Quite a bit of speculation has circulated in the scientific community questioning whether a subset of people could be hypersensitive to the effects of the TASER. Although this hypothesis is a valid consideration, multiple studies conducted have demonstrated that the shock produced by a TASER is far below the level necessary to cause a heart to fibrillate. Pacemakers must comply with the Active Implantable Medical Device Requirement, which specifies that pacemakers must be individually tested to withstand very high shocks from external defibrillators. The TASER delivers 0.36–1.7 joules per pulse; whereas the pacemaker must be able to withstand 360 joules per pulse, a considerably higher load.

For some, though, it is a matter of public perception. When a TASER has been used on an older person, public perception of the event is often negative. While it is beyond the scope of this text to offer an opinion on the use of the TASER in older people, one principle remains: As with all applications of force, law enforcement officers using less lethal options are expected to use necessary and reasonable force to effect a lawful purpose. Necessary and reasonable uses are defined by the totality of the circumstances and the exercise of reasonable judgment. One solid recommendation that can be made is that any older person who has been tased should then be evaluated by EMS and transported to the emergency department to have the probes removed and for further evaluation.

OLDER INMATES

Corrections, prisons, and the study of prison populations are a separate discipline. The study of the aging prison population in the United States has received much attention recently in the academic literature. The focus of this section is to discuss housing older arrestees in local or county jails for a short period of time and those age-related considerations that must be taken when housing older people. However, a brief overview is provided on older people in the prison population.

Older Inmates in Correctional Facilities

There has been a remarkable growth in the absolute number and proportion of older prisoners in the U.S. prison population.

According to the National Corrections Reporting System, in 2009 there were 68,764 people in state prisons over age 55, representing an average of 7.2% of all inmates in state prisons. Further stratified by age, those over 60 years of age represented 3.4%, those over 65 years of age represented 1.5%, those over 70 years of age represented 0.6%, and those over 75 years of age represented 0.2% of the total state prison population.[13]

The Bureau of Justice Statistics, Federal Justice Statistics Program reported that in 2009, the number of inmates in the federal prison system over the age of 61 was 6,593, representing 3.5% of the 185,273 prisoners in the federal system. Further stratified by age, those age 61–70 years totaled 5,646 (or 3.0% of the total prison population in the federal prison system); those age 71–80 years totaled 877 (or 0.5%); and those over age 80 totaled 70 (or 0.03%).[14]

From 1995–2010 (as reported by the Bureau of Justice Statistics, Prisoner Series, 1995–2010) the growth in state and federal prisoners age 55 and older grew by 282%. During that same period, the total prison population grew by only 42.1%. In 2010, there were 124,400 prisoners over the age of 55 in state and federal prisons.[15]

Correctional facilities are designed to house and manage inmates who are young when they enter and young when released. Older inmates, due to the effects of aging, have different needs, and thus, place a far greater demand on the correctional system than do younger inmates. This is especially true of healthcare needs.

Most corrections systems have set a specific chronological age to serve as a proxy for the physical and mental changes and conditions that correlate with aging. Their definitions of "older" inmates range from 50 years of age to 70 years.[16]

Research shows prison medical expenditures for older inmates range from three to nine times higher than those for the average inmate. Like their community-dwelling counterparts, older prisoners are susceptible to the chronic diseases and infirmities associated with age, including heart and lung problems, diabetes, hypertension, cancer, ulcers, poor hearing and eyesight, and a range of physical disabilities. A recent survey found that 46% of male inmates 50 years or older and 82% of inmates 65 years or older have a chronic physical problem.[17]

Given the age range of what constitutes an elderly offender (50–70), local jails and facilities should focus on an older prisoner's overall health condition and functional limitations when considering special needs.

HOUSING OLDER ARRESTEES

Housing older arrestees, even on a temporary basis, can be challenging for local law enforcement agencies. Issues such as frailty, comorbidities, assistive devices, and medication administration are the major challenges to be confronted. Also, housing older arrestees with the general population (or in a common holding area) may also pose issues for the older arrestee.

Many law enforcement agencies are not equipped to handle older arrestees with any of the challenges they pose. For legal reasons, administering prescribed medications to an older detainee may not be permitted, even though the older arrestee may need these medications daily—even several times a day. State and county jails often have segregated areas to house older or infirmed detainees; local jails and precinct facilities do not.

Prison systems have already had to face the challenges of housing older inmates with many developing special needs programs, special housing, prison nursing homes, and prison hospice programs. Local facilities must also direct special attention to this issue. While it is beyond the scope of this text to offer specific policies on these issues, several broad guidelines can be offered when considering the issues involving housing older arrestees:

1. If an older perpetrator is arrested who presents sensory deficits, ensure that the detainee has his or her hearing aid and/or eye glasses. If not, the arrestee may not be able to communicate effectively and understand the processes that will occur.
2. If an older perpetrator who is arrested has an assistive device (cane, walker, or wheelchair), these devices should be transported with the older arrestee. While these devices may not be permitted in the holding area, they should be available to the older arrestee to aid with movement.
3. If the older arrestee requires assistance with activities of daily living, determine what assistance is required. Depending upon the level of assistance needed, alternative housing may be needed.
4. If the older arrestee presents with multiple comorbidities and appears in any way to be in distress, this detainee should be evaluated in the emergency department prior to being transported to the jail.
5. If the older arrestee advises that he or she has medications that must be taken daily (or multiple times a day), these medications must be provided to the older arrestee. This is a particularly challenging issue. Some law enforcement agencies are not permitted to dispense medications. Others transport the older detainee to the emergency department to have needed medications dispensed. Some agencies have the medications verified by a physician and dispense them to the detainee at the specified times.
6. Frequently, older people have specific dietary needs. If possible, ensure that these dietary needs are met.

The following tips may also be helpful when housing older arrestees:

1. Have a separate intake form for older people. This form should address the specific needs of older arrestees. For example, the ability of the older detainee to perform his or her activities of daily living, use of an assistive device, need for hearing aid or glasses, dietary needs, and specific medication needs.
2. A physician should evaluate an older arrestee being housed longer than 48 hours.
3. Ensure that the older arrestee has sufficient dietary intake when in custody.
4. Ensure that the cell bunk or bed is accessible for the older arrestee (older arrestees should be housed on a lower bunk).

Case Study 3

Your 911 center has received a call from an elderly male stating that he has just killed his wife. The caller states that his wife was very ill and he could not bear to see her suffer any longer.

When you and another unit arrive at the caller's residence, you are greeted by an 80-year-old male, Lawrence Pinder. Mr. Pinder states that his wife has had Parkinson's disease for many years and had become bedridden over the last 6 months. During that time, Mr. Pinder states she also had been declining mentally. He tearfully tells you and your partner that he simply could not bear to see his wife of over 50 years suffer anymore. Mr. Pinder states his own medical problems and frailty have prevented him from caring for his wife. He continues that he was unable to get outside help. Mr. Pinder says that he placed a pillow over her face and smothered her so she would not suffer any longer.

How do you handle this?

What considerations do you make regarding arrest procedures?

---

5. Consider allowing the older arrestee to have his or her own shoes (as opposed to issued slippers). One of the biggest causes of falls in jail is the slippers that are usually issued.

6. Ensure the older arrestee is warm enough in the cell. When older people are cold, this can be medically stressful.

7. Keep a watchful eye on older arrestees (suicide watch). The chronically ill and older people have a higher suicide rate than the general population.

8. If possible, house the older arrestee in a county or regional facility (even before a bail review) that has a medical staff and facility conducive to older detainees.

Older offenders are considered special needs offenders. It is recommended that local law enforcement agencies have plans in place that consider each of the challenges mentioned above. This can be accomplished using a team approach. Members who may be helpful include representatives of the local department of aging, public health nurses, and geriatricians. State prison officials (specifically the medical unit) may also be helpful in assisting local jails with formulating plans for holding older arrestees.

When housing older arrestees, consider the senior CAN DO approach:[18]

C   Consider and care for an older arrestee's age-related and healthcare needs.

A   Apply proactive methods. The goal is to plan for how to accommodate the older arrestee when entering a holding area or jail.

N   Needs assessment. Develop an individual needs assessment for every older detainee.

D Develop relationships with other agencies that work with and understand older people and their needs. Such agencies include the local departments of aging and social services. Individuals with expertise that could provide valuable assistance include geriatricians and/or geriatric health nurses.

O Organize data collection and management to improve efficiency when housing older arrestees. Share this data with other law enforcement agencies to develop a "best practices" approach.

PREVENTING ELDERLY CRIME[19]

Preventing crime from occurring is an integral function of any law enforcement agency. In 2009, those age 65 and older made up only 0.8% of all who were arrested. While crime in old age has been described as atypical and abnormal, there are certain preventive strategies that law enforcement officials must consider with respect to elder crime.

Improved Mental Health

Mental health problems seem to play a significant role in crimes committed by first-time elderly offenders (recall the discussion "A Typology of Geriatric Offenders" earlier in this chapter). Therefore, one effective prevention strategy must include the improvement of mental health for older people. This strategy also includes alcohol screening and prevention in older people, as alcohol seems to play an important role in elder criminality.

Strengthening Elders' Social Network

Older people are more likely to live alone. It has been postulated that this social isolation may act as a victimogenic and/or as a criminogenic factor. Strengthening the social networks of older people may reduce crime by, and victimization against, older people.

For those older people who have already come into contact with the criminal justice system, the role of self-help groups and self-help activities may be an alternative to conventional probation and parole models. A program run by older volunteers to provide advice, assistance, and support to older offenders may prevent a relapse into crime. Older volunteers may be more likely than younger professionals to understand the stressors, frustrations, and problems that led the older person to commit the crime.

Improving Social Services and Social Support Systems for the Elderly

Many offenses committed by older people can be traced directly or indirectly to the difficulties encountered in coping with various age-related changes. A policy aimed at reducing elder crimes should include providing the social services needed to help older people cope with such problems.

Changing the Structure of Opportunity

A social policy aimed at improving the quality of life of older people may reduce elder crime. It has been suggested that a great deal of leisure time, boredom, and lack of meaningful activities have a criminogenic effect and are responsible, wholly or in part, for crimes committed by retired people.

The Role of Law Enforcement

While improving mental health, strengthening the elderly's social networks, improving social services and social support systems for the elderly, and changing the structure of opportunity may not appear to be the primary role of law enforcement, there must be a crucial shift in thinking with respect to preventing elder crime. Preventing elder crime is a multidisciplinary approach in which law enforcement is a key stakeholder. Multi-agency crime prevention teams can be created and should include law enforcement, the department of aging, social services, mental health teams, and the participation of local hospitals. Many local hospitals provide outreach and health screening to older people.

Emergency medical services (EMS) should also be considered for inclusion on the team. A significant portion of patients transported by EMS involves older people. EMS providers are being taught to evaluate not only the medical needs of older people, but also their social and psychological needs. EMS providers play a crucial role in the evaluation and referral of older people with social, psychological, and environmental needs. The goal of the team is to identify at-risk elders who may require health and social services, thereby reducing the propensity to commit crime.

Law enforcement agencies have long been involved in the lives of youth with the goal of crime prevention. The same must now be the goal for older people. Ensuring that older people receive the services they require will help them continue to live productive and active lives, and may prevent elder crime.

A MODEL INTERVENTIONAL PROGRAM

While it is beyond the scope of this text to address sentencing issues and the older perpetrator, one model interventional program is worthy of mention—the Broward County Senior Intervention and Education (BSIE) Program. Established in the spring of 1979 in Broward County, Florida, the program has two major objectives: (1) to prevent the recurrence of shoplifting by the elderly, and (2) to provide the courts with humanitarian and socially constructive sanctions for elderly shoplifters. The BSIE is a three-dimensional rehabilitation program designed to reduce the likelihood of recidivism among elderly shoplifters. The first dimension of the program emphasizes counseling, including an opportunity to reduce the trauma of the shoplifting event and accompanying pretrial anxieties, as well as addressing more long-standing family, economic, social, and personal issues, especially those regarded as causing or motivating the shoplifting behavior. The second dimension of the program focuses on getting the client involved in certain social activities, including participating in lecture series, learning new crafts, teaching a skill to others, and so on. The third dimension is an externship with a community service organization, such as a local hospital or a food delivery service for shut-ins. This is especially designed for those diagnosed as overly concerned with their own problems and unable to transcend or see their own situation in perspective. To be eligible, the client must meet the following criteria:

1. Be 60 years of age or older
2. Be charged with only one count of misdemeanor shoplifting
3. Enter a plea of guilty
4. Be a first-time offender
5. Voluntarily agree to participate in the program

Typically, all clients have appeared as defendants before a judge in open court, have been apprised of the nature of the misdemeanor shoplifting charge against them, and have entered a plea of guilty. The judge then explains that the court will withhold judgment, thereby avoiding a criminal record, if the defendant agrees to participate in the BSIE program. If the defendant agrees to participate in the program, a representative counselor is introduced to the defendant who explains the goals and objectives of the program.

The program is organized as a special service component of the Jewish Community Centers of South Broward. These centers have traditionally offered services to older residents. The court system filters clients into the program. Counselors work directly with the elderly clients to achieve the goals of the program. Acceptance into the program depends on the consent of the presiding judge, and then a memorandum of understanding and a waiver of speedy trial are filed with the court and state's attorney. The client is informed that arraignment will be continued and sentence deferred until completion of the program. The client is also informed of the program requirements. The older offender is advised of what participation in the BSIE offers: (1) It will remove the offender from the criminal justice system into a social agency trained to deal with the problems of aging; (2) it will provide counseling; (3) the agency will offer the ability to plug into social services as needed; and (4) successful completion of participation will result in dismissal of charges with no court costs and no criminal record. According to available statistics from the BSIE program, there is a less than 2% recidivism rate.[20]

SUMMARY

Whether it be a chronic perpetrator or a first time offender, law enforcement officials will encounter older people who present to the criminal justice system as offenders. The biggest challenge to law enforcement is the first time older offender. Understanding the nature of first time offenses committed by older people and the reasons they are committed provide an opportunity for officials to intervene and provide needed services and resources that may prevent a reoccurrence.

Older offenders are special needs offenders. Even if housing the older arrestees for a short amount of time, understanding age related changes, the chronic conditions common in the older population, and the daily needs older people require will aid law enforcement officials when housing older arrestees.

CASE STUDY SUMMARIES

Case Study 1 Summary

You know that shoplifting is the most common offense for which older people are arrested. You also know the major motive in older shoplifting is not real economic hardship, but that it does occur in a percentage of older shoplifting cases. Unfortunately, this is one of these cases—a frail 76-year-old female has attempted to shoplift several over-the-counter medications valued at $21.09. The suspect is remorseful, advising you that she cannot afford these items, but requires them for her medical conditions. Under the eyes of the law, this case is no different than any other larceny. There may be, however, circumstances that you may take to mitigate the effects of the crime. If the owner or manager of the convenience store does not wish to press charges, your options are greater. There is an opportunity for you to assist the older person with obtaining needed resources that may enable her to afford medications. A referral to social services is appropriate. If the owner or manager wishes to press charges, you will be forced to arrest the suspect. If this is the case, there still remains an opportunity to refer the woman to social services. When sentencing occurs, if the woman is receiving necessary aid, a judge may be lenient or a plea bargain may be entered.

Case Study 2 Summary

The 74-year-old woman is acting aggressively and threatening the staff. The staff is unable to speak to the woman or control her aggressive behavior. As you attempt to speak to the woman, she screams profanities at you and swings her cane. The woman rises from a chair, proceeds to her room, striking a staff member with her cane as she does so. The center director advises that the woman cannot remain in the facility while displaying this type of behavior. The question to ask is whether this is a medical situation or a crime. Along with the EMS crew, you will want to determine what, if anything, may have precipitated the situation. Additionally, attempt to determine if this behavior is atypical for the woman. In any event, the woman must be transported to the emergency department (by EMS) for a medical evaluation. A sudden change in mental status and behavior is a medical emergency and should be treated as such. You and the EMS crew should attempt to negotiate with the woman to allow transport to the emergency department.

Case Study 3 Summary

In this case study, your duty as a law enforcement officer is clear. Mr. Pinder advises you that he has just killed his ailing wife by smothering her with a pillow. He must be taken into custody and charged accordingly. Homicide investigators will interview Mr. Pinder and ascertain the facts surrounding and leading up to the event. The medical examiner will determine the cause of death. The considerations you make in arresting Mr. Pinder must reflect his frailty and overall health. If he requires a walker, it should be brought with him. If Mr. Pinder requires glasses, a hearing aid, and medications, these items must be transported with him. This will be an emotionally charged event for everyone involved, especially the suspect. Mr. Pinder, if housed even for a short time pending a bail review, should be placed on suicide watch. If it is anticipated that he will be housed longer than 48 hours before a bail review, a physician should evaluate him. The sentencing Mr. Pinder receives will be a matter for the court.

ENDNOTES

1. Rothman, M. B., Dunlop, B. D., & Entzel, P. (2000). *Elders, crime, and the criminal justice system: Myth, perception, and reality in the 21st century.* New York: Springer; p. 46.
2. Lewis, C. F., Fields, C., & Rainey, E. (2006). A study of geriatric forensic evaluees: Who are the violent elderly? *Journal of American Academy of Psychiatry Law, 34,* 324–332.
3. Fattah, E. A., & Sacco, V. F. (1989). *Crime and victimization of the elderly.* New York: Springer-Verlag; pp. 61–62.
4. Ibid., pp. 62–63.
5. Ibid., pp. 63–66.
6. Alston, L. T. (1986). *Crime and older Americans.* Springfield, IL: Charles C. Thomas Publishers; pp. 143–145.
7. Aday, R. H. (2003). *Aging prisoners, crisis in American corrections.* Westport, CT: Praeger; pp. 48–51.
8. Newman, E. S., Newman, D. J., & Gerwitz, M. L. (1984). *Elderly criminals.* Cambridge, MA: Oelgeschlager, Gunn & Hain Publishers; pp. 83–89.
9. Fazel, S., Bond, M., Gulati, G., &; O'Donnell, I. (2007). Elderly homicide in Chicago, IL: A research note. *Behavioral Sciences and the Law, 25,* 629–639.
10. McCarthy, B., & Langworthy, R. (1988). *Older offenders, perspectives in criminology and criminal justice.* New York: Praeger; p. 68.
11. Fattah, E. A., & Sacco, V. F. (1989). *Crime and victimization of the elderly.* New York: Springer-Verlag, pp. 105–112.
12. Maryland Police and Correctional Training Commissions. (n.d.). *Response to allegations of criminal activity by nursing home patients.*

13. Bureau of Justice Statistics, Office of Justice Programs. (2009). *National corrections reporting program, 2009—Statistical tables.* Retrieved from http://bjs.ojp.usdoj.gov/index.cfm?ty=pbdetail&iid=2174.
14. Human Rights Watch. (2012). Old behind bars: The aging prison population in the United States. Retrieved April 12, 2012, from http://www.hrw.org/sites/default/files/reports/usprisons0112webwcover_0.pdf; p. 104.
15. Ibid., p. 7.
16. Ibid., p. 17.
17. Ibid., pp. 72–73.
18. Modified from the Florida Department of Corrections 2009–2010 Annual Report, p. 20.
19. Fattah, E. A., & Sacco, V. F. (1989). *Crime and victimization of the elderly.* New York: Springer-Verlag; pp. 124–127.
20. Newman, E. S., Newman, D. J., & Gerwitz, M. L. (1984). *Elderly criminals.* Cambridge, MA: Oelgeschlager, Gunn & Hain Publishers; pp. 177–183.

RESOURCES
Website
National Institute of Corrections (http://nicic.gov/)

Books and Articles
Collins, D. R., & Bird, R. (2007). The penitentiary visit—a new role for geriatricians? *Age and Ageing, 36,* 11–13.

Maryland State Commission on Criminal Sentencing Policy. *Aging offenders and the criminal justice system.*

Yorston, G. A., & Taylor, J. (2006). Commentary: Older offenders–no place to go? *Journal of American Academy of Psychiatry Law, 34,* 333–337.

KEY TERMS
booster: A type of shoplifter who steals for resale, concentrating on higher priced goods

snitch: A type of shoplifter, an amateur, stealing for his or her own use

Appendix A

Aging Resources

The Aging Resources appendix is designed to help law enforcement officials find the information they need about older people and agencies and organizations who serve the needs of older people. The appendix is listed alphabetically by topic.

A

Adult Day Care

National Council on Aging (www.ncoa.org)

Advocacy

American Association of Retired Persons (www.aarp.org)

Better Business Bureau (www.bbb.org)

African American Health

National Caucus and Center on Black Aged (www.ncba-aged.org)

National Urban League (www.nul.org)

Aging Research

Administration on Aging (www.aoa.gov)

Alliance for Aging Research (www.agingresearch.org)

Alzheimer's Association (www.alz.org)

Alzheimer's Disease Education and Referral Center
(www.nia.nih.gov/alzheimers)

American Federation for Aging Research (www.afar.org)

American Geriatrics Society (www.americangeriatrics.org)

American Society on Aging (www.asaging.org)

Gerontological Society of America (www.geron.org)

National Institute on Aging (www.nih.gov/nia)

AIDS

National Institute of Allergy and Infectious Diseases (www.niaid.nih.gov)

New England Association on HIV Over Fifty (www.hivoverfifty.com)

Alaska Native Health

Indian Health Service (www.ihs.gov)

National Indian Council on Aging (www.nicoa.org)

National Resource Center on Native American Aging
(http://ruralhealth.und.edu/projects/nrcnaa)

Alcohol Abuse

National Council on Alcoholism and Drug Dependence (www.ncadd.org)

National Institute on Alcohol Abuse and Alcoholism (www.niaaa.nih.gov)

Substance Abuse and Mental Health Services Administration
(www.samhsa.gov)

Alzheimer's Disease

Alzheimer's Association (www.alz.org)

Alzheimer's Disease Education and Referral Center
(www.nia.nih.gov/alzheimers)

American Academy of Neurology (www.aan.com)

American Health Assistance Foundation (www.ahaf.org)

National Institute of Mental Health (www.nimh.nih.gov)

National Institute of Neurological Disorders and Stroke
(www.ninds.nih.gov)

National Institute on Aging (www.nih.gov/nia)

Arthritis

American Academy of Orthopaedic Surgeons (www.aaos.org)

Arthritis Foundation (www.arthritis.org)

National Institutes of Arthritis and Musculoskeletal and Skin Diseases (www.niams.nih.gov)

Asian Pacific American Health

Japanese American Citizens League (www.jacl.org)

National Asian Pacific Center on Aging (www.napca.org)

OCA National (www.ocanational.org)

Assisted Living

American Health Care Association (www.ahca.org)

Assisted Living Federation of America (www.alfa.org)

LeadingAge (www.leadingage.org)

National Council on Aging (www.ncoa.org)

National Resource Center on Supportive Housing and Home Modifications (www.homemods.org)

Autoimmune Diseases

Lupus Foundation of America (www.lupus.org)

National Institutes of Arthritis and Musculoskeletal and Skin Disease (www.niams.nih.gov)

B

Balance Disorders

American Academy of Otolaryngology—Head and Neck Surgery (www.entnet.org)

National Institute on Deafness and Other Communication Disorders (www.nidcd.nih.gov)

Vestibular Disorders Association (www.vestibular.org)

Blindness

See Eyes

Brain Diseases

Alzheimer's Association (www.alz.org)

Alzheimer's Disease Education and Referral Center (www.nia.nih.gov/alzheimers)

American Academy of Neurology (www.aan.com)

American Parkinson Disease Association (www.apdaparkinson.org)

National Institute of Neurological Disorders and Stroke
(www.ninds.nih.gov)

C

Cancer

American Cancer Society (www.cancer.org)

Leukemia and Lymphoma Society (www.lls.org)

National Cancer Institute (http://cancer.gov)

The Skin Cancer Foundation (www.skincancer.org)

Caregiving

Administration on Aging (www.aoa.gov)

Alzheimer's Association (www.alz.org)

Brookdale Center for Healthy Aging & Longevity of Hunter College
(www.brookdale.org)

Children of Aging Parents (www.caps4caregivers.org)

Eldercare Locator (www.eldercare.gov)

ElderWeb (www.elderweb.com)

National Association of Professional Geriatric Care Managers
(www.caremanager.org)

National Council on Aging (www.ncoa.org)

National Family Caregivers Association (www.nfcacares.org)

National Osteoporosis Foundation (www.nof.org)

National Resource Center: Diversity and Long-Term Care
(www.sihp.brandeis.edu)

Well Spouse Foundation (www.wellspouse.org)

Catholic Organizations

Catholic Charities USA (www.catholiccharitiesusa.org)

Chinese American Health

OCA National (www.ocanational.org)

Communication Disorders

American Speech-Language-Hearing Association (www.asha.org)

American Tinnitus Association (www.ata.org)

Better Hearing Institute (www.betterhearing.org)

Described and Captioned Media Program (www.dcmp.org)

Hearing Loss Association of America (www.hearingloss.org)

International Hearing Society (www.ihsinfo.org)

National Association of the Deaf (www.nad.org)

National Institute on Deafness and Other Communication Disorders (www.nidcd.nih.gov)

Community-Based Care

Administration on Aging (www.aoa.gov)

Center for the Advancement of State Community Service Programs (www.nasuad.org)

Central Plains Geriatric Education Center (http://coa.kumc.edu/cpgec)

Eldercare Locator (www.eldercare.gov)

Indian Health Service (www.ihs.gov)

National Association of Area Agencies on Aging (www.n4a.org)

National Association of States United for Aging and Disability (www.nasuad.org)

Long-Term Care Resource Center (www.hpm.umn.edu/ltcresourcecenter)

Project Aliento (www.anppm.org)

Visiting Nurse Associations of America (www.vnaa.org)

Community Service

Elder Craftsmen (www.eldercraftsmen.org)

Gray Panthers (www.graypanthers.org)

National Council on Aging (www.ncoa.org)

National Urban League (www.nul.org)

Computer Literacy

Generations on Line (www.generationsonline.com)

SeniorNet (www.seniornet.org)

Consumer Information

Federal Citizen Information Center (www.pueblo.gsa.gov)

National Consumers League (www.natlconsumersleague.org)

Counseling

American Association for Geriatric Psychiatry (www.aagponline.org)

American Counseling Association (www.counseling.org)

National Association of Social Workers (www.naswdc.org)

Mental Health America (www.nmha.org)

National Organization for Victim Assistance (www.try-nova.org)

Crime

Clearinghouse on Abuse and Neglect of the Elderly
(www.cane.udel.edu)

Department of Justice (www.justice.gov)

National Center on Elder Abuse (www.ncea.aoa.gov)

National Organization for Victim Assistance (www.try-nova.org)

National Policy and Resource Center on Women and Aging
(www.brandeis.edu/heller/national)

D

Databases

Alzheimer's Disease Education and Referral Center
(www.nia.nih.gov/alzheimers)

American Association of Retired Persons (www.aarp.org)

Census Bureau (www.census.gov)

Clearinghouse on Abuse and Neglect of the Elderly
(www.cane.udel.edu)

Gerontological Society of America (www.geron.org)

National Center for Health Statistics (www.cdc.gov/nchs)

National Institute of Diabetes and Digestive and Kidney Diseases
(www.niddk.nih.gov)

National Digestive Disease Information Clearinghouse
(http://digestive.niddk.nih.gov)

National Health Information Center (www.health.gov/NHIC)

National Rehabilitation Information Center (www.naric.com)

Death and Dying

National Hospice and Palliative Care Organization (www.nhpco.org)

National Hospice Foundation (www.nationalhospicefoundation.org)

Caring Connections (www.caringinfo.org)

Diabetes

American Diabetes Association (www.diabetes.org)

National Institute of Diabetes and Digestive and Kidney Diseases
(www.niddk.nih.gov)

Digestive Disorders

National Institute of Diabetes and Digestive and Kidney Diseases (www.niddk.nih.gov)

Disabilities

Disabled American Veterans (www.dav.org)

National Legal Support for Elderly People with Mental Disabilities (www.bazelon.org)

National Rehabilitation Information Center (www.naric.com)

National Resource Center: Diversity and Long-Term Care (www.sihp.brandeis.edu)

Dizziness

American Academy of Otolaryngology—Head and Neck Surgery (www.entnet.org)

Vestibular Disorders Association (www.vestibular.org)

Drug Abuse

National Council on Alcoholism and Drug Dependence (www.ncadd.org)

National Institute on Drug Abuse (www.nida.nih.gov)

Substance Abuse and Mental Health Services Administration (www.samhsa.gov)

E

Education

Association for Gerontology in Higher Education (www.aghe.org)

Legal Counsel for the Elderly (www.aarp.org)

Elder Abuse

Clearinghouse on Abuse and Neglect of the Elderly (www.cane.udel.edu)

Department of Justice (www.justice.gov)

National Center on Elder Abuse (www.ncea.aoa.gov)

National Organization for Victim Assistance (www.try-nova.org)

Emergency Assistance

American Red Cross (www.redcross.org)

MedicAlert Foundation (www.medicalert.org)

Employment

Disabled American Veterans (www.dav.org)

National Association for Hispanic Elderly (www.anppm.org)

National Caucus and Center on Black Aged (www.ncba-aged.org)

National Council on Aging (www.ncoa.org)

National Urban League (www.nul.org)

Senior Service America (www.seniorserviceamerica.org)

Epilepsy

Epilepsy Foundation (www.epilepsyfoundation.org)

National Institute of Neurological Disorders and Stroke
(www.ninds.nih.gov)

Exercise

American Heart Association (www.americanheart.org)

Arthritis Foundation (www.arthritis.org)

Centers for Disease Control and Prevention (www.cdc.gov)

Eyes

American Academy of Ophthalmology (www.eyenet.org)

American Council of the Blind (www.acb.org)

American Foundation for the Blind (www.afb.org)

American Health Assistance Foundation (www.ahaf.org)

Better Vision Institute (www.thevisioncouncil.org/bvi)

Glaucoma Research Foundation (www.glaucoma.org)

Lighthouse International (www.lighthouse.org)

National Eye Health Education Program (www.nei.nih.gov)

Opticians Association of America (www.oaa.org)

Prevent Blindness America (www.preventblindness.org)

F

Faith-Based Organizations

National Interfaith Coalition on Aging (www.ncoa.org)

Foot Care

American Podiatric Medical Association (www.apma.org)

Fraud

Department of Justice (www.justice.gov)

Food and Drug Administration (www.fda.gov)

National Bar Association (www.nationalbar.org)

National Consumers League (www.natlconsumersleague.org)

National Council Against Health Fraud (www.ncahf.org)

G

Geriatrics

American Association for Geriatric Psychiatry (www.aagponline.org)

American Geriatrics Society (www.americangeriatrics.org)

National Association of Professional Geriatric Care Managers
(www.caremanager.org)

Gerontology

Association for Gerontology in Higher Education (www.aghe.org)

Gerontological Society of America (www.geron.org)

National Gerontological Nursing Association (www.ngna.org)

Guardianship

American Health Care Association (www.ahca.org)

Brookdale Center for Healthy Aging & Longevity of Hunter College
(www.brookdale.org)

Center for Social Gerontology (www.tcsg.org)

H

Health Care

American Academy of Dermatology (www.aad.org)

American Academy of Family Physicians (www.aafp.org)

American Academy of Neurology (www.aan.com)

American Academy of Orthopaedic Surgeons (www.aaos.org)

American Academy of Otolaryngology-Head and Neck Surgery, Inc.
(www.entnet.org)

American College of Physicians-American Society of Internal Medicine
(www.acponline.org)

American College of Surgeons (www.facs.org)

American Dental Association (www.ada.org)

American Geriatrics Society (www.americangeriatrics.org)

American Medical Association (www.ama-assn.org)

American Podiatric Medical Association (www.apma.org)

Department of Veterans Affairs (www.va.gov)

Hearing Loss

American Academy of Otolaryngology—Head and Neck Surgery (www.entnet.org)

American Speech-Language-Hearing Association (www.asha.org)

Better Hearing Institute (www.betterhearing.org)

Described and Captioned Media Program (www.dcmp.org)

Hearing Loss Association of America (www.hearingloss.org)

International Hearing Society (www.ihsinfo.org)

National Association of the Deaf (www.nad.org)

National Institute on Deafness and Other Communication Disorders (www.nidcd.nih.gov)

Heart Diseases

American Association of Cardiovascular and Pulmonary Rehabilitation (www.aacvpr.org)

American Health Assistance Foundation (www.ahaf.org)

American Heart Association (www.americanheart.org)

American Lung Association (www.lung.org)

National Heart, Lung, and Blood Institute Health Information Center (www.nhlbi.nih.gov)

Hispanic Health

National Alliance for Hispanic Health (www.hispanichealth.org)

National Association for Hispanic Elderly (www.anppm.org)

National Hispanic Council on Aging (www.nhcoa.org)

Project Aliento (www.anppm.org)

Home Health Care

National Association for Home Care and Hospice (www.nahc.org)

National Association of Area Agencies on Aging (www.n4a.org)

Vestibular Disorders Association (www.vestibular.org)

Visiting Nurse Associations of America (www.vnaa.org)

Hospice

Caring Connections (www.caringinfo.org)

National Association for Home Care and Hospice (www.nahc.org)

National Hospice and Palliative Care Organization (www.nhpco.org)

National Hospice Foundation (www.nationalhospicefoundation.org)

Visiting Nurse Associations of America (www.vnaa.org)

Hospitals

Centers for Medicare and Medicaid Services (www.medicare.gov)

Department of Veterans Affairs (www.va.gov)

Housing

American Health Care Association (www.ahca.org)

Assisted Living Federation of America (www.alfa.org)

CARF—Continuing Care Accreditation Commission (www.carf.org)

National Council on Aging (www.ncoa.org)

National Long-Term Care Ombudsman Resource Center (www.ltcombudsman.org)

LeadingAge (www.leadingage.org)

Long-Term Care Resource Center (www.hpm.umn.edu/ltcresourcecenter)

National Resource Center on Supportive Housing and Home Modifications (www.homemods.org)

Huntington's Disease

Huntington's Disease Society of America (www.hdsa.org)

National Institute of Neurological Disorders and Stroke (www.ninds.nih.gov)

I

Immunizations

National Foundation for Infectious Diseases (www.nfid.org)

National Institute of Allergy and Infectious Diseases (www.niaid.nih.gov)

Incontinence

National Association for Continence (www.nafc.org)

National Kidney and Urologic Diseases Information Clearinghouse (www.kidney.niddk.nih.gov)

Simon Foundation for Continence (www.simonfoundation.org)

Infectious Diseases

Centers for Disease Control and Prevention (www.cdc.gov)

National Foundation for Infectious Diseases (www.nfid.org)

National Institute of Allergy and Infectious Diseases (www.niaid.nih.gov)

Insurance

Agency for Healthcare Research and Quality (www.ahrq.gov)

American Association of Retired Persons (www.aarp.org)

Centers for Medicare and Medicaid Services (www.medicare.gov)

America's Health Insurance Plans (www.hiaa.org)

Medicare Rights Center (www.medicarerights.org)

Social Security Administration (www.ssa.gov)

Intergenerational Programs

Generations on Line (www.generationsonline.com)

Generations Together (www.gt.pitt.edu)

Gray Panthers (www.graypanthers.org)

National Council on Aging (www.ncoa.org)

National Urban League (www.nul.org)

J

Japanese American Health

Japanese American Citizens League (www.jacl.org)

Jewish Service Organizations

Associated Jewish Charities (www.associated.org)

B'nai B'rith (www.bnaibrith.org)

Joint and Bone Diseases

American Academy of Orthopaedic Surgeons (www.aaos.org)

National Institute of Arthritis and Musculoskeletal and Skin Diseases (www.niams.nih.gov)

National Osteoporosis Foundation (www.nof.org)

NIH Osteoporosis and Related Bone Diseases National Resource Center (www.bones.nih.gov)

Paget Foundation for Paget's Disease of Bone and Related Disorders (www.paget.org)

K

Kidney Diseases

American Foundation for Urologic Disease (www.urologyhealth.org)

National Kidney and Urologic Diseases Information Clearinghouse (www.kidney.niddk.nih.gov)

National Kidney Foundation (www.kidney.org)

L

Legal Issues

American Bar Association Commission on Law and Aging (www.americanbar.org/groups/law_aging.html)

Brookdale Center for Healthy Aging & Longevity of Hunter College (www.brookdale.org)

Center for Social Gerontology (www.tcsg.org)

Eldercare Initiative in Consumer Law (www.consumerlaw.org)

Legal Counsel for the Elderly (www.aarp.org)

National Academy of Elder Law Attorneys (www.naela.org)

National Association of States United for Aging and Disability (www.nasuad.org)

National Bar Association (www.nationalbar.org)

Sargent Shriver National Center on Poverty Law (www.povertylaw.org)

National Legal Support for Elderly People with Mental Disabilities (www.bazelon.org)

Long-Term Care Resource Center (www.hpm.umn.edu/ltcresourcecenter)

National Senior Citizens Law Center (www.nsclc.org)

Pension Rights Center (www.pensionrights.org)

Leukemia

Leukemia and Lymphoma Society (www.lls.org)

National Cancer Institute (http://cancer.gov)

Long-Term Care

See Nursing Homes

Low Vision

See Eyes

Lung Diseases

American Association of Cardiovascular and Pulmonary Rehabilitation (www.aacvpr.org)

American Lung Association (www.lung.org)

National Heart, Lung, and Blood Institute Health Information Center (www.nhlbi.nih.gov)

Pulmonary Fibrosis Foundation (www.pulmonaryfibrosis.org)

Lupus

Arthritis Foundation (www.arthritis.org)

Lupus Foundation of America (www.lupus.org)

National Institute of Arthritis and Musculoskeletal and Skin Diseases (www.niams.nih.gov)

M

Medicaid

Centers for Medicare and Medicaid Services (www.medicare.gov)

Medicare

Centers for Medicare and Medicaid Services (www.medicare.gov)

Medical Care

See Health Care

Medicines

American Association of Retired Persons (www.aarp.org)

American Pharmacists Association (www.pharmacist.com)

Food and Drug Administration (www.fda.gov)

National Council on Patient Information and Education (www.talkaboutrx.org)

Men's Health

American Cancer Society (www.cancer.org)

American Foundation for Urologic Disease (www.urologyhealth.org)

Menopause

National Heart, Lung, and Blood Institute Health Information Center (www.nhlbi.nih.gov)

National Osteoporosis Foundation (www.nof.org)

North American Menopause Society (www.menopause.org)

Mental Health

American Association for Geriatric Psychiatry (www.aagponline.org)

American Counseling Association (www.counseling.org)

National Association of Social Workers (www.naswdc.org)

National Institute of Mental Health (www.nimh.nih.gov)

Mental Health America (www.nmha.org)

Substance Abuse and Mental Health Services Administration (www.samhsa.gov)

Minority Health

Administration on Aging (www.aoa.gov)

Indian Health Service (www.ihs.gov)

Japanese American Citizens League (www.jacl.org)

National Alliance for Hispanic Health (www.hispanichealth.org)

National Asian Pacific Center on Aging (www.napca.org)

National Association for Hispanic Elderly (www.anppm.org)

National Caucus and Center on Black Aged (www.ncba-aged.org)

National Hispanic Council on Aging (www.nhcoa.org)

National Resource Center: Diversity and Long-Term Care (www.sihp.brandeis.edu)

National Resource Center on Native American Aging (http://ruralhealth.und.edu/projects/nrcnaa)

National Urban League (www.nul.org)

OCA National (www.ocanational.org)

Project Aliento (www.anppm.org)

Mouth Care

American Dental Association (www.ada.org)

National Institute of Dental and Craniofacial Research (www.nidcr.nih.gov)

Multiple Sclerosis

National Institute of Neurological Disorders and Stroke (www.ninds.nih.gov)

National Multiple Sclerosis Society (www.nationalmssociety.org)

N

Native American Health

Indian Health Service (www.ihs.gov)

National Association of Area Agencies on Aging (www.n4a.org)

National Indian Council on Aging (www.nicoa.org)

National Resource Center on Native American Aging
(http://ruralhealth.und.edu/projects/nrcnaa)

Native Hawaiian Health

National Resource Center on Native American Aging
(http://ruralhealth.und.edu/projects/nrcnaa)

Nurses

National Gerontological Nursing Association (www.ngna.org)

Visiting Nurse Associations of America (www.vnaa.org)

Nursing Homes

American Geriatrics Society (www.americangeriatrics.org)

American Health Care Association (www.ahca.org)

Centers for Medicare and Medicaid Services (www.medicare.gov)

National Citizens' Coalition for Nursing Home Reform (www.nccnhr.org)

National Long-Term Care Ombudsman Resource Center
(www.ltcombudsman.org)

LeadingAge (www.leadingage.org)

Long-Term Care Resource Center (www.hpm.umn.edu/ltcresourcecenter)

Nutrition

Academy of Nutrition and Dietetics (www.eatright.org)

American Heart Association (www.americanheart.org)

Food and Drug Administration (www.fda.gov)

Food and Nutrition Information Center (www.nal.usda.gov/fnic)

Meals on Wheels Association of America (www.mowaa.org)

National Association of Nutrition and Aging Services Programs
(www.nanasp.org)

National Association of States United for Aging and Disability
(www.nasuad.org)

National Policy and Resource Center on Nutrition, Physical Activity and
Aging (http://nutritionandaging.fiu.edu/)

O

Occupational Therapy

Visiting Nurse Associations of America (www.vnaa.org)

Osteoporosis

American Academy of Orthopaedic Surgeons (www.aaos.org)

National Institute of Arthritis and Musculoskeletal and Skin Diseases (www.niams.nih.gov)

National Osteoporosis Foundation (www.nof.org)

NIH Osteoporosis and Related Bone Diseases National Resource Center (www.bones.nih.gov)

P

Paget's Disease

National Institute of Arthritis and Musculoskeletal and Skin Diseases (www.niams.nih.gov)

NIH Osteoporosis and Related Bone Diseases National Resource Center (www.bones.nih.gov)

Paget Foundation for Paget's Disease of Bone and Related Disorders (www.paget.org)

Parkinson's Disease

American Parkinson Disease Association (www.apdaparkinson.org)

National Institute of Neurological Disorders and Stroke (www.ninds.nih.gov)

Parkinson's Disease Foundation (www.pdf.org)

Pensions

Department of Veterans Affairs (www.va.gov)

Disabled American Veterans (www.dav.org)

Employee Benefits Security Administration (www.dol.gov/ebsa)

Older Women's League (www.owl-national.org)

Pension Rights Center (www.pensionrights.org)

Social Security Administration (www.ssa.gov)

Physical Therapy

Visiting Nurse Associations of America (www.vnaa.org)

Prostate Diseases

American Foundation for Urologic Disease (www.urologyhealth.org)

National Kidney and Urologic Diseases Information Clearinghouse (www.kidney.niddk.nih.gov)

Psoriasis

National Psoriasis Foundation (www.psoriasis.org)

Psychiatry

American Association for Geriatric Psychiatry (www.aagponline.org)

R

Rehabilitation

American Association of Cardiovascular and Pulmonary Rehabilitation (www.aacvpr.org)

American Council of the Blind (www.acb.org)

Better Hearing Institute (www.betterhearing.org)

Department of Veterans Affairs (www.va.gov)

Lighthouse International (www.lighthouse.org)

National Rehabilitation Information Center (www.naric.com)

National Stroke Association (www.stroke.org)

Respite Care

Brookdale Center for Healthy Aging & Longevity of Hunter College (www.brookdale.org)

Well Spouse Foundation (www.wellspouse.org)

Retirement Planning

American Association of Retired Persons (www.aarp.org)

CARF—Continuing Care Accreditation Commission (www.carf.org)

Employee Benefits Security Administration (www.dol.gov/ebsa)

SPRY Foundation (www.spry.org)

Rural Health

Central Plains Geriatric Education Center (http://coa.kumc.edu/cpgec)

National Council on Aging (www.ncoa.org)

National Resource Center on Native American Aging (http://ruralhealth.und.edu/projects/nrcnaa/)

National Rural Health Association (www.ruralhealthweb.org)

S

Safety

American Red Cross (www.redcross.org)

Department of Transportation (www.dot.gov)

Food and Drug Administration (www.fda.gov)

National Consumers League (www.natlconsumersleague.org)

National Council on Patient Information and Education (www.talkaboutrx.org)

Skin Diseases

American Academy of Dermatology (www.aad.org)

American Cancer Society (www.cancer.org)

National Institute of Arthritis and Musculoskeletal and Skin Diseases (www.niams.nih.gov)

National Cancer Institute (http://cancer.gov)

The Skin Cancer Foundation (www.skincancer.org)

Sleep Disorders

National Heart, Lung, and Blood Institute Health Information Center (www.nhlbi.nih.gov)

National Sleep Foundation (www.sleepfoundation.org)

Social Security

National Committee to Preserve Social Security and Medicare (www.ncpssm.org)

Social Security Administration (www.ssa.gov)

Speech Therapy

American Speech-Language-Hearing Association (www.asha.org)

Visiting Nurse Associations of America (www.vnaa.org)

Stroke

American Academy of Neurology (www.aan.com)

American Health Assistance Foundation (www.ahaf.org)

American Heart Association (www.americanheart.org)

American Stroke Association (www.strokeassociation.org)

National Heart, Lung, and Blood Institute Health Information Center (www.nhlbi.nih.gov)

National Institute of Neurological Disorders and Stroke (www.ninds.nih.gov)

National Stroke Association (www.stroke.org)

T

Therapy

American Association for Geriatric Psychiatry (www.aagponline.org)

Mental Health America (www.nmha.org)

Transportation

American Cancer Society (www.cancer.org)

Department of Transportation (www.dot.gov)

National Association of Area Agencies on Aging (www.n4a.org)

Tremor

International Essential Tremor Foundation (www.essentialtremor.org)

U

Urologic Disease

American Foundation for Urologic Disease (www.urologyhealth.org)

National Kidney and Urologic Diseases Information Clearinghouse (www.kidney.niddk.nih.gov)

V

Veterans Health

Department of Veterans Affairs (www.va.gov)

Disabled American Veterans (www.dav.org)

W

Women's Health

National Osteoporosis Foundation (www.nof.org)

North American Menopause Society (www.menopause.org)

Older Women's League (www.owl-national.org)

Source: Updated and modified from U.S. Department of Health and Human Services, National Institute on Aging. (2001, June). *Resource Directory for Older People*. NIH Publication No. 01–738.

Appendix B

State Agencies on Aging

Alabama

Alabama Department of Senior Services
770 Washington Avenue
RSA Plaza, Suite 470
Montgomery, Alabama 36130
Telephone: (334) 242-5743
Fax: (334) 242-5594
Website: www.alabamaageline.gov

Alaska

Alaska Commission on Aging
Division of Senior Services
Department of Administration
150 Third Street
Juneau, Alaska 99811
Telephone: (907) 465-3250
Fax: (907) 465-1398
Website: www.alaskaaging.org

American Samoa Government

Territorial Administration on Aging
A.P. Lutali Executive Office Building
Pago Pago, American Samoa 96799
Telephone: 011-684-633-1251
Fax: 011-864-633-2533
Website: www.americansamoa.gov

Arizona

Arizona Department of Economic Security
Division of Aging and Adult Services
1789 West Jefferson Street
Phoenix, Arizona 85007
Telephone: (602) 542-4446
Fax: (602) 542-6575
Website: www.azdes.gov

Arkansas

Division of Aging and Adult Services
Arkansas Department of Human Services
700 Main Street
PO 1437-Slot S-530
Little Rock, Arkansas 72203
Telephone: (501) 682-2441
Fax: (501) 682-8155
Website: www.daas.ar.gov

California

California Department of Aging
1300 National Drive, Suite 200
Sacramento, California 95834
Telephone: (916) 419-7500
Fax: (916) 928-2267
Website: www.aging.ca.gov

Colorado

Colorado Department of Human Services
Division of Aging and Adult Services
1575 Sherman Street, 10th Floor
Denver, Colorado 80203
Telephone: (303) 866-2800
Fax: (303) 866-2696
Website: www.colorado.gov/cdhs

Connecticut

Department of Social Services
Aging Services Division—State Unit on Aging
25 Sigourney Street, 10th Floor
Hartford, Connecticut 06106
Telephone: (860) 424-5274
Fax: (860) 424-5301
Website: www.ct.gov/agingservices

Delaware

Delaware Division of Services for Aging and Adults with
Physical Disabilities
Department of Health and Social Services
1901 North DuPont Highway, Main Bldg
New Castle, Delaware 19720
Telephone: (800) 233-9074
Fax: (302) 255-4445
Website: www.dsaapd.com

District of Columbia

District of Columbia Office on Aging
500 K Street, NE
Washington, DC 20002
Telephone: (202) 724-5622
Fax: (202) 727-4979
Website: www.dcoa.dc.gov

Florida

Department of Elder Affairs
4040 Esplanade Way
Tallahassee, Florida 32399
Telephone: (850) 414-2000
Fax: (850) 414-2004
Website: www.elderaffairs.state.fl.us

Georgia

Department of Human Resources
Division of Aging Services
Two Peachtree Street, NW, 33rd Floor
Atlanta, Georgia 30303
Telephone: (404) 657-5258
Fax: (404) 657-5285
Website: www.aging.dhr.georgia.gov

Guam

Division of Senior Citizens
Department of Public Health and Social Services
130 University Drive, Suite 8
University Castle Mall
Mangilao, Guam 96923
Telephone: 011-671-735-7011
Fax: 011-671-735-7516
Website: www.dphss.guam.gov/content/division-senior-citizens

Hawaii

Hawaii Executive Office on Aging
No. 1 Capital District
250 South Hotel Street, Suite 406
Honolulu, Hawaii 96813
Telephone: (808) 586-0100
Fax: (808) 586-0185
Website: www.hawaii.gov/health/eoa

Idaho

Idaho Commission on Aging
341 W. Washington
Boise, Idaho 83720
Telephone: (208) 334-3833
Website: www.aging.idaho.gov

Illinois

Illinois Department on Aging
One Natural Resources Way, Suite 100
Springfield, Illinois 62702
Telephone: (217) 785-3356
Fax: (217) 785-4477
Website: www.state.il.us/aging

Indiana

Family & Social Services Administration
Division of Aging
402 West Washington Street, #W454
PO Box 7083, MS21
Indianapolis, Indiana 46204
Telephone: (317) 232-7867
Fax: (317) 233-2182
Website: www.in.gov/fssa/da

Iowa

Iowa Department on Aging
Jessie M. Parker Building
510 East 12th Street, Suite 2
Des Moines, Iowa 50319
Telephone: (515) 725-3333
Website: www.aging.iowa.gov

Kansas

Department on Aging
New England Building
503 South Kansas Avenue
Topeka, Kansas 66603
Telephone: (785) 296-4986
Fax: (785) 296-0256
Website: www.agingkansas.org/kdoa

Kentucky

Cabinet for Health and Family Services
Department for Aging and Independent Living
Commonwealth of Kentucky
275 East Main Street
Frankfort, Kentucky 40621
Telephone: (502) 564-6930
Fax: (502) 564-4595
Website: www.chfs.ky.gov

Louisiana

Governor's Office of Elderly Affairs
PO Box 61
Baton Rouge, Louisiana 70821
Telephone: (225) 342-7100
Fax: (225) 342-5261
Website: www.goea.louisiana.gov

Maine

Office of Elder Services
Maine Department of Health and Human Services
11 State House Station
32 Blossom Lane
Augusta, Maine 04333
Telephone: (207) 287-9200
Fax: (207) 287-9229
Website: www.maine.gov/dhhs/oes

Maryland

Maryland Department of Aging
301 West Preston Street, Suite 1007
Baltimore, Maryland 21201
Telephone: (410) 767-1100
Fax: (410) 333-7943
Website: www.aging.maryland.gov

Massachusetts

Massachusetts Executive Office of Elder Affairs
One Ashburton Place, 5th Floor
Boston, Massachusetts 02108
Telephone: (617) 727-7750
Fax: (617) 727-9368
Website: www.mass.gov/elders

Michigan

Michigan Office of Services to the Aging
300 East Michigan Avenue, 3rd Floor
PO Box 30676
Lansing, Michigan 48909
Telephone: (517) 373-8230
Fax: (517) 373-4092
Website: www.michigan.gov/miseniors

Minnesota

Minnesota Board on Aging
PO Box 64976
St. Paul, Minnesota 55164
Telephone: (651) 431-2500
Fax: (651) 431-7453
Website: www.mnaging.org

Mississippi

Division of Aging and Adult Services
750 North State Street
Jackson, Mississippi 39202
Telephone: (601) 359-4929
Fax: (601) 359-4370
Website: www.mdhs.state.ms.us/aas.html

Missouri

Department of Health and Senior Services
912 Wildwood
PO Box 570
Jefferson City, Missouri 65109
Telephone: (573) 751-6400
Fax: 573-751-6010
Website: www.health.mo.gov

Montana

Department of Public Health and Human Services
Senior and Long Term Care Division
2030 11th Avenue
Helena, Montana 59620
Telephone: (406) 444-4077
Fax: (406) 444-7743
Website: www.dphhs.mt.gov

Nebraska

Department of Health and Human Services
State Unit on Aging
PO Box 95026
Lincoln, Nebraska 68509
Telephone: (402) 471-4624
Fax: (402) 471-4619
Website: dhhs.ne.gov/medicaid/Pages/ags_agsindex.aspx

Nevada

Nevada Department of Health and Human Services
Aging and Disability Services Division
State Mail Room Complex
3416 Goni Road, Building D-132
Carson City, Nevada 89706
Telephone: (775) 687-4210
Fax: (775) 687-4264
Website: www.aging.state.nv.us

New Hampshire

Bureau of Elderly and Adult Services
State Office Park South
129 Pleasant Street
Concord, New Hampshire 03301
Telephone: (603) 271-9203
Fax: (603) 271-4643
Website: www.dhhs.nh.gov

New Jersey

Department of Health and Senior Services
PO Box 360
Trenton, New Jersey 08625
Telephone: (800) 792-8820
Website: www.state.nj.us/health

New Mexico

Aging and Long-Term Care Services Department
Toney Anaya Building
2550 Cerrillos Road
Santa Fe, New Mexico 87505
Telephone: (505) 476-4799
Website: www.nmaging.state.nm.us

New York

New York State Office for the Aging
2 Empire State Plaza
Albany, New York 12223
Telephone: (800) 342-9871
Website: www.aging.ny.gov

North Carolina

Division of Aging
Department of Health and Human Services
2101 Mail Service Center
Raleigh, North Carolina 27699
Telephone: (919) 855-3400
Fax: (919) 733-0443
Website: www.ncdhhs.gov/aging

North Dakota

Aging Services Division
Department of Human Services
1237 W. Divide Ave., Suite 6
Bismarck, North Dakota 58501
Telephone: (701) 328-4601
Fax: (701) 328-8744
Website: www.nd.gov/dhs/services/adultsaging/

North Mariana Islands

CNMI Office on Aging
PO Box 2178
Commonwealth of the Northern Mariana Islands
Saipan, MP 96950
Telephone: (670) 233-1320
Fax: (670) 233-1327
Website: www.gov.mp

Ohio

Ohio Department of Aging
50 West Broad Street, 9th Floor
Columbus, Ohio 43215
Telephone: (614) 466-5500
Fax: (614) 466-5741
Website: www.aging.ohio.gov

Oklahoma

Department of Human Services
Aging Services Division
2401 N.W. 23rd Street, Suite 40
Oklahoma City, Oklahoma 73107
Telephone: (405) 521-2281
Fax: (405) 521-2086
Website: www.okdhs.org/divisionsoffices/visd/asd/

Oregon

Seniors and People with Disabilities
500 Summer Street, NE E12
Salem, Oregon 97301
Telephone: (503) 945-5921
Fax: (503) 373-7823
Website: www.oregon.gov

Pennsylvania

Commonwealth of Pennsylvania
Department of Aging
Forum Place
555 Walnut Street, 5th Floor
Harrisburg, Pennsylvania 17101
Telephone: (717) 783-1550
Fax: (717) 783-6842
Website: www.aging.state.pa.us

Puerto Rico

Governor's Office for Elderly Affairs
1064 Ponce de Leon Ave.
PO Box 191170
San Juan, Puerto Rico 00919
Telephone: (787) 721-6121
Fax: (787) 721-6510
Website: www.pr.gov

Rhode Island

Division of Elderly Affairs
74 West Road
Cranston, Rhode Island 02920
Telephone: (401) 462-3000
Website: www.dea.ri.gov

South Carolina

Lieutenant Governor's Office on Aging
1301 Gervais Street, Suite 350
Columbia, South Carolina 29201
Telephone: (803) 734-9900
Fax: (803) 734-9886
Website: www.aging.sc.gov

South Dakota

Division of Aging and Adult Services
Richard F. Kneip Building
700 Governors Drive
Pierre, South Dakota 57501
Telephone: (605) 773-3165
Fax: (605) 773-4085
Website: www.dss.sd.gov

Tennessee

Commission on Aging and Disability
Andrew Jackson Building, 9th Floor
500 Deaderick Street
Nashville, Tennessee 37243
Telephone: (615) 741-2056
Fax: (615) 741-3309
Website: www.tn.gov/comaging

Texas

Texas Department of Aging and Disability Services
701 W. 51st Street
Austin, Texas 78751
Telephone: (512) 438-3011
Website: www.dads.state.tx.us

U.S. Virgin Islands

Department of Human Services
1303 Hospital Ground
Knud Hansen Complex, Building A
St. Thomas, Virgin Islands 00802
Telephone: (340) 774-0930
Fax: (340) 774-3466
Website: www.dhs.gov.vi

Utah

Aging and Adult Services
195 North 1950 West
Salt Lake City, Utah 84116
Telephone: (801) 538-3910
Fax: (801) 538-4395
Website: www.hsdaas.utah.gov

Vermont

Department of Disabilities, Aging and Independent Living
103 South Main Street
Weeks Building
Waterbury, Vermont 05671
Telephone: (802) 241-2401
Fax: (802) 241-2325
Website: www.dail.vermont.gov

Virginia

Virginia Department for the Aging
1610 Forest Avenue, Suite 100
Richmond, Virginia 23229
Telephone: (804) 662-9333
Fax: (804) 662-9354
Website: www.vda.virginia.gov

Washington

Aging and Disability Services Administration
Department of Social and Health Services
PO Box 45130
Olympia, Washington 98504
Telephone: (800) 737-0617
Website: www.aasa.dshs.wa.gov

West Virginia

West Virginia Bureau of Senior Services
1900 Kanawha Boulevard East
Charleston, West Virginia 25305
Telephone: (304) 558-3317
Fax: (304) 558-5609
Website: www.wvseniorservices.gov

Wisconsin

Aging and Disability Resource Centers
Department of Health Services
1 West Wilson Street
Madison, Wisconsin 53703
Telephone: (608) 266-1865
Website: www.dhs.wisconsin.gov/aging

Wyoming

Aging Division
Wyoming Department of Health
6101 Yellowstone Road
Cheyenne, Wyoming 82002
Telephone: (307) 777-7986
Fax: (307) 777-5340
Website: www.health.wyo.gov/aging

Source: U.S. Department of health and Human Services, National Institute on Aging. (2001, June). *Resource Directory for Older People*. NIH Publication No. 01–738. Updated January 2012.

Appendix C

Death Investigation and Older People

INTRODUCTION

Many law enforcement agencies have homicide detectives who investigate murders; crime lab technicians who search for, collect, and process information; and personnel from the medical examiner's/coroner's office who will respond to the scene and assist with investigations. Other law enforcement agencies that may not have these resources within their agencies have access to them. However, in the time it takes for these resources to respond to the scene, the initial arriving officer can begin the crucial first steps in the investigation. In some agencies, the initial arriving officer may be the investigator. This appendix is offered as a brief refresher in death investigation. Additionally, items for consideration when conducting a death investigation of an older person are presented.

SIGNS OF DEATH[1]

There are certain changes that take place to the body when one dies. These changes are described as follows.

- *The pupils dilate and become nonreactive.* Corneal reflexes are absent and the cornea becomes cloudy.

- *Rigor mortis*. The muscles become flaccid after death; however, within 1 to 3 hours, they become increasingly rigid and the joints freeze. Rigor is affected by body temperature—the higher the temperature, the faster rigor occurs. Conversely, rigor is slowed by cooling. The body stiffens from the head down, from the muscles of mastication (jaws) to the elbows and then to the knees. A body is in complete rigor when the jaws, elbows, and knees are immovable, a process that takes 10 to 12 hours in an environmental temperature of 70–75°F. The body remains rigid for 24 to 36 hours before the muscles start to loosen in the same order they stiffened.
- *Livor mortis*. Discoloration due to the settling of blood no longer being circulated through the body (sometimes referred to as venous pooling). Blood settles in vessels by gravity in dependent areas and colors the skin purple-red; however, the skin may not discolor if it is pressed against a bony prominence. Livor is noticed 1 hour after death. The color increases intensity and becomes fixed in 8 hours. Fixed blood in nondependent areas means the body was moved after death. Carbon monoxide or cyanide poisoning may cause bright cherry red livor, while extensive blood loss may leave a very light or nonexistent livor.
- *Algor mortis*. The body cools after death to the surrounding environmental temperature.
- *Decomposition*. As rigor passes, the body first turns green in the abdomen, and the color spreads to the rest of the trunk. The body swells due to bacterial methane gas production. Rates and types of decomposition depend on the environment.

DEATH INVESTIGATION

This section is adapted from the National Institute of Justice *Death Investigation: A Guide for the Scene Investigator*.[2]

Arriving at the Scene

1. *Introduce and identify self and role*. Introductions aid in establishing a collaborative investigative effort.
2. *Exercise scene safety*. The safety of all investigative personnel is essential to the investigative process. Risks of environmental and physical injury must be removed prior to initiating a scene investigation.
3. *Confirm or pronounce death*. Appropriate personnel must make a determination of death prior to the initiation of the death investigation. Confirmation determines jurisdictional responsibilities.
4. *Participate in scene briefing with attending agency representatives*. Scene investigators must recognize jurisdictional and statutory responsibilities that apply to each agency representative. Determining each agency's responsibility is essential in planning the scope and depth of each scene investigation and the release of information to the public.

5. *Conduct scene walkthrough.* The walkthrough provides an overview of the entire scene and gives the investigator the first opportunity to locate and view the body, identify valuable and fragile evidence, and determine initial investigative procedures that will allow for systematic examination and documentation of the scene and body.

6. *Establish chain of custody.* This ensures the integrity of the evidence and safeguards against subsequent allegations of tampering, theft, planting, and contamination of evidence.

7. *Follow laws of evidence.* All agencies must follow local, state, and federal laws for the collection of evidence to ensure its admissibility to court. The death investigator works with law enforcement and the legal authorities to determine laws regarding collection of evidence.

Documenting and Evaluating the Scene

1. *Photograph the scene.* Photographic documentation creates a permanent historical record of the scene. Photographs provide detailed corroborating evidence that constructs a system of redundancy should questions arise concerning the report, witness statements, or position of evidence at the scene.

2. *Develop descriptive documentation of the scene.* The narrative report provides a permanent record that may be used to correlate with and enhance photographic documentation, refresh recollections, and record observations.

3. *Establish probable location of injury or illness.* The death scene may not be the actual location where the injury/illness that contributed to the death occurred. It is imperative that the investigator attempt to determine the locations of any and all injuries/illnesses that may have contributed to the death. Physical evidence at these locations may be pertinent in establishing the cause, manner, and circumstances of death.

4. *Collect, inventory, and safeguard property and evidence.* The investigator must safeguard the decedent's valuables/property to ensure proper processing and eventual return to next of kin.

5. *Interview witnesses at the scene.* Documented comments of witnesses allow the investigator to obtain primary source data regarding discovery of the body, witness corroboration, and terminal history.

Documenting and Evaluating the Body

1. *Photograph the body.* Photographic documentation of the body creates a permanent record that preserves essential details of body position, appearance, identity, and final movements. Photographs also allow sharing of information with other agencies investigating the death.

2. *Conduct superficial external body examination.* This provides the investigator with objective data regarding the single most important piece of

evidence at the scene, the body, by giving detailed information regarding the decedent's physical attributes, the person's relationship to the scene, and possible cause, manner, and circumstances of death. This examination is performed in a manner that does not contaminate or destroy evidence.

3. *Preserve evidence on the body.* Photographic and narrative documentation of evidence on the body allows the investigator to obtain a permanent historical record of the evidence. Evidence must be collected, preserved, and transported properly and the chain of custody maintained. All of the physical evidence visible on the body (such as blood and other body fluids) must be photographed and documented prior to collection and transport. Fragile evidence (that which can be easily contaminated, lost, or altered) must be collected and preserved, and the chain of custody maintained.

4. *Establish decedent identification.* Conformation of the decedent's identity is paramount to the death investigation to allow notification of next of kin, settlement of estates, resolution of criminal and civil litigation, and the proper completion of the death certificate.

5. *Document postmortem changes.* Documenting postmortem changes assists the investigator in explaining body appearance in the interval following death. Inconsistencies between postmortem changes and body location may indicate movement of the body and validate or invalidate witness statements. Postmortem changes to the body, when correlated with circumstantial information, can also assist the investigators in estimating the approximate time of death.

6. *Participate in scene debriefing.* Scene debriefing helps investigators from all agencies to establish post-scene responsibilities. Scene debriefing provides each agency the opportunity for input regarding special requests for assistance, additional information, special examinations, and other requests requiring inter-agency communication, cooperation, and education.

7. *Determine notification procedures (next of kin).* Every reasonable effort should be made to notify the next of kin as soon as possible. This helps initiate closure for the family and disposition of remains, and facilitates the collection of additional information relative to the case.

8. *Ensure security of the remains.* Ensuring security of the body requires the investigator to supervise the labeling, packaging, and removal of the remains. An appropriate identification tag is placed on the body to preclude misidentification upon receipt at the examining agency. This function also includes safeguarding all potential physical evidence and/or property and clothing that remains on the body.

Establishing and Recording Decedent Profile Information

1. *Document the discovery history.* The decedent profile includes documenting a discovery history and circumstances surrounding the discovery.

The basic profile will dictate subsequent levels of investigation, jurisdiction, and authority, as well as the focus (breadth/depth) of further investigation.

2. *Determine terminal episode history.* Preterminal circumstances play a significant role in determining cause and manner of death. Documentation of medical intervention and/or procurement of antemortem specimens helps to establish the decedent's condition prior to death.

3. *Document decedent medical history.* Most deaths referred to the medical examiner/coroner are natural deaths. Establishing the decedent's medical history helps focus the investigation. Documenting the decedent's medical signs or symptoms prior to death determines the need for subsequent examinations, since the relationship between disease and injury may play a role in the cause, manner, and circumstances of death.

4. *Document decedent mental health history.* The decedent's mental health history can provide insight into his or her behavior/state of mind. That insight may produce clues that will aid in establishing the cause, manner, and circumstances of the death.

5. *Document social history.* Social history includes marital, family, sexual, educational, employment, and financial information, just as it does in the social history in the living. Daily routines, habits and activities, and friends and associates of the decedent help develop the decedent's profile and aid in establishing the cause, manner, and circumstances of death.

Completing the Scene Investigation

1. *Maintain jurisdiction over the body.* This helps the investigator to protect the chain of custody as the body is transported from the scene for autopsy, specimen collection, or storage.

2. *Release jurisdiction of the body* Prior to releasing jurisdiction of the body to an authorized receiving agent or funeral director, it is necessary to determine the person responsible for certification of the death. Information to complete the death certificate includes demographic information and the date, time, and location of death.

3. *Perform exit procedures.* Bringing closure to the scene investigation ensures that important evidence has been collected and the scene has been fully processed. A systematic review of the scene ensures that artifacts or equipment are not inadvertently left behind and that any dangerous materials or conditions have been reported.

4. *Assist the family.* The death investigator provides the family with a timetable so it can arrange for final disposition. The death investigator also provides information on available community and professional resources that may assist the family.

HOMICIDE INVESTIGATION OF AN OLDER PERSON

In addition to standard death investigation procedures, the following items are crucial to homicide investigation involving an older person:

1. *Medical history.* It is important to determine the medical history of the older decedent. While it may be a logical conclusion to assume that an older person with an extensive medical history has died of one or a combination of conditions, this may not always be the case. The investigator should speak with the decedent's primary care physician. While an older person with multiple comorbidities may have several physicians (cardiologist, pulmonologist, urologist), the primary care physician should be consulted initially, for it is often the primary care physician who can speak to the decedent's overall health status and the physician is likely to have seen the decedent the most. Information that should be obtained from the primary care physician includes: complete medical history, date last seen, overall health status at last visit, prognosis (based on conditions), medications prescribed by the physician, level of independent functioning (in community dwelling and nursing home decedents), and any additional problems the decedent may have been having or expressed at last visit.

   For decedents in long-term care facilities, medical information can be obtained from the decedent's chart. It is still important to speak with the decedent's attending physician. When reviewing the decedent's chart, read the nurses' notes over the last several weeks. Observe for any changes in the decedent's medical condition or behavior.

2. *Medications.* Obtain a list of the decedent's medications. Document the names, dosages, and prescribing physician(s). Note the date each prescription was filled and how often the medication was to be taken. Does the amount of medication remaining in each bottle correspond to the date filled and how often it should have been taken? If not, attempt to ascertain why. For decedents in long-term care facilities, this information can be obtained from the decedent's chart.

3. *Observe the body and environment for signs of abuse and neglect.* With any suspicious death involving an older person, elder abuse or neglect must be considered. Observe the decedent's living environment. An easy initial question to ask is: Is this an adequate living environment for the older person? While there may be extenuating circumstances such as eccentricities if the older person was of sound mind and capable of understanding his or her circumstances, an environmental assessment must be made. If there are signs from the environmental assessment of abuse or neglect, the scene should be photographed.

   If the decedent was a resident of a long-term care facility, observe the living area (particularly the decedent's bed and bathroom).

An initial postmortem examination should be made of the decedent's body, observing for signs of abuse or neglect. Photograph any wounds, suspicious marks, or physical indication of abuse or neglect.

If the decedent is a resident of a long-term care facility and appears malnourished, intake should be documented in the decedent's medical record.

4. *Caregiver*. Determine if the decedent required a caregiver for assistance with activities of daily living. If so, the caregiver must be interviewed in order to ascertain if the caregiver's involvement was consistent with the needs of the decedent.

When conducting a death investigation of an older person, contact should be made with adult protective services in order to determine if a referral was ever made on behalf of the decedent. If the decedent was a resident of a long-term care facility, review the state inspection records for the facility in order to determine if a pattern of inadequate care exists in the facility.

Assistance with review of medical records can be obtained from medical professionals and regulatory agencies in order to provide expert medical opinion on the appropriateness of care.

ENDNOTES

1. Brown, K. M., & Muscari, M. E. (2010). *Quick reference to adult and older adult forensics, a guide for nurses and other health care professionals.* New York: Springer; p. 375.
2. U.S. Department of Justice, Office of Justice Programs, National Institute of Justice. (1999). *Death investigation: A guide for the scene investigator.* Washington, DC: Author. Retrieved April 13, 2012, from https://www.ncjrs .gov/pdffiles/167568.pdf.

Glossary

abandonment: As it relates to elder abuse, a situation in which an older person is left at the emergency department by a family member or caretaker

acidosis: An actual or relative increase in the acidity of blood due to an accumulation of acids or an excessive loss of bicarbonate; the hydrogen ion concentration of the fluid is increased, lowering the pH

active adult community: A community that offers age-restricted housing specifically for seniors who enjoy participating in physical and social activities; also called active adult living and active retirement community

active neglect: The refusal or failure to fulfill a caretaking obligation; a conscious or intentional attempt to inflict physical or emotional stress; examples include abandonment and denial of food or health-related services

activities of daily living (ADLs): Basic, everyday activities needed to sustain life, such as feeding oneself, walking, dressing, getting up from a chair, and toileting

advance directive: Written documentation that specifies medical treatment for a competent person should the person become unable to make decisions

ageism: Stereotyping of, and discrimination against, people who are old

alopecia: Hair loss, especially from the head, suggestive of normal aging (as opposed to traumatic alopecia, indicative of abuse)

alveoli: Air sacs in the lungs

Alzheimer's care facilities: Specialized facilities for those with signs of Alzheimer's disease or dementia

andropause: A lessening of testosterone and sexual activity in males later in life; also known as male menopause

arrhythmia: An abnormal or irregular heart rhythm resulting from an electrical disturbance in conduction

apraxia: An impairment in carrying out purposeful movements, which can also manifest as a speech impairment, with inability to produce speech with the correct rhythm and timing, as well as highly inconsistent errors

assisted living: A residential facility that provides residents with assistance with activities of daily living; also known as residential care, board and care, and boarding house

asthma: An acute spasm of the smaller air passages, called bronchioles, associated with excessive mucous production and with swelling of the mucous lining of the respiratory passages

atherosclerosis: A disorder in which cholesterol and calcium build up inside the walls of the blood vessels, forming plaque, which eventually leads to partial or complete blockage of blood flow. An atherosclerotic plaque can also become a site where blood clots can form, break off, and embolize elsewhere in the circulation

atrophy: Wasting or shrinkage of an organ

autonomy: The right of an individual to make choices freely, in accordance with the individual's own goals and values

booster: A type of shoplifter who steals for resale, concentrating on higher priced goods

bradykinesia: Slowness of movement

bronchi: The two main branches leading from the trachea to the lungs

bronchitis: An acute or chronic inflammation of the lung that may damage lung tissue; usually associated with cough and production of sputum and, depending on its cause, sometimes fever

capacity: The ability to perform a task

cardiac output: Amount of blood pumped out of the heart in 1 minute

chronic obstructive pulmonary disease (COPD): A slow process of dilation and disruption of the airways and alveoli caused by chronic bronchial obstruction

cohort: Persons who experience the same significant life event (i.e., birth, marriage) within a specified period of time

collagen: The substance that makes the skin and other connective tissues strong; both collagen and elastin decrease with age

communication: The transmitting of information from a sender to receiver and verification that the receiver received and understood the information

dependency theory: A theory that attempts to explain the cause of elder abuse; maintains that frailty and medical illness set up the older person for abuse and neglect

depression: Persistent mood of sadness, despair, discouragement; depression may be a symptom of many different mental and physical disorders, or it may be a disorder on its own

do not resuscitate (DNR) order: Written documentation giving permission to medical personnel not to attempt resuscitation in the event of cardiac arrest

dura matter: A fibrous connective tissue membrane, the outermost of the meninges covering the spinal cord and brain

durable power of attorney: A type of advance directive that names a future decision maker and anticipates a future situation in which decisions about CPR and other forms of life-sustaining treatment must be made, but the person is unable at that time to make them; also called healthcare proxy or a healthcare agent

dysarthria: A disorder of speech production, resulting from weakness, slowness, or incoordination of the speech mechanism due to damage to the nervous system; speech errors are highly consistent from one occasion to the next

edema: The presence of large amounts of fluid between the cells in body tissues, causing swelling of the affected area

elastin: The substance that makes the skin pliable; both elastin and collagen decrease with age

elder abuse: An all inclusive term representing all types of mistreatment toward older adults; can be an act of commission (abuse) or omission (neglect), intentional or unintentional, and of one or more types: physical, psychological (or emotional), sexual, or financial, resulting in unnecessary suffering, injury, pain, loss or violation of human rights, and decreased quality of life

emphysema: A disease of the lungs in which there is extreme dilation and eventual destruction of the pulmonary alveoli with poor air exchange of oxygen and carbon dioxide; it is one form of chronic obstructive pulmonary disease

eschar: A covering of black, dead tissue; this can form over a pressure ulcer, making it difficult to determine how deep the ulcer is

excoriation: Abrasion of the epidermis or of the coating of any organ by trauma, chemicals, burns, or other causes

financial/material exploitation: Illegal or improper use of an older person's funds, property, or assets; examples include cashing checks without permission, forging signatures, misusing money or possessions, forcing or deceiving into signing legal documents, and improper use of guardianship or power of attorney

gerontology: The study of aging

gerophile: A sexual predator who targets older people

hemothorax: A collection of blood in the pleural cavity

hospice care: In-home or hospice care facility services provided to patients with a terminal illness; services include supportive medical, social, and spiritual services to patients, and support for the patient's family

hypercarbia: Increased carbon dioxide in the bloodstream

incontinence: Involuntary leakage of urine or feces

infestation: The harboring of animal parasites; common infestations in the setting of abuse and neglect are "bed bugs" (*Cimex lectularius*); can cause hemorrhages in the skin, or wheals

informed consent doctrine: Allows a person to decide against unwanted medical interventions

isolation theory: A theory that attempts to explain the cause of elder abuse; maintains that the older person's diminishing social network is a major risk factor in elder abuse

kyphosis: A condition in which the back becomes hunched over due to an abnormal increased curvature of the spine

listening: The act of receiving information; includes observation of more than just the words; also includes the volume, pitch, inflection, tone, and nonverbal aspects

living will: A type of advance directive that documents decisions about particular end-of-life treatments in particular situations should the patient become incompetent; depending on the law in each state, it can cover CPR and other forms of life-sustaining treatment in the event of terminal condition, permanent unconsciousness, and fatal illness prior to the terminal phase; also called an instructional directive

maceration: The process of softening a solid by steeping in a fluid

macular degeneration: Deterioration of the central portion of the retina

medication misuse: Unintentional or willful use of a medication in a way that differs from the prescribed dose or intent

medication/substance abuse: Deliberate use of a drug for nonmedicinal uses

melanin: The pigment that provides color to the hair and skin

Meniere's disease: A disease affecting the membranous inner ear characterized by deafness, dizziness (vertigo), and ringing in the ear (tinnitus)

menopause: The process later in a woman's life during which menstruation ceases

micrographia: Small handwriting

myocardial infarction (MI): Death of heart muscle caused by hypoxia as a result of obstruction of blood flow to the heart

neglect: Refusal or failure on the part of the caregiver to provide life necessities, such as food, water, clothing, shelter, personal hygiene, medicine, comfort, and personal safety

neurons: Cells that make up nerve tissue and receive and transmit impulses

nonblanching erythema: Tissue redness that does not blanch (turn white) when pressed with a finger

nonverbal communication: Includes eye contact, hand gestures, body position, facial expression, and touch

nursing home: A facility where residents receive 24-hour nursing care; also known as a skilled nursing facility, convalescent home, or long-term care facility

old-age dependency ratio: The number of older people for every 100 adults between the ages of 18 and 64

oropharynx: The central portion of the pharynx (the passageway for air from the nasal cavity to the larynx and for food from the mouth to the esophagus) lying between the soft palate and the upper portion of the epiglottis (the uppermost cartilage of the larynx, located immediately posterior to the root of the tongue)

osteoporosis: A condition characterized by a decrease in bone mass, leading to a reduction in bone strength and a greater susceptibility to fracture, even after minimal trauma

otosclerosis: A disease involving the middle ear capsule, specifically affecting the movement of the stapes (one of the three tiny bones in the middle ear)

ototoxic: Any drug with the potential to cause toxic reactions to structures of the inner ear

Parkinson's disease: A chronic nervous disease characterized by a fine, slowly spreading tremor, muscle weakness and rigidity, and a peculiar gait

palliative care: Care of persons whose disease is not responsive to curative treatment. Such care can include providing relief from pain and other distressing symptoms; neither hastening nor prolonging death; offering a supportive system to help the family cope; and integrating psychological and spiritual aspects of care

passive neglect: An unintentional refusal or failure to fulfill a caretaking obligation, which results in physical or emotional distress to the older person; examples include abandonment and the nonprovision of food and health services that are the result of the caretaker's lack of knowledge, laziness, infirmity, or addiction to drugs or alcohol

peripheral edema: Swelling in the abdomen or lower extremities; can be a sign of right-sided heart failure

PERLS: A concept developed to assist the law enforcement officer when responding to calls for service to older people. PERLS has five components: P—prevention; E—elder population; R—responsiveness, resources, referrals; L—life issues; S—social issues

physical abuse: Force resulting in bodily injury—that is, from hitting, slapping, burning, unwarranted administration of drugs and physical restraints, force feeding, or physical punishment

pneumothorax: A partial or complete accumulation of air in the pleural spaces

presbycusis: Hearing loss associated with aging

psychological or emotional abuse: Infliction of anguish, emotional pain, or distress; includes verbal assaults, threats, intimidation, harassment, and forced social isolation

psychopathology of the abuser theory: A theory that attempts to explain the cause of elder abuse; maintains that the abuser's problems (such as personality disorders or substance abuse) can lead to the abuse or neglect

pulmonary edema: A build up of fluid in the lungs, usually as a result of congestive heart failure

residual volume: The amount of air left in the lungs after the maximum possible amount of air has been expired

self-neglect: Behaviors on the part of the older person that threaten his or her own health or safety; generally manifests itself in refusal or failure to provide oneself with adequate food, shelter, or personal safety

sexual abuse: Nonconsensual sexual contact of any kind, including with a person incapable of giving consent; includes, but is not limited to, unwanted touching, sexual assault, or battery such as rape, sodomy, coerced nudity, and sexually explicit photographing

social learning theory: A theory that attempts to explain the cause of elder abuse;

maintains that violence is learned—if a person was abused as a child, that person will abuse his or her parents; also called transgenerational theory

snitch: A type of shoplifter, an amateur, stealing for his or her own use

stressed caregiver theory: A theory that attempts to explain the cause of elder abuse; maintains that when the caretaker reaches a certain stress level, abuse and neglect will occur

stroke volume: The amount of blood pumped out of the heart in one beat

subdural hematoma: Bleeding into the area between the brain and the meningeal layer called the dura matter

tamponade: Closing or blockage in order to stop bleeding

trachea: The windpipe; the main trunk for air passing to and from the lungs

tramline: A bruise appearing as a pale linear central area lined on either side by linear bruising

transgenerational theory: *See* social learning theory

transient ischemic attack (TIA): A disorder of the brain in which brain cells temporarily stop working because of insufficient oxygen, causing stroke-like symptoms that resolve completely within 24 hours of onset

undue influence: The substitution of one person's will for the true desires of another

urine burn: Reddening of the skin that occurs around the inner thighs and buttocks when the older person is allowed repeatedly to lie for prolonged periods of time in his or her own urine

ventilation: Movement of air in and out of the lungs produced by chest wall motion

verbal communication: Includes words, volume, pitch, inflection, and tone

vital capacity: Volume of air moved during the deepest inspiration and expiration

Index

THE PERLS SCALE

PREVENTION

- What are the crime prevention programs and strategies that are best suited for the older population?
- How can they be implemented?

ELDER POPULATION

- Treat the older person with respect and dignity.
- Older people are different and will present differently than younger adults.
- Older people have specific fears and concerns.
- Think about the changes that occur with age.
- Remember how to effectively communicate with the older person

RESPONSIVENESS, RESOURCES, REFERRALS

- Be responsive to the older person's needs.
- What resources are available for older people?
- Taking the time to make referrals will help to improve the quality of the lives of older people.

LIFE ISSUES

- What are the unique characteristics of the older population you are serving?

SOCIAL ISSUES

- Does the older person have a social network? Does the older person have ways to interact socially with others on a daily basis?
- Evaluate activities of daily living (eating, bathing, dressing, toileting).
- Evaluate the older person's surroundings, and be on guard for the possibility of elder abuse and neglect.